CARS

CARS

igloo

Published in 2009
by Igloo Books Ltd.
Cottage Farm
Sywell
NN6 0BJ
www.igloo-books.com

10 9 8 7 6 5 4 3

ISBN: 978 1 84817 720 8

Project managed by BlueRed Press Ltd
Cover design by Stephen Croucher
Design by Jon Morgan

Printed and manufactured in China

Contents

6	*Introduction*
8	**Dream Cars**
10	Alfa Romeo 8C Competizione
12	Alfa Romeo Montreal
14	Alfa Romeo SZ
16	Aston Martin DB7 Vantage Zagato Coupe
18	Aston Martin DB9
22	Audi S8
24	Bentley Azure T
26	Bentley Brooklands
30	Bentley R-Type Continental
34	BMW Hydrogen 7
36	BMW Z8
40	Bugatti EB 16/4 Veyron
44	Bugatti EB110 SS
46	Bugatti Type 35
50	Cadilac Allante
52	Cadillac Eldorado Convertible
54	Cadillac XLR-V
56	Chevrolet Camaro Z28
60	Chevrolet Corvette Sting Ray
64	Citroen SM
66	DeLorean DMC-12
70	Ferrari 246 GT Dino
74	Ferrari 250 GTO
78	Ferrari 365 GTB/4 Daytona
80	Ferrari California
84	Fisker Karma
88	Ford GT40 Mark I Production
92	Ford Mustang
94	Ford Thunderbird
98	Infiniti FX50
100	Iso Grifo
102	Jaguar D-Type
106	Jaguar E-Type
110	Jaguar XFR
114	Jensen FF
116	Lamborghini Miura P400
120	Land Rover Range Rover
122	Lexus LS460
124	Lincoln Continental Mark IV
126	Maserati GranTurismo S
130	Maserati Quattroporte
132	Maybach 62
134	Mercedes-Benz 300 SL
136	Mercedes-Benz S65 AMG
138	Plymouth Superbird
140	Porsche Panamera
144	Rolls Royce Phantom Drophead Coupe
148	Rolls Royce Phantom
152	Spyker C8 Laviolette
156	Volkswagen Phaeton W12 4 Motion
158	**Fast Cars**
160	AC Cobra 427
164	Ascari KZ1
166	Aston Martin DB5
168	Aston Martin V8 Vantage
170	Audi quattro
174	Audi R8
176	Bentley Continental Supersports
178	BMW M1
180	BMW M3 CSL
182	BMW M5
186	Caterham Superlight R300
188	Chevrolet Camaro SS
190	Chevrolet Corvette ZR-1
194	De Tomaso Pantera
196	Dodge Challenger SRT8
198	Dodge Charger 500 Daytona
202	Dodge Viper SRT-10
206	Ferrari Enzo
210	Ferrari F40
214	Ford GT
218	Gumpert Apollo
220	Honda NSX
222	Jaguar XJ220
226	Konigsegg CCX
230	Lamborghini Countach
234	Lamborghini Gallardo
236	Lamborghini Murcielago
240	Lancia Delta HF Integrale Evoluzione II
242	Lancia Stratos
244	Lotus Elise
246	Lotus Esprit Turbo
248	Maserati Bora
252	McLaren F1
256	Mercedes-Benz SLR McLaren Roadster
258	Mercedes-Benz SLR McLaren Stirling Moss
262	Mitsubishi Lancer EVO X
264	Morgan Aero 8
266	Morgan Plus 8
268	Nissan 370Z
272	Nissan GT-R
274	Noble M15
276	Pagani Zonda
278	Porsche 911
282	Porsche 911 GT3
284	Porsche 959
286	Porsche Carrera GT
290	Shelby Mustang GT350
292	Subaru Impreza WRX STI
296	Toyota 2000GT
300	TVR Griffith
303	*Picture Credits*
304	*Index*

Introduction

The world has had a passionate love affair with the car ever since Gottlieb Daimler and Karl Benz invented gasoline-powered vehicles, the event which started the age of the modern automobile. And nothing reflects this passion more than the dream cars and fast cars that make drivers stop and stare when one of these special cars pulls up next to them.

Clean lines, elegant designs, special finishing and exclusivity all help to make a dream car. These are the classic cars; the cars that never look dated. A car doesn't have to be old to be a classic. It's a combination of the way a car looks and the way it handles on the road, but if a car is sleek, graceful and has a touch of glamour, it will qualify as a dream car. If a car makes a pulse race, if buying one means a decision made by the heart instead of the head, it's a dream car.

Fast cars exude power. They're all about acceleration, engines, speed, transmission, grip, handling: the car that can do 200 mph (320 kph) - easily – and the car that can take the corners and bends.

Dream cars and fast cars – one of a kind, special, attention grabbing and head turning. Cars that set your heart racing. Cars worth the passion.

DREAM CARS

Alfa Romeo 8C Competizione

There's a Maserati chassis under the skin and a Maserati-designed engine under the bonnet, but the 8C Competizione sports Alfa Romeo badges – and it's arguably the most beautiful car ever to do so. It started life as a concept car, which was shown at the Frankfurt Motor Show in 2003, but in the three years it took to prepare the 8C for production, it lost none of its grace, elegance and sheer power. It's still got the gaping air intakes and the fared-in headlights at the front and it's still got the four exhaust pipes and twin circular tail lights at the rear.

The 8C shares its name with the eight-cylinder Alfa Romeo sports cars that dominated Europe's racetracks before World War II, and especially with the 8C 2900, which not only clocked up scores of victories but also became one of the great Grand Tourers of its age. It also draws inspiration from other past masters, including the Tipo 33 Stradale and Giulia TZ2, though the modern 8C's design – by Wolfgang Egger at Alfa's own Centro Stile – resists any temptation of falling into the retro trap.

Instead, it has a thoroughly modern supercar design, with a long bonnet and a short tail. There's a prominent horizontal furrow cut into the side above the wheel arch, which adds visual dynamism, while the massive wheels and muscular rear wings emphasize the performance potential of Alfa's latest supercar. Aerodynamic efficiency was a keystone of the body design, with all surfaces optimized for smooth airflow, though the clever bits are hidden underneath, where there's an aerodynamic undertray that ensures plenty of downforce at high speeds without the need for intrusive spoilers or wings on top.

Under the bonnet of the 8C Competizione is a 4,691 cc V8 producing 450 bhp at 7,000 rpm and 470 Nm of torque at 4,750 rpm. It drives the rear wheels via a six-speed electro-hydraulic manual transmission. Operated by paddles behind the steering wheel, the gearbox can be used in manual or automatic modes and in normal and sport modes. The all-independent suspension uses double wishbones, variable gas dampers, coil springs and an anti-roll bar front and rear, while stopping power is provided by massive cross-drilled discs.

Performance is electric: from a standstill, it reaches 60 mph in 4.1 seconds and 100 mph in 9.3 seconds, and has a top

ALFA ROMEO 8C COMPETIZIONE 2006		WIDTH: 74½ in / 1,894 mm
ENGINE: 4,691 cc V8		HEIGHT: 52¾ in / 1,341 mm
MAXIMUM POWER: 450 bhp at 7,000 rpm		WHEELBASE: 104¼ in / 2,646 mm
MAXIMUM TORQUE: 470 Nm at 4,750 rpm		MANUFACTURE DATE: 2006–present
MAXIMUM SPEED: 181 mph / 291 km/h		BRAKES: disc (f and r)
0–60 MPH ACCELERATION: 4.1 secs		SUSPENSION: double wishbone (f and r)
TRANSMISSION: 6-speed electro-hydraulic manual		WHEELS: alloy, 20 in
LENGTH: 168½ in / 4,381 mm		TIRES: 245/35 R-20 (f and r)

speed of 181 mph / 291 km/h. That's quicker than the Maserati GranTurismo, from which it borrows the suspension, or the Maserati Coupé, from which it borrows elements of its structure. It's very nearly as fast as a Ferrari F430, thanks to its lightweight carbon-fibre body, which is 176 lb / 80 kg lighter than that of its Maserati cousins. On the road, the Alfa 8C is not just fast, it's also very noisy, with its rumbling exhaust note and crackling from the tail pipe on the overrun.

Inside the two-seater cabin, carbon fibre and the finest leathers abound. Owners can even specify special leather luggage to fit in the rear shelf behind the drive and passenger. In other respects, the interior is classically simple with large cowls over the speedometer and rev counter and a prominent starter button on the fascia.

Some may question whether it is a true Alfa Romeo, given that it has a Maserati chassis and suspension system, its engine is developed from an existing Maserati unit and built by Ferrari, and the car itself is put together not in an Alfa factory in Milan or

Turin but by Maserati in Modena. But does it really matter? The 8C Competizione is frankly so wonderful, so desirable, and so classically elegant that it's enough that it exists – albeit at a list price of some £111,000. Alfa announced in advance that it only intended to make 500 examples of the 8C coupé, and a further 500 examples of the 8C Competizione Spyder convertible, so this will forever remain a rare supercar.

Alfa Romeo Montreal

The stunning Alfa Romeo Montreal was created to showcase Italian engineering and design flair in the Italian Pavilion at Expo '67 in Montreal, Canada. It was so well received that it went into production in 1970 and was still being made in 1977, by which time nearly 4,000 examples of the 2+2 coupé had been sold. Ironically, however, not a single one was sold in Montreal. Production was strictly limited to European markets because of emissions restrictions in North America.

Styling of the Alfa Montreal was the work of Marcello Gandini at coachbuilders Bertone – the man who later in his career would later design the Lamborghini Countach. He penned the sleek body with its four headlights under slatted front panels and its side air scoops that suggested this might be a mid-engined design – though in fact the ducts only provided cabin ventilation. The body was fitted on top of a standard production Alfa Giulia 1750 GTV chassis, complete with its double wishbone front suspension and live axle at the back – something that was to prove the Montreal's Achilles heel.

Although the original Montreal show car was fitted with Alfa's 1.6-liter twin-cam engine, a far more serious powerplant had been chosen by the time the car was put into production: a 2,593 cc fuel-injected V8, which produced 200 bhp at 6,500 rpm and 235 Nm of torque at 4,750 rpm. The engine was an arresting

development, as up until then, Alfa Romeo had never specified a V8 engine in a production car. It drove the rear wheels via a five-speed manual transmission and limited slip differential.

This was a truly race-bred engine, as it had first seen the light of day in the Tipo 33/2 racing car. When detuned, it made a great roadcar engine, offering not just a relatively high output for a normally aspirated unit, but also very spirited performance, thanks to its free-revving spirit and high red line. The brakes were significantly upgraded from the standard Alfa Giulia, with ventilated discs fitted front and rear to ensure adequate stopping power.

Performance was good for its day: it had a top speed of 132 mph / 212 km/h and 0–60 mph acceleration in under eight seconds, despite the car weighing some 470 lb / 213 kg – more than the Giulia GTV upon which it was based.

But it wasn't excess weight that let the Montreal down. The problem was its unsophisticated rear suspension, which compromised the handling. It was simply too softly sprung, so cornering was never going to be as precise as it might have been with a fully independent set-up. The Montreal also suffered from its rather agricultural recirculating ball steering, which was geared to make the car driveable at low speeds rather than sharp and agile at higher speeds.

And yet the Montreal was a very special car that worked wonders for Alfa Romeo's image at the time. It had style, power and presence in a way that Alfa's normal road cars in 1970 – such as the Spider and GTV – could never hope to emulate. It had power and a race-bred soul, and it turned heads wherever it went, making it one of the most desirable cars of its generation. It was a true Grand Tourer with a price tag to match: it cost around £5,000 in the UK in 1970, which was a serious amount of money at that time.

At that price level, the Alfa Montreal briefly competed with the likes of the Mercedes-Benz 350 SL and BMW 3.0 CS in a sector of the market that was previously alien to the Italian brand. It can't be said to have been a commercial success, but it gave a massive boost to the brand in the 1970s in just the same way as the 8C Competitzione has done in the early years of the 21st century.

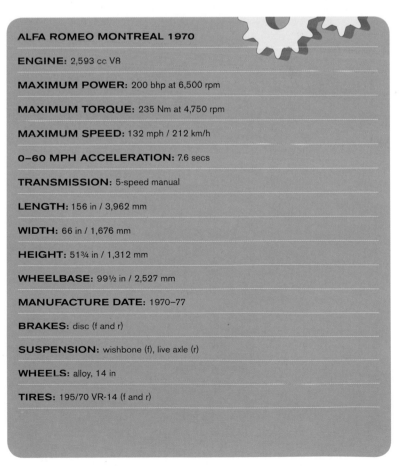

ALFA ROMEO MONTREAL 1970

ENGINE: 2,593 cc V8

MAXIMUM POWER: 200 bhp at 6,500 rpm

MAXIMUM TORQUE: 235 Nm at 4,750 rpm

MAXIMUM SPEED: 132 mph / 212 km/h

0–60 MPH ACCELERATION: 7.6 secs

TRANSMISSION: 5-speed manual

LENGTH: 156 in / 3,962 mm

WIDTH: 66 in / 1,676 mm

HEIGHT: 51¾ in / 1,312 mm

WHEELBASE: 99½ in / 2,527 mm

MANUFACTURE DATE: 1970–77

BRAKES: disc (f and r)

SUSPENSION: wishbone (f), live axle (r)

WHEELS: alloy, 14 in

TIRES: 195/70 VR-14 (f and r)

Alfa Romeo SZ

The Alfa Romeo SZ is a car that truly polarizes opinion. To some observers, it is a unique example of automotive style, unsullied by focus groups, and self-consciously determined not to be perceived as yet another anodyne, anonymous design. To others, the Alfa SZ is just plain ugly.

The car first saw the light of day at the Geneva Motor Show in 1989 as a prototype on the Zagato stand. Zagato and Alfa had a long history of collaboration, starting in 1929, when Zagato made the bodies for the racing Alfa Romeo 6C 1750 Gran Sport. Zagato had also already produced an SZ model for Alfa – the Giulietta Sprint Zagato (SZ) in 1959. At that Geneva Show, the latter-day SZ was called something else – the ES-30 – and initial interest was strong enough to persuade Alfa Romeo to put the car into limited production of 1,000 examples. As a reminder of past collaborations between Alfa and Zagato, it was decided to revive the SZ name.

Production started quickly with the first few cars being built in 1989, followed by 289 in 1990 and a final batch of 736 in 1991. Customers had no trouble deciding on a final specification – every car was produced with red paint and a dark grey roof section, with one exception: a special black version with black-tinted glass was made for Andrea Zagato.

The SZ was powered by Alfa's light alloy 3.0-liter V6 that was already fitted to the Alfa 75 model. It was tuned by Alfa's motor sport division Alfa Corse to boost the power output to 210 bhp at 6,200 rpm and the torque to 245 Nm at 4,500 rpm. It powered the rear wheels via a five-speed transmission fitted to the rear transaxle for optimum weight balance.

Front and rear suspension was also based on standard Alfa 75 units, with independent coil springs at the front and a de Dion rear axle, though uniball joints and adjustable Koni dampers were specified for the SZ. Large ventilated disc brakes were fitted to all four corners.

The SZ was equipped with an extremely strong steel shell, to which were bonded plastic body panels. Thanks to this rigidity and the relatively stiff suspension setting, the SZ's handling and grip was outstanding. On its Pirelli P-Zero tires it was capable of cornering at more than 1G – the sort of performance expected of a racing car on a track. In fact, all-round performance of the SZ was truly commendable: it raced from 0 to 62mph in seven seconds and had a top speed of 152 mph / 245 km/h. It was loud and it was raucous – in short, it offered a great driving experience.

Though the SZ was always intended to be a driver's car, the cabin was smart and comfortable and, with its large glass area, provided excellent visibility. Unlike the Alfa 75, whose interior controls seemed to be fitted wholly at random, the SZ had been subjected to a modicum of ergonomic design.

Despite many people's continuing concerns about the appearance of the SZ, it certainly achieved one aim – that of providing visibility and publicity for the Alfa Romeo brand. To maintain this momentum, a second range of convertibles, called the RZ, was launched in 1992. Because of its added weight, the RZ was inevitably not as sprightly as the SZ, even though it was powered by the same engine. Its 0–62mph acceleration was 7.5 seconds and its top speed was 143 mph / 230 km/h. This time, there were some colour options – red, black or yellow, though three silver and one white car were also built – but despite this, the RZ did not sell well. Alfa announced a run of 350 cars but only 278 were made.

ALFA ROMEO SZ 1989

ENGINE: 2,959 cc V6

MAXIMUM POWER: 210 bhp at 6,200 rpm

MAXIMUM TORQUE: 245 Nm at 4,500 rpm

MAXIMUM SPEED: 152 mph / 245 km/h

0–62 MPH ACCELERATION: 7.0 secs

TRANSMISSION: 5-speed manual

LENGTH: 182½ in / 4,635 mm

WIDTH: 68 in / 1,730 mm

HEIGHT: 51¼ in / 1,300 mm

WHEELBASE: 98¾ in / 2,510 mm

MANUFACTURE DATE: 1989–91

BRAKES: disc (f and r)

SUSPENSION: independent coil spring (f), de Dion tube (r)

WHEELS: alloy, 16 in

TIRES: 205/55 ZR-16 (f), 225/50 ZR-16 (r)

Aston Martin DB7 Vantage Zagato Coupé

Aston Martin's relationship with Italian styling house Zagato began in 1961 when Zagato was commissioned to build the DB4 Zagato, a purpose-built racer intended to compete on the track with the likes of the Ferrari 250. Later in the 1980s, Zagato produced special bodies for a limited run of V8 coupés and convertibles for Aston Martin.

In 2002, Aston Martin renewed the partnership with the unveiling of the DB7 Zagato and the announcement at the Pebble Beach Concours d'Elegance that it would go into production. Andrea Zagato and Ulrich Bez, CEO of Aston Martin, had both been judges at the Pebble Beach Concours the previous year, and the idea had been spawned there of relaunching the collaboration between the two companies.

Unlike the original DB4 Zagato, the DB7 Zagato was never intended to race, but rather to be a highly exclusive run of 99 cars built on a shortened Vantage Volante floor pan. It was not just a more compact car but also at least 132 lb / 60 kg lighter than its predecessor.

Power came from a tuned 440 bhp derivative of Aston Martin's V12, which was mated to a six-speed manual transmission. Bespoke wheels, upgraded brakes and the same sports suspension as the DB7 Vantage were also part of the full specification. That suspension uses double wishbones with coil springs and an anti-roll bar at the front and a multi-link rear suspension with coil springs and anti-roll bar.

The svelte aluminium bodies were manufactured by Zagato in Italy then shipped to Aston Martin's factory at Bloxham, near Oxford, where final assembly took place. Zagato's genius in creating this body lies in the incorporation of traditional styling cues from the DB4 Zagato within a thoroughly modern design. The car has the traditional long bonnet and short tail of all Astons and also features the famous 'double-bubble' roof and Zagato's trademark radiator grille and broad rear wheel arches. The double bubble was extended from the roof right down the rear screen, which made for some complicated but highly distinctive glasswork at the rear.

The cabin is as luxurious as that of any Aston Martin and features a hand-stitched quilted-leather design that is unique to this car, and unique carbon fibre panels. As might be expected, it's a masterpiece of craftsmanship. All the DB7 Zagatos were strictly two seaters, with a luggage shelf replacing the rear seats of the standard car.

The all-alloy, twin-cam 48-valve V12 has the same capacity as the standard DB7 at 5,939 cc, but its power has been upgraded to 440 bhp at 6,000 rpm with peak torque of 556 Nm at 5,000 rpm. Though the gearbox is standard DB7, the Zagato is given a special final drive ratio to boost performance and a short shift gear level for snappier changes. Needless to say, performance is impressive: 0–60 mph in 4.9 seconds and a top speed of 186 mph / 299 km/h.

Just 99 examples of the DB7 Zagato were built, in 2002 and 2003, at a list price of £160,000. In 2003, a new model, the Aston Martin DB AR1, was launched, again with a production run of only 99 examples. This car was specifically designed for the US market, hence its name (which stood for American Roadster 1). Though it looked like a convertible version of the DB7 Zagato, it was actually a separate model designed by Zagato on a standard wheelbase, which went on sale in the USA at $226,000. That was less than the $250,000 charged for the DB7 Zagato coupé, but then the AR1 roadster didn't even have a roof as part of its specification; it truly was a vehicle designed for the Californian sunshine. The DB AR1 was one of the last DB7s to be made: the car went out of production during 2003 to be replaced by the DB9 model.

ASTON MARTIN DB7 VANTAGE ZAGATO COUPÉ 2002

ENGINE: 5,939 cc V12

MAXIMUM POWER: 440 bhp at 6,000 rpm

MAXIMUM TORQUE: 556 Nm at 5,000 rpm

MAXIMUM SPEED: 186 mph / 299 km/h

0–60 MPH ACCELERATION: 4.9 secs

TRANSMISSION: 6-speed manual

LENGTH: 176½ in / 4,481 mm

WIDTH: 48¼ in / 1,224 mm

HEIGHT: 73¼ in / 1,861 mm

WHEELBASE: 99½ in / 2,531 mm

MANUFACTURE DATE: 2002–03

BRAKES: disc, (f and r)

SUSPENSION: double wishbone (f), multi-link (r)

WHEELS: alloy, 18 in

TIRES: 245/40 ZR-18 (f), 265/35 ZR-18 (r)

Aston Martin DB9

The DB9 was the model that was supposed to assure the future of Aston Martin. The company had been through a number of different owners, but now, as part of Ford's Premier Automotive Group (which also included Jaguar, Land Rover and Volvo), it had secured the investment to create an all-new manufacturing facility at Gaydon in Warwickshire to replace the antiquated sheds at Newport Pagnell from which it had operated for so many years.

When the DB9 appeared, the future looked bright indeed: the new 2+2 was not only stunningly good looking, but it also had all the power it needed to compete at the top end of the supercar league, a suspension set-up that gave it breathtaking agility, and a simply gorgeous hand-crafted cockpit. Indeed, at the time of its launch in 2004, the Aston Martin DB9 was one of the most advanced and technically sophisticated cars of all.

Its bonded aluminium frame is light, strong and highly efficient structurally: despite the fact that the bodyshell is some 25 per cent lighter than that of the DB7, its frame has twice the torsional rigidity. The engine, transmission and suspension are mounted on the frame, then the body panels are bonded to the frame, increasing the stiffness of the whole structure but also eliminating squeaks and rattles. The front wings, bonnet and roof are made of aluminium, while the rear wings and boot lid are constructed from lightweight composites. The DB9's front suspension is mounted on a separate aluminium subframe, while the rear suspension and transaxle is mounted on its own subframe. Forged aluminium wishbones and aluminium-bodied shock absorbers are used front and rear. Braking is by disc front and rear, incorporating a host of electronic aids, including Electronic Brakeforce Distribution, Brake Assist and ABS.

At the heart of the DB9 is a V12 developed from the Vanquish unit, a 48-valve quad-cam 5,953 cc engine that produces 450 bhp at 6,000 rpm and 570 Nm of torque at 5,000 rpm, some 80 per cent of which is available as low as 1,500 rpm, which makes the car immensely tractable at low speeds and wonderfully responsive at higher speeds. The DB9 achieves 0–60 mph in just 4.7 seconds and has a top speed of 186 mph / 299 km/h. The engine is mounted as far back as possible and is connected to the rear transaxle by a carbon-fibre propshaft inside an aluminium torque tube, an arrangement that ensures the optimal 50:50 weight distributions. The gearbox is available as either a six-speed manual or six-speed automatic, the latter being one of the world's first shift-by-wire arrangements, which allows the driver to select park, reverse, drive or neutral by pressing a dashboard button. The driver can also shift gears manually using paddles on the steering column.

But perhaps more important than its mechanical specification is the appearance of the DB9. Its design is a thoroughly modern reinterpretation of classic Aston Martin sports car style: curved, elegant, clean and smooth, while at the same time hinting at the power potential and the lithe agility of the car.

Very soon after the launch of the DB9 came the introduction of the DB9 Volante, which features a fully retractable hood that is then stored within the body of the car to avoid spoiling its elegant lines. Operated with the push of a button, it takes just 17 seconds to open or close. Mechanically, the Volante is very similar to the DB9 coupé, though it does feature extra roll-over sensors that detect an imminent rollover and deploy two hoops from the rear seat headrests, which operate in tandem with the front windscreen to withstand weight more than twice that of the car.

ASTON MARTIN DB9 2004

ENGINE: 5,953 cc V12

MAXIMUM POWER: 450 bhp at 6,000 rpm

MAXIMUM TORQUE: 570 Nm at 5,000 rpm

MAXIMUM SPEED: 186 mph / 299 km/h

0–60 MPH ACCELERATION: 4.7 secs

TRANSMISSION: 6-speed manual or 6-speed automatic

LENGTH: 184¾ in / 4,691 mm

WIDTH: 73¾ in / 1,875 mm

HEIGHT: 51½ in / 1,305 mm

WHEELBASE: 107¾ in / 2,740 mm

MANUFACTURE DATE: 2004–present

BRAKES: disc (f and r)

SUSPENSION: double wishbone (f and r)

WHEELS: alloy, 19 in

TIRES: 235/40 ZR-19 (f), 275/35 ZR-19 (r)

Audi S8

The vast majority of Audi cars are fairly normal, though well-engineered saloons and hatchbacks. But the company has a habit of offering at least one model in each of its product ranges that is a genuine performance car. There's the S4 and even more potent RS4 versions of the Audi A4 series and the S6 and RS6 of the A6 series. So it's no surprise that there should also be a wilder derivative of the flagship A8 saloon range.

Actually, until 2005, the Audi S8 was quick, but never offered anything like supercar standards of performance. Its purpose remained to offer comfortable, cosseted travel rather than out-and-out speed. But since Audi owns Lamborghini, the opportunity arose to borrow the Gallardo's V10 powerplant and plumb it into a beefed-up A8 chassis.

Audi's engineers increased the capacity of the Lambo engine from 5,000 to 5,200 cc and added its FSI direct fuel-injection system. And because an Audi S8 still needs to offer refinement levels unnecessary in a Lamborghini, an extra balancer shaft was added to reduce vibrations under heavy acceleration.

After Audi's adaptations, the all-aluminium V10 produced 450 bhp at 7,000 rpm and 540 Nm of torque at 3,500 rpm. A full 90 per cent of that peak torque is available as low down as 2,300 rpm, which means that the S8 is not only fast, it's also extremely flexible in traffic. Acceleration from 0 to 60 mph takes 5.0 seconds and the top speed is electronically limited to 155 mph / 249 km/h – highly respectable performance figures for a large luxury saloon.

To cope with the extra power, the S8 has firmer, lowered suspension, uprated brakes (with a ceramic brakes option) and a quicker steering rack. Permanent Quattro four-wheel drive is standard, with the torque bias set at 40:60 front to rear. The result is agile handling, enormous levels of grip and, thanks to the adjustable air suspension, very acceptable ride quality, despite the 20-inch wheels, low-profile tires and sports-oriented damper settings that might normally be expected to result in a harsher feel. A six-speed Tiptronic automatic transmission with paddle-operated steering wheel controls is standard, with the output directed via a Torsen center differential to the front and rear wheels.

From the outside, the S8 does little to reveal its true potential. There's a V10 badge mounted on the wing and larger air intakes at the front to keep the V10 cool. There's also a small spoiler on the rear boot lid to provide extra downforce at higher speeds, as well as other modest body adaptations. But for the most part, the S8 looks just like a standard A8 saloon. Once under way, however, the difference soon makes itself felt. Not only is the S8 much faster than its stablemate, but it also sounds unique, thanks to the deep metallic howl of the V10 engine.

There are also changes in the cabin, which retains all the space and elegance of the standard saloons, but adds a sportier

touch with two-tone leather seats and extensive use of carbon fibre and brushed aluminium.

The Audi A8's launch price of around £70,000 meant buyers could enjoy the heart of a £130,000 Lamborghini for little more than half the cost of the original. This isn't the first time this sort of thing has happened, because in the 1980s, the Lancia Thema 8:32 had a Ferrari engine under its bonnet. What's different about the Audi S8 is that it retains the raw acceleration and howling V10 tone of the Lamborghini.

The S8 faces plenty of competition in the market from the likes of the Maserati Quattroporte, the BMW M5 and the Mercedes-Benz S55 AMG. It's understated, beautifully engineered and smooth and luxurious when driven gently, but once the throttle is applied, it's clear that this is a car with serious firepower under its bonnet.

AUDI S8 2005

ENGINE: 5,204 cc V10

MAXIMUM POWER: 450 bhp at 7,000 rpm

MAXIMUM TORQUE: 540 Nm at 3,500 rpm

MAXIMUM SPEED: 155 mph / 249 km/h

0–60 MPH ACCELERATION: 5.0 secs

TRANSMISSION: 6-speed automatic

LENGTH: 199¼ in / 5,062 mm

WIDTH: 74½ in / 1,895 mm

HEIGHT: 57 in / 1,445 mm

WHEELBASE: 116 in / 2,944 mm

MANUFACTURE DATE: 2005–present

BRAKES: disc (f and r)

SUSPENSION: wishbone (f), multi-link (r)

WHEELS: alloy, 20 in

TIRES: 265/35 ZR-20 (f and r)

Bentley Azure T

The first Bentley Azure – a top of the range convertible – was on sale between 1995 and 2002, and the first hint that a replacement might be in the pipeline came at the Los Angeles Auto Show in 2005, when Bentley displayed an Arnage Drophead Coupé concept. Potential customers were so enthusiastic – some even tried to place deposits on the stand there and then – that Bentley rushed it into production, and the first cars were delivered as early as spring 2006.

This second-generation car is clearly derived from the Arnage saloon and shares its platform, engine, suspension and front-end appearance, but the Azure is far more than an Arnage with its roof chopped off. The entire cabin and rear section of the car are newly designed, and incorporate a complex folding roof operated hydraulically at the touch of a switch, which enables the impressive, three-layer fabric assembly to be elegantly stowed beneath a hide-trimmed tonneau in less than 30 seconds.

The twin-turbocharged Bentley V8 engine, double-wishbone suspension and extremely rigid body structure of the Arnage provided a fine basis for the new Azure, whose 6,750 cc twin-turbocharged intercooled V8 engine was tuned to deliver 450 bhp and 875 Nm of torque. Until recently, neither Bentley nor Rolls-Royce ever divulged power and torque figures, but instead merely stated they were 'sufficient'. In the Azure, they were more than sufficient to offer 0–60 mph acceleration in 5.9 seconds and a top speed of 168 mph / 270 km/h.

And that's just in the standard version of the Azure. In late 2008, Bentley unveiled an even more powerful Azure T. Fitted with a 500 bhp high-performance version of Bentley's 6,752 cc V8 engine, it's the latest in a line of Bentley models to bear the 'T' legend. The 1996 Continental coupe, the first modern Bentley 'T', was followed in 2002 by the Arnage T,

both flagship models with a distinctive sporting character and thunderous performance.

In the Azure T, power is up 11 per cent to 500 bhp at 4,200 rpm and torque is up 14 per cent to a breathtaking 1,000 Nm at 3,200 rpm. As a direct result, performance is significantly raised, giving the car a top speed of 170 mph / 274 km/h, a 0–60 mph time of 5.9 seconds and 0–100 mph acceleration in 12.1 seconds – astonishing results for a large and weighty four-seater convertible.

The massive V8 engine is mated to a six-speed ZF automatic transmission, which offers optimum flexibility, response and refinement. Three transmission modes (Drive, Sport and Manual) allow the driver to take full advantage of the powerful 500 bhp V8 engine.

The Azure's double wishbone front and rear suspension is carried over to the Azure T unaltered. Fine-tuned to give a refined ride that best suits the character of this convertible Bentley, the system features coil springs with computer-controlled, adaptive electro-hydraulic dampers and automatic ride-height control with auto-load compensation.

The Azure T can be identified by its larger 20-inch five-spoke alloy wheels, Le Mans-style lower front-wing air vents, dark-tinted

upper and lower grilles, retractable Flying 'B' mascot and 'jewel' fuel-filler cap that's made from milled aluminium.

The cabin has also been tweaked, in tune with the Azure T's sporting pretensions. It now has diamond quilted leather seats and door panels, drilled aluminium pedals, a turned aluminium dashboard reminiscent of 1920s racing Bentleys and a prominent chrome gear knob. As would be expected of Bentley, craftsmanship and bespoke finishing are to the fore in the interior, which, by the very nature of a convertible, is often on display. And Bentley owners are given every opportunity to make their own mark in creating a uniquely personal car, with a choice of 42 exterior colours, 25 interior hides, and a wide range of premium veneers.

The Bentley Azure T is among the world's most elegant convertibles and is destined to become a future classic.

BENTLEY AZURE T 2008

ENGINE: 6,752 cc V8

MAXIMUM POWER: 500 bhp at 4,200 rpm

MAXIMUM TORQUE: 1,000 Nm at 3,200 rpm

MAXIMUM SPEED: 170 mph / 274 km/h

0–60 MPH ACCELERATION: 5.9 secs

TRANSMISSION: 4-speed automatic

LENGTH: 210¼ in / 5,342 mm

WIDTH: 81 in / 2,057 mm

HEIGHT: 58 in / 1,476 mm

WHEELBASE: 120½ in / 3,061 mm

MANUFACTURE DATE: 2008–present

BRAKES: disc (f and r)

SUSPENSION: independent wishbone (f), independent strut (r)

WHEELS: alloy, 17 in

TIRES: 255/55 W-17 (f and r)

Bentley Brooklands

This is not just any old car. It's not even just any old Bentley. It's the very latest Bentley Brooklands coupé, a two-door version of the venerable Arnage/Azure range, and, until the Arnage is finally replaced, the latest flagship model of the Bentley family. But to see it as either an Arnage coupé or an Azure with a hard top is missing the point. The Brooklands is faster, sportier and more aggressively styled than either of its brethren and has a character all of its own, such that it's virtually an all-new model.

This ultimate Bentley is a stylish, four-seat, grand touring coupé, with classic British proportions and muscular performance. It's a true hardtop, with no center window post to spoil its flowing, elegant lines. Sporting design cues are matched by the phenomenal performance engineering of Bentley's legendary Crewe-built V8 engine. Under the long sweeping bonnet of the Bentley Brooklands lies the most powerful V8 the company has ever produced – a 530 bhp, twin-turbocharged 6.75-liter unit that also produces a prodigious 1,050 Nm of torque.

Amazingly, Bentley's V8 was first launched in the Bentley S2 saloon way back in 1959, with a capacity of 1.37 gallons / 6.23 liters. It was very advanced for its time, with an all-aluminium construction, a five-bearing crankshaft and a well-supported camshaft, producing nearly 200 bhp and 400 Nm of torque. The result was a light and supple powertrain that produced maximum torque at low engine speeds – the hallmark of every Bentley ever produced.

In 1969, the capacity was increased to 6.75 liters (and this has remained constant), but by far the most significant change came in 1982, with the introduction of a turbocharger to create the near-300 bhp Mulsanne Turbo, a car that transformed the image of Bentley. Twin turbos arrived in the Arnage in 2002, developing up to 450 bhp.

For the 2007 model Arnage, the V8 engine saw a step-change in performance and refinement, which became the starting point for the new Bentley Brooklands. A reprofiled camshaft and new, low-inertia turbochargers, which operate with greater efficiency at lower engine speeds, have resulted in reduced turbo lag, enhancing that prodigious wave of torque at any revs. For the Bentley Brooklands, further component optimization and engine calibration ensure record power and torque levels from this hand-assembled engine, which is matched to a six-speed automatic transmission.

BENTLEY BROOKLANDS 2007

ENGINE: 6,751 cc V8

MAXIMUM POWER: 530 bhp at 4,000 rpm

MAXIMUM TORQUE: 1,050 Nm at 3,200 rpm

MAXIMUM SPEED: 184 mph / 296 km/h

0–62 MPH ACCELERATION: 5.3 secs

TRANSMISSION: 6-speed automatic

LENGTH: 213 in / 5,411 mm

WIDTH: 81¾ in / 2,078 mm

HEIGHT: 58 in / 1,473 mm

WHEELBASE: 122¾ in / 3,116 mm

MANUFACTURE DATE: 2007

BRAKES: disc (f and r)

SUSPENSION: double wishbone (f and r)

WHEELS: alloy, 20 in

TIRES: 255/40 ZR-20 (f and r)

Each Brooklands coupé is lovingly hand-assembled, employing traditional coach-building techniques and the craftsmanship skills in wood veneer and leather hide for which Bentley has long been renowned. As an example of attention to details, the flowing line where the roof meets the rear wings is hand-welded, and Bentley insist that's the only way of making the join imperceptible. The Brooklands costs a cool £236,500, and as if that alone wasn't enough to ensure exclusivity, lifetime production will be strictly limited to just 550 cars.

Bentley's plan in developing the Brooklands was to offer 'exhilarating, effortless, accessible performance for those truly passionate about their driving'. It has certainly achieved that aim, even though the bare figures don't suggest the ultimate in performance. The 0–62mph acceleration time, for example, is 5.0 seconds – respectable, but no longer in the supercar league. Similarly, its 184 mph / 296 km/h top speed is fast, but by no means the fastest available.

But in no other car can you sit in such sumptuous comfort and feel such an explosion of raw power as under acceleration the bonnet lifts and the Brooklands sits down on its haunches. Considering that it weighs around 2.56 tons / 2.6 tonnes, it's also astonishing how swiftly the huge car can be hustled around corners. Reassuringly, it stops as well as it goes, too, thanks to massive carbon brakes in each of the 20-inch wheels.

The Bentley Brooklands is a fantastic *tour de force* – a fact that has clearly been recognized by potential customers. Of the 550 cars that the company vowed would be made, 500 had been sold before the first one had rolled off the production line.

Bentley R-Type Continental

One of the 1953 Bentley R-Type Continental's chief claims to fame was that, at the time of its launch, it was comfortably the most expensive car in the world. But far more importantly, it was also one of the world's most elegant, beautiful and desirable cars. After World War II, Bentley badly needed a flagship model that would re-establish the marque in its own right. Bentley had been taken over by Rolls-Royce in 1931, and since then, Bentley models had been based on Rolls-Royce designs. They might have been a little sportier than the stately Rolls models, but Bentleys were never allowed to shine, because that might have undermined the Rolls-Royce claim to be the top car brand in the world.

In 1952, the Bentley R-Type was launched to replace the earlier Mark VI. Powered by a 4,566 cc straight-six engine, the R-Type saloon was spacious, luxurious and showed a fair turn of speed – the 0–60 mph time of 13.25 seconds seems sedate

BENTLEY R-TYPE CONTINENTAL 1952

ENGINE: 4,566 cc inline 6-cylinder

MAXIMUM POWER: 150 bhp at 4,500 rpm (est)

MAXIMUM TORQUE: not disclosed

MAXIMUM SPEED: 102 mph / 164 km/h

0–62 MPH ACCELERATION: 13.25 secs

TRANSMISSION: 4-speed manual

LENGTH: 199½ in / 5,067 mm

WIDTH: 70 in / 1,778 mm

HEIGHT: 66 in / 1,676 mm

WHEELBASE: 120 in / 3,048 mm

MANUFACTURE DATE: 1952–55

BRAKES: hydraulic (f), mechanical (r)

SUSPENSION: independent (f), semi-elliptic (r)

WHEELS: steel, 16 in

TIRES: 6.5x16 radial

saloon's, and significantly more aerodynamic. As a result, the Continental's performance was transformed. At that time, Bentley chose not to reveal the power output of its engines, but instead allowed the performance to tell the story. In this case, the top speed was increased to 115 mph / 185 km/h – at the time, an impressively high figure.

And the fortunate owners of a Continental enjoyed its performance in style. The cabin was awash with leather, wood and deep carpets, while, as might be expected from a Bentley, the quality of every component was top notch.

With its high cost, the Bentley R-Type Continental was never going to sell in huge numbers. In the mid-1950s, a small standard car such as a Morris Minor cost just under £600, less than a twelfth of the price of a Continental. In any case, the coachbuilding firm Mulliners could not have coped with large volumes. Of the 2,320 R-Type Bentleys produced, only around 200 were Continentals.

The R-Type Continental marked a renaissance for the Bentley marque. For the first time since the company had been taken over by Roll-Royce, a Bentley was more than a somewhat watered-down version of the group's main product. Once again, Bentley had become a genuine alternative to a Rolls-Royce.

by today's standards, but the car's top speed of 102 mph / 164 km/h was entirely respectable.

If the saloon cost a great deal of money in those days – £4,481 – that was nothing compared to the cost of a special coachbuilt two-door version produced by H.J. Mulliner. The R-Type Continental cost a massive £7,608. It was the first time that Bentley had used the name 'Continental', though it was to be by no means the last: this was the first of a long, honourable line of high-speed Grand Tourers that continues to this day.

The R-Type Continental had the same engine as the saloon, and indeed as the Rolls-Royce Silver Dawn, upon which the R-Type was based. But for the Continental, the compression ratio was raised, larger carburettors were installed, the inlet and exhaust manifolds were modified, and a close-ratio manual gearbox was specified in place of the saloon's auto box to ensure better acceleration. For good measure, a higher final drive ratio was adopted to allow for relaxed high-speed cruising.

As for the bodywork that Mulliner created, this was something truly special. While the front of the car was relatively conventional, the sloping rear was unique at the time. This was the world's first fastback design, in which the body sweeps straight down from the roofline to the bumper, with the rear window and the boot lid in a single unbroken plane.

But the sensuous, sweeping bodywork was more than just fabulously stylish. It was also considerably lighter than the

BMW Hydrogen 7

As concern for the environment increases, so does interest in hydrogen-powered cars. And the reason is simple: when hydrogen is burnt, the only emissions from the tailpipe are water vapour. This makes it potentially the perfect fuel. In developing the Hydrogen 7 model, BMW engineers set out to prove that hydrogen can realistically be used as a source of energy for a production car, and that the dream of sustainable mobility without using fossil-fuel resources and without impacting the earth's climate can become a reality.

However, there are major difficulties on the road to a hydrogen-fuelled future. Safety is certainly an issue: many people still associate hydrogen with the Hindenburg airship disaster, during which many lives were lost as the massive airship burst into flames shortly after landing in New Jersey in 1937. Another problem is the sheer cost of the technology. Some motor manufacturers are developing fuel-cell cars, in which hydrogen is chemically converted to produce electricity, which then in turn powers the vehicle. BMW's solution in its Hydrogen 7 vehicle is rather different, in that it directly burns the hydrogen, which is produced from water and renewable energy – wind, sun or hydropower – in place of petrol in an internal-combustion engine.

The V12 engine in the Hydrogen 7 is the same as the petrol unit in the BMW 7-Series saloons, though it has been modified to allow it to burn hydrogen as well as petrol, the driver switching from one fuel to the other using a button on the steering wheel. The hydrogen used is not a gas, so BMW insist there is no

danger of a Hindenburg-type accident. Instead the hydrogen is cooled to 487°F / 253°C to create liquid hydrogen, which is stored in a specially insulated tank, which contains enough of the fluid to run the car for around 125 miles / 201 km. A conventional petrol tank provides an additional 300 miles / 483 km range. According to BMW figures, the Hydrogen 7 engine produces 260 bhp and is capable of providing acceleration from 0 to 62 mph in 9.5 seconds and reaching an electronically limited top speed of 143 mph / 230 km/h.

Burning hydrogen directly is a far cheaper solution technologically than investing in fuel cells, but there is a payback: the Hydrogen 7, which is some 529 lb / 250 kg heavier than the standard 7-Series saloon, has a fuel consumption of around 17 mpg / 7.2 km/l on petrol and less than 5 mpg / 2.1 km/l on hydrogen. By comparison, the Honda FCX Clarity car returns more than 80 mpg / 34 km/l when operating in fuel-cell mode. However, the cost of developing fuel-cell technology and manufacturing it is so high that it's impossible to envisage its widespread use in the short or even medium term. It's also difficult to see how directly powered hydrogen cars can realistically be sold on a volume basis as there's currently no infrastructure allowing drivers to refuel. And again, the need to keep the hydrogen supercooled to ensure it remains in a liquid state will inevitably mean creating a refueling infrastructure that will be extremely costly.

BMW claims its Hydrogen 7 is the world's first production-ready hydrogen vehicle, and to prove its potential, it has leased 100 examples to prominent businessmen, politicians and media figures. But as the need to protect the environment grows, so pressure on manufacturers to find a no-emissions solution will increase. One day, it's possible that all cars on the road will be powered by hydrogen. And then people will be able to look back and remember the BMW Hydrogen 7 as having led the way.

BMW HYDROGEN 7 2007

ENGINE: 5,976 cc V12

MAXIMUM POWER: 260 bhp at 5,100 rpm

MAXIMUM TORQUE: 390 Nm at 4,300 rpm

MAXIMUM SPEED: 143 mph / 230 km/h

0–60 MPH ACCELERATION: 9.5 secs

TRANSMISSION: 6-speed automatic

LENGTH: 204 in / 5,180 mm

WIDTH: 74¼ in / 1,900 mm

HEIGHT: 58¾ in / 1,490 mm

WHEELBASE: 123¼ in / 3,130 mm

MANUFACTURE DATE: 2007–present

BRAKES: disc (f and r)

SUSPENSION: strut (f), multi-arm (r)

WHEELS: alloy, 19 in

TIRES: 245/45 R-19 (f), 275/40 R-19 (r)

BMW Z8

The BMW 507 Roadster of 1956 is reckoned by many to be one of the most beautiful cars ever conceived. BMW's designers decided to see if they could recreate a modern interpretation of that earlier car, and duly unveiled a Z09 concept car at the 1997 Tokyo Motor Show. It was so well received that it re-appeared at the 1998 Detroit Show, where once again the reaction was universally favourable, so BMW took the decision to put the car into production.

The production car, the BMW Z8 that appeared in 2000, had its engine at the front under a long, low bonnet, a cockpit set towards the rear of the car, tapered overhangs, and a low beltline – all reminiscent of the 507 – and its rounded, curvaceous style was very different to the more angular designs that were popular at the turn of the millenium. The original designer of the classic 507, Count Albrecht Goertz, was certainly impressed: 'If I were to design the 507 today, it would look like the Z8', he said.

The Z8 had a retro air, but the technology underneath the sensuous body was absolutely state of the art. Its 4,941 cc V8 engine produced a storming 394 bhp and drove the rear wheels through a six-speed transmission, while its suspension system – MacPherson struts at the front and a multi-link set up at the back

BMW Z8 2000

ENGINE: 4,941 cc V8

MAXIMUM POWER: 394 bhp at 6,600 rpm

MAXIMUM TORQUE: 492 Nm at 3,800 rpm

MAXIMUM SPEED: 155 mph / 249 km/h

0–60 MPH ACCELERATION: 4.3 secs

TRANSMISSION: 6-speed manual

LENGTH: 172¼ in / 4,374 mm

WIDTH: 72 in / 1,831 mm

HEIGHT: 52 in / 1,318 mm

WHEELBASE: 98½ in / 2,504 mm

MANUFACTURE DATE: 2000–03

BRAKES: disc (f and r)

SUSPENSION: MacPherson strut (f), multi-link (r)

WHEELS: alloy, 18 in

TIRES: 245/45 ZR-18 (f), 275/40 ZR-18 (r)

bodies were built and painted in one factory, the front and rear bumpers at another. The engine and transmission came from a third BMW plant. All the parts were then brought together to Munich, where the cars were virtually hand-built by craftsmen. In all, the Z8 took ten times longer to assemble than a normal BMW saloon.

In 2003, the year the Z8 went out of production, an even faster Alpina version was launched, with a five-speed automatic transmission in place of the standard six-speed manual. This was mated to a tuned 4.8-liter V8 that produced less power (375 bhp) but more torque (519 Nm instead of 492 Nm), for more relaxed cruising.

BMW had no trouble selling the Z8, despite its hefty £80,000 price tag, perhaps because the car gained worldwide publicity just before its official launch when it appeared, driven by Pierce Brosnan, in the 1999 James Bond movie *The World Is Not Enough.*

– was lifted off the M5 saloon, generally reckoned to be one of the best-handling cars in the world. Better still, the engine was set well back in the chassis to provide perfect 50:50 weight distribution.

The Z8's body was constructed in lightweight aluminium and it was mounted to an aluminium spaceframe that was both light and incredibly stiff, which gave the car superb performance: it accelerated from 0 to 60 mph in 4.3 seconds, from 0 to 100 mph in 10.5 seconds, and had an electronically limited top speed of 155 mph / 250 km/h. The Z8 was as quick as any Porsche or Ferrari, but in many ways far more civilized. For example, it had an infinitely variable electronically controlled valve timing system, and this ensured that at low speeds the car was as tractable and easy to drive as any BMW saloon.

The Z8 was a true convertible, with a powered soft top as standard, though every car was also offered with a body-coloured hardtop too. The cabin offered its occupants luxury and comfort levels of a high order. Electric windows, cruise control, a navigation system and climate control were all standard equipment. So although it promised supercar performance, the Z8 could also be used as a day-to-day car. It was a heady combination of speed and beauty, sophisticated modern technology and classic elegance.

Building the Z8 was a study in complicated logistics: the

Bugatti EB 16/4 Veyron

Many extravagant claims are made at motor shows, but none
were more radical than those made by Ferdinand Piech at the
Frankfurt Show in 1999. Standing in front of a concept called
the Bugatti 18/4 Veyron, the boss of the Volkswagen Group
(which by now owned Bugatti) said the car would go into
production by 2000. He also claimed it would have over 1,000
bhp, which would make it the most powerful production car
ever. And, just for good measure, he assured listeners that it
would also be the fastest and most expensive, too.

Amazingly, the car that was eventually produced in 2005 was
very similar to that original concept, though in the intervening
years, the W18 engine with three banks of six cylinders had
been amended to a W16 with four banks of four cylinders.
To boost the power to the magic 1,000 bhp mark, four
turbochargers were specified.

It was an incredible feat of engineering, though it came
to market five years later than Piech had promised because
of difficulties over cooling, aerodynamics and tires. Good
aerodynamics meant smooth airflow, but in order to get cooling
air to the engine, vents or ducts were required, and these
increased drag and lowered the top speed. The solution – to
give an example of the hurdles that had to be overcome – was
to give the Veyron ten different radiators: three for the engine,
two for the air conditioning, the others for the intercooler, engine
oil, transmission oil, differential oil and hydraulic oil. The problem
with the tires was that none existed that were capable of
carrying the weight of the Veyron at speeds of up to 250 mph /
402 km/h. The solution was found with the help of Michelin, who
created a special Pilot Sport tire especially for the Veyron.

Eventually, much hard work paid off, and a pre-production
prototype took to a test track and recorded 253 mph / 407 km/h.
This speed was possible not only because of the awesome
power of the engine but also because at higher speeds, above
137 mph / 220 km/h, the car comes alive – an adjustable
spoiler at the back is raised, a diffuser at the rear provides the
necessary downforce to maintain stability, and the hydraulic
dampers lower the car to reduce ground clearance. But to
achieve the very highest speeds, the driver has to use a special
key to put the car into High Speed Mode. It is this that allows the
ground clearance to be reduced still further, from the standard
5 in / 125 mm to just 2½ in / 65 mm, for the spoiler to retract,
and for the air diffusers to close to reduce aerodynamic drag.

So, the Veyron had fulfilled Piech's claim that it would be
the fastest car in the world – for good measure it was recorded
at an eye-watering 2.4 seconds for 0–60 mph acceleration –
and it produced 1,001 bhp, breaking the 1,000 bhp mark that
had been promised. All that was left was for the price to be
announced. Sure enough, the final promise was fulfilled: the
new car cost €1,000,000.

In fact, just about everything else about the Veyron is extreme,
too: its brakes are ventilated and drilled carbon rotors with

titanium calipers, but when even more stopping power is needed, the rear wing deploys to act as an extra air brake. It has four-wheel drive and a seven-speed transmission that can be driven in either manual or auto mode. It is created from aluminium panels fitted to a carbon fibre monocoque with an aluminium front subframe and a stainless-steel rear subframe.

The Bugatti Veyron is truly a unique machine. There is nothing else like it in the world and it's difficult to conceive that there will ever be anything like it again.

BUGATTI EB 16/4 VEYRON 2006

ENGINE: 7,993 cc W16

MAXIMUM POWER: 1,001 bhp at 6,000 rpm

MAXIMUM TORQUE: 1,250 Nm at 3,300 rpm

MAXIMUM SPEED: 253 mph / 407 km/h

0–60 MPH ACCELERATION: 2.4 secs

TRANSMISSION: 7-speed semi automatic

LENGTH: 175¾ in / 4,463 mm

WIDTH: 78¾ in / 1,999 mm

HEIGHT: 47¾ in / 1,212 mm

WHEELBASE: 106¾ / 2,710 mm

MANUFACTURE DATE: 2006–present

BRAKES: disc (f and r)

SUSPENSION: control arm (f and r)

WHEELS: alloy, 20 in (f), 21 in (r)

TIRES: 265/680 ZR500A (f), 365/710 ZR540A (r)

Bugatti EB110 SS

When Bugatti, one of the motor industry's most famous and revered names, was acquired by Italian businessman Romano Artioli in 1987, he announced ambitious plans to produce the most technically sophisticated supercar the world had ever seen. Artioli employed Marcello Gandini, who had designed the Lamborghini Countach, and Mauro Forghieri, one of the most famous racing car engineers, to head up the development team. Between them, they came up with a stunning mid-engined design powered by a 60-valve 3,449 cc V12 with four turbochargers to boost the power output to a peak of 560 bhp. That gave the new car, the Bugatti EB110, acceleration from 0 to 62mph in 4.5 seconds and a top speed of 213 mph / 343 km/h, which was absolutely outstanding in its day, and truly worthy of the Bugatti name. (Incidentally, the car was named after the company's founder, Ettore Bugatti – his initials plus the number of year's since his birth.)

The new car had a carbon-fibre monocoque chassis manufactured by the French aeronautics company Aerospatiale, which had learnt about the material in developing its rockets. This in itself set the EB110 apart from any car that had gone before – it was the first to use this construction technique. The body was composed of aluminium panels bonded to the monocoque and, unusually, it incorporated a glass panel over the engine so owners

BUGATTI EB110 SS 1992

ENGINE: 3,498 cc V12

MAXIMUM POWER: 603 bhp at 8,000 rpm

MAXIMUM TORQUE: 637 Nm at 4,200 rpm

MAXIMUM SPEED: 217 mph / 349 km/h

0–60 MPH ACCELERATION: 3.2 secs

TRANSMISSION: 6-speed manual

LENGTH: 157¾ in / 4,400 mm

WIDTH: 76½ in / 1,940 mm

HEIGHT: 44¼ in / 1,125 mm

WHEELBASE: 100½ in / 2,550 mm

MANUFACTURE DATE: 1992–95

BRAKES: disc (f and r)

SUSPENSION: double wishbone (f and r)

WHEELS: alloy, 18 in

TIRES: 245/40 ZR 18 (f), 325/30 ZR-18 (r)

could view the bespoke powerplant. Forward-lifting scissor doors ensured a small piece of theatre every time the car was parked, though on the road, the view most people would have had was of the back of the car, with its speed-sensitive rear wing, which rose at higher velocities. To ensure all that power could be evenly transmitted to the road, the EB110 was fitted with a permanent four-wheel drive system that directed 27 per cent of the power to the front and the remaining 73 per cent to the rear. Massive stopping power was provided by Brembo brakes, while the huge tires were specially made by Michelin. For good measure, French oil company Elf provided a unique organic lubricant, which had originally been developed for the Benetton F1 team.

The EB110 was launched in 1991, but just a year later, it was improved still further in the EB110 SS (Supersport) model, which was was introduced at a price of £281,000. This car was lighter and produced even more power (up to 603 bhp). The result was a slightly higher top speed of 217 mph / 349 km/h, but markedly quicker acceleration through the six-speed gearbox: 0–62 mph now took a mere 3.2 seconds. The Supersport retained the EB110's original four-wheel drive system, but the aluminium bonnet, engine cover and venturi undertray were replaced with even lighter carbon-fibre panels, the wheels were changed from aluminium alloy to magnesium, and the moveable rear wing became a fixed unit. The extra power had been squeezed out of the engine by installing bigger injectors and a revized electronic control unit, and by removing two of the energy-sapping catalytic converters in the exhaust. On the open road, the EB110 SS was even more extreme that the EB110. Indeed, it was so outstanding that F1 champion Michael Schumacher bought one for himself

and kept it for many years, even after he moved to become a Ferrari driver.

Sadly, Artioli's dream wouldn't last long. He over-extended himself by developing a four-door EB112 model, and at the same time, bought the British company Lotus. Bankruptcy followed in 1995, which brought to an end the production of the mighty EB110 after only 139 had been built. Volkswagen Group bought the rights to the Bugatti marquee in the late 1990s, but the original EB110 remains one of the rarest and finest supercars ever made.

Bugatti Type 35

When he was just 19, Ettore Bugatti designed his first car, which won a gold medal at the 1901 Milan trade fair. During the early years of the 20th century, he build a handful of models, but it was not until after World War 1 that he started to make a real name for himself.

The breakthrough came in 1921, when five Bugattis entered the Voiturette Grand Prix at Brescia and took the first four places. In the following years, private entrants bought his cars as Bugatti became known as the top manufacturer of racing cars in Europe. Unfortunately, the period of success didn't last long: Fiat and others introduced supercharging and the Bugattis became uncompetitive.

This led Ettore Bugatti to create the car that made him a legend and his Bugatti marque as a world leader. To replace the earlier Type 30 and Type 32 cars, he introduced the Type 35, for which he further developed the 2.0-liter eight-cylinder in-line engine that had been used in earlier cars by adopting five main bearings instead of three. This allowed the engine to be revved harder, up to 6,000 rpm, and for the power output to increase to 95 bhp. Normally, this might not have been enough power to be truly competitive on the racetrack, but Bugatti had created a car that was light, nimble and handled beautifully. It

was also extremely reliable, which in the early days of racing was an extraordinary achievement.

A four-speed manual gearbox was used on the Type 35. The suspension was basic leaf springs front and rear, but there were other innovations, such as cable-operated drum brakes and a hollow front axle to reduce unsprung weight and improve the handling. The Type 35 also featured innovative cast-alloy wheels that had the drum brakes integrated within them, so that as the wheel was removed, so were the brakes. The car had an elegant aluminium body with a distinctive horseshoe-shaped radiator at the front – the first occurence of what has since become a Bugatti trademark.

The Type 35's first appearance was at the 1924 Lyons Grand Prix, where tire problems led to the car being retired. At the next Grand Prix, in San Sebastian, wider tires were fitted and the car took second place. After that there was no stopping the Type 35, which won over 2,000 races in the next five years.

As time went on, Bugatti had to continue developing the Type 35 to ensure it remained competitive, but he also introduced other models of the Type 35. The 35A, launched in 1925, was the first of these. It was never really intended for racing and had a simplified engine to decrease maintenance requirements.

Then, in 1926, came the 35C, which was fitted with a Rootes supercharger that boosted the power output to 128 bhp and ensured Bugattis remained at the front of the GR grids. The 35T, a special model intended to compete in the Targa Florio, was launched same year. Its capacity was increased to 2.3 liters, which made it ineligible for Grands Prix, where capacity was still limited to 2.0 liters. However, when GP regulations changed, Bugatti introduced the most powerful Type 35 of all, the 35B. It had the same 2.3-liter engine as the 35T but had a supercharger bolted to it to raise peak output to 138 bhp.

In all, around 340 Bugatti Type 35 cars were built between 1924 and 1929. Quite apart from creating Bugatti's reputation, the Type 35 can fairly claim to be the most successful racing car of all time, not only because of the sheer number of victories it won – although 2,000 is undoubtedly impressive – but also because they came in so many different areas of motorsport, from Grands Prix to endurance races and even hillclimbs and sprints.

BUGATTI TYPE 35 1924

ENGINE: 1,991 cc inline 8-cylinder

MAXIMUM POWER: 95 bhp at 6,000 rpm

MAXIMUM TORQUE: not quoted

MAXIMUM SPEED: 118 mph / 190 km/h

0–60 MPH ACCELERATION: not disclosed

TRANSMISSION: 4-speed manual

LENGTH: 145¾ in / 3,700 mm

WIDTH: 52 in / 1,320 mm

HEIGHT: 38¾ in / 985 mm

WHEELBASE: 94½ in / 2,400 mm

MANUFACTURE DATE: 1924–29

BRAKES: drum (f and r)

SUSPENSION: rigid axle (f), live axle (r)

WHEELS: alloy

TIRES: 27x4.40 (f and r)

Cadillac Allante

The Cadillac Allante was unique in the history of both the motor industry and the commercial aviation industry. Its body was built in Italy, near Turin, then air freighted by Lufthansa to the Hamtramck, Michigan, in the USA, where final assembly took place. It may seem difficult to fathom why anyone would choose such a convoluted and expensive production process, but in 1987, Cadillac wanted to regain its position at the pinnacle of the US premium luxury market and felt that an association with Pininfarina – designer of the majority of post-war Ferraris – could help it in that quest.

The specification of the car looked encouraging. Pininfarina had created an elegant two-seater convertible design and a suitably upmarket interior for the car. It was a full convertible, with an integral folding softtop, though a detachable aluminium hardtop was also supplied with the car. Despite, or perhaps because of, its production process – it was described as having a 9,000 mile production line – every single Allante was track tested and evaluated by Cadillac technicians, who had to sign off each unit to ensure it met Cadillac's high quality standards. And as a mark of the company's confidence in the vehicle, a seven-year warranty was offered on the car.

Unusually for an American car of that time, it was front-wheel drive, which lead to some problems with torque steer in the early days, though traction control was added later to improve matters somewhat. Crucially, all the Allante's main competitors

– the Mercedes-Benz SL, Jaguar XJ-S and Porsche 911, for example – were rear-wheel drive designs.

At launch, the Allante was powered by GM's 4.1-liter V8, which, despite its size, its multi-port fuel injection, high-flow cylinder head and tuned inlet manifold, produced only 170 bhp at 4,300 rpm and 319 Nm of torque at 3,200 rpm. It was mounted transversely and mated to a four-speed automatic transmission. Suspension was fully independent, with MacPherson struts at the front and a transverse leaf spring at the rear, and four-wheel disc brakes were standard, along with ABS.

Though the main body and frame of the Allante were constructed from galvanized steel, the bonnet and boot were aluminium to save weight. However, this was not enough to conceal the biggest disappointment about the Allante – it was simply not very quick. Official figures state that 0–60 mph acceleration took 9.3 seconds, but early road tests suggested 10 seconds was nearer the mark, and its top speed was an uninspiring 119 mph / 192 km/h. Other disappointments were the Allante's weird electronic digital instrumentation and the fact that the folding roof was a wholly manual operation. At the price of the Allante, customers expected a powered unit.

Cadillac did its best to rectify the shortcomings, switching to analogue instruments in 1988 and fitting a 200 bhp 4.5-liter V8 with a more aggressive final drive ratio to improve the 0–60 mph acceleration to 8.5 seconds. Later, in 1993, the new 4,565 cc

Northstar V8 was adopted, pushing 295 bhp through a new four-speed automatic box. The Allante's 0–60 mph acceleration was now down to under seven seconds and the car was transformed with a new rear suspension, improved traction control and speed-sensitive steering.

By this time, the Allante was the car it should have been at the start – it had the performance, the handling and the image to compete with the best in the world. Sadly, it was too late. When Cadillac launched the Allante in 1987 it was by far the company's most expensive product, with a list price of $54,700 at a time when the Cadillac De Ville cost around $21,000. Even so, the company planned to sell between 6,000 and 8,000 Allantes a year. But sales had been slow from day one, and the last Allante travelled on that air bridge between Italy and the USA in July 1993, by which time 21,430 had been manufactured, an average of just over 3,000 a year.

CADILLAC ALLANTE 1993

ENGINE: 4,565 cc V8

MAXIMUM POWER: 295 bhp at 5,600 rpm

MAXIMUM TORQUE: 393 Nm at 4,400 rpm

MAXIMUM SPEED: 145 mph / 233 km/h

0–60 MPH ACCELERATION: 6.7 secs

TRANSMISSION: 4-speed automatic

LENGTH: 178¾ in / 4,539 mm

WIDTH: 73½ in / 1,864 mm

HEIGHT: 51½ in / 1,308 mm

WHEELBASE: 99½ in / 2,525 mm

MANUFACTURE DATE: 1987–93

BRAKES: disc (f and r)

SUSPENSION: independent MacPherson strut (f and r)

WHEELS: alloy, 16 in

TIRES: 225/55 VR-16 (f and r)

Cadillac Eldorado Convertible

Eldorado is the mythical City of Gold that enticed thousands of European sailors and explorers to cross the Atlantic in search of treasures in South America. It's also the Cadillac model that, more than any other, represents the hopes and aspirations of the late 1950s. The very first Cadillac Eldorado was a concept car shown at GM's Motorama Show in the ballroom of a swanky New York hotel, an annual event at which all GM's brands put their latest models and their ideas for the future on display. (First staged in 1949, Motorama was the USA's first major motor show.)

It was an enormous convertible vehicle, 220¾ in / 5,610 mm long and 78¾ in / 2,000 mm wide, and available in only four special colours – red, white, yellow and blue, with either a white or black folding convertible roof. It was powered by GM's 5,424 cc V8 that produced a relatively modest 210 bhp.

Though billed as a concept car, the 1953 Eldorado was for sale – to those with pockets deep enough to afford its high price tag. At $7,750, it was easily the most expensive Cadillac on the market at the time. Nevertheless, more than 500 were sold and the Eldorado became a mainstream model, still at the top end of the price range, but slightly more affordable and with a less opulent specification than the first Motorama cars.

As the 1950s progressed, the Cadillac Eldorado was refined and improved. But what made it especially iconic was its use of extravagant rear fins. They were first used on the 1955 Eldorado Brougham Town Car and over the next few years they became bigger, higher and more extreme.

And so, by the time the 1959 Cadillac Eldorado was launched, with its larger and far more powerful engine, the Caddy flagship became a symbol for the new jet-age era that worshipped both speed and modernity.

Under the massive bonnet was a 6,396 cc V8 producing 345 bhp and providing a top speed of 120 mph / 193 km/h despite its enormous bulk and 5,000 lb / 2,268 kg weight. The engine was mated to a three-speed Hydra-Matic automatic transmission that drove the rear wheels via a 2.94:1 rear axle gear ratio.

This was a car built for comfort and cruising rather than out-and-out performance, and although it was available as both a coupé and a convertible, it is the convertible that represents that classic era of rock and roll, drive-in diners and drive-in movies.

With its jutting rear fins, acres of chrome, quad headlights and rather bulbous bodywork, the 1959 Cadillac Eldorado cannot be described as beautiful, elegant or sophisticated. It wasn't even

that distinctive mechanically by 1959, because its triple carburettor engine was by then available as an option on every other Cadillac in the range, whereas previously, the rest of the Cadillac range had had to make do with a lower-powered single-carburettor engine.

Yet it is the 1959 Eldorado that has gained near-iconic status as the years have passed. Just 1,320 convertibles and 975 coupés were built during that famous model year, and sold at a factory price of $7,401 – considerably less than the original 1953 model. The specification included air suspension and electric windows with air conditioning as an added-cost option.

Today, at auction, the best examples of a Cadillac Eldorado are reaching around $230,000, a clear sign that the iconic finned monster remains one of the most potent symbols of an era of excitement, extravagance and excess. It may not have been pretty, it may even have been rather tasteless, but it was certainly flamboyant, and it was exactly what the public wanted then and what still gets car enthusiasts' hearts beating faster today.

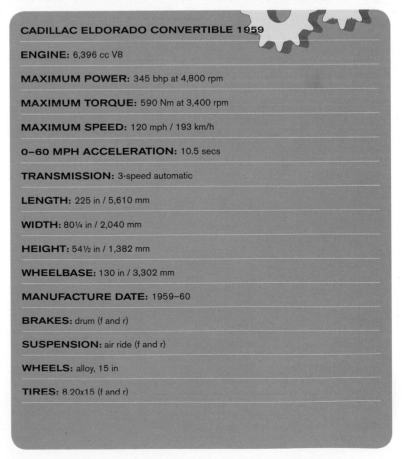

CADILLAC ELDORADO CONVERTIBLE 1959

ENGINE: 6,396 cc V8

MAXIMUM POWER: 345 bhp at 4,800 rpm

MAXIMUM TORQUE: 590 Nm at 3,400 rpm

MAXIMUM SPEED: 120 mph / 193 km/h

0–60 MPH ACCELERATION: 10.5 secs

TRANSMISSION: 3-speed automatic

LENGTH: 225 in / 5,610 mm

WIDTH: 80¼ in / 2,040 mm

HEIGHT: 54½ in / 1,382 mm

WHEELBASE: 130 in / 3,302 mm

MANUFACTURE DATE: 1959–60

BRAKES: drum (f and r)

SUSPENSION: air ride (f and r)

WHEELS: alloy, 15 in

TIRES: 8.20x15 (f and r)

Cadillac XLR-V

Cadillac launched the XLR two-seater sports car in 2003 in an attempt to prove that it really could compete on an equal footing with the best that the European and Japanese car manufacturers could produce. Its sharply angular style was derived from the razor lines of the Evoq concept that was first shown at the Detroit Motor Show in 1999 and the Vizion shown in 2001. By the time the car had been put into production in 2003, the extreme lines of these concept cars had been toned down, but the XLR was still a highly distinctive, dynamic design that was claimed at the time to be the lightest and most powerful vehicle in its class.

It shares its platform with the Corvette but it's a very different sort of car. While the Corvette is designed for out-and-out performance, the XLR is more of a grand tourer, more refined and more relaxed than the uncompromising Corvette. So while the Corvette's V8 was pushing out 436 bhp, the Cadillac XLR's Northstar V8 was tuned to produce 320 bhp, which was more than sufficient to provide good performance – 0–60 mph in 5.9 seconds and an electronically limited top speed of 155 mph / 249 km/h – but not the sort of output that encourages laying

rubber on the road from standing starts. Not surprisingly then, while there were Cadillac fans who appreciated the XLR's elegant styling and cosseting cabin, others dismissed the XLR as a poor substitute for other, 'proper' sports cars.

In February 2005, Cadillac chose the Super Bowl to reveal the higher performance XLR-V for the first time and to provide an answer to those seeking better performance. Like the standard XLR, the XLR-V is a two-seater, retractable hardtop convertible, offering distinctive styling with what Cadillac describes as 'contemporary luxury' and rear-wheel-drive performance.

But the XLR-V is rather different to the standard XLR in that it's fitted with a supercharged Northstar engine 4,371 cc V8 producing 440 bhp at 6,400 rpm and 576 Nm of torque at 3,600 rpm. The supercharger and four intercoolers are all integrated within the inlet manifold – an elegant packaging job.

For optimum weight distribution, its six-speed automatic transmission is mounted on the rear transaxle and the XLR-V is fitted with larger 19-inch wheels, more powerful brakes borrowed from the Corvette, and an uprated suspension system. It uses

double wishbones with upper and lower control arms, transverse leaf springs and monotube shock absorbers at the front and rear, and it also features Magnetic Ride Control (MR) system, which instantly adapts the dampers according to the way in which the car is being driven, firming up the ride when the car is being pushed hard into a corner.

The engine is one of the most powerful ever fitted to a Cadillac, and the aggressive torque curve produced by the supercharged engine gives the XLR-V 0–60 mph acceleration in 4.9 seconds, according to Cadillac – considerably quicker than the standard XLR. In fact, Cadillac's figures understate the actual performance, according to some tests, which quote the car's acceleration time as 4.6 seconds from 0 to 60 mph and 11.3 seconds from 0 to 100 mph.

At a base price of $98,000 in 2006, when the XLR-V actually went on sale, the flagship Cadillac is not cheap. But for the money, it does provide outstanding performance, together with high levels of comfort and technology. The cabin boasts hand-cut leather and upmarket wood and metallic trims, and a specification that includes a head-up display, adaptive cruise control that maintains the car a set distance from the vehicle in front, and an Adaptive Forward Lighting system, a first-time application on a Cadillac, which automatically adjusts headlamp direction up to 15 degrees for improved night driving vision.

For the ultimate in Cadillac performance, the CTS-V, with its 556 bhp supercharged V8 and blistering 0–60 mph time of 3.9 seconds might seem the obvious choice, particularly as it costs some $40,000 less than the XLR-V.

But the XLR-V, with its combination of effortless performance, luxurious interior and power retractable hardtop makes a strong case for itself despite its price.

CADILLAC XLR-V

ENGINE 4,371 cc V8

MAXIMUM POWER: 440 bhp at 6,400 rpm

MAXIMUM TORQUE: 576 Nm at 3,600 rpm

MAXIMUM SPEED: 155 mph / 259 km/h

0–60 MPH ACCELERATION: 4.9 secs

TRANSMISSION: 6-speed automatic

LENGTH: 177¾ in / 4,514 mm

WIDTH: 72¼ in / 1,836 mm

HEIGHT: 50½ in / 1,280 mm

WHEELBASE: 105¾ in / 2,685 mm

MANUFACTURE DATE: 2006–present

BRAKES: disc (f and r)

SUSPENSION: double wishbone (f and r)

WHEELS: alloy, 19 in

TIRES: 235/50 WR-18 (f and r)

Chevrolet Camaro Z28

In 1967, Chevrolet was looking for a muscle car that could challenge the all-conquering Ford Mustang in the Trans-Am race series. To be eligible, the car would have to be based on a production vehicle with at least 1,000 street-legal examples sold, and its engine would have to be restricted to no more than 305 cu in in capacity. Chevvy already had 5,359 cc and 4,638 cc V8s, and by putting a 283 crankshaft into the 5,359 cc block it created a 4,949 cc unit, well within the Trans-Am regulations. But to make up for the power lost in reducing the capacity, Chevrolet's engineers then specified a Holley four-barrel carburettor, specially tuned inlet manifold, a reprofiled camshaft and other modifications to give the new engine an official output of 290 bhp at 5,800 rpm and 393 Nm of torque at 4,200 rpm. In fact, the power output was considerably more and could have been close to 400 bhp, depending on which inlet and exhaust manifolds were used.

The Camaro, a new model that shared the GM F-Body platform with the Pontiac Firebird, was chosen as the production model, but bizarrely, Chevrolet never advertized what became known as the Z28 version. Those in the know had to go to a dealership and order a base Camaro and then specify the Z28 package from a long list of options. This then transformed a fairly ordinary vehicle into one of the great muscle cars of the 1960s. It gained not only the 4,949 cc engine but also wider tires on lightweight Corvette alloy wheels, disc brakes, a quicker ratio steering rack, upgraded radiator and what was described as the F-41 suspension package – basically firmer coil springs and upgraded shock absorbers. There was no choice over the transmission, as only a four-speed Muncie manual was available.

The total cost of the Z28 package was $2,966 – just $500 more than the base six-cylinder Camaro. For this, buyers didn't even get any Z28 badges (they were first introduced in 1968), merely wide racing stripes on the bonnet and bootlid. A rear bootlid spoiler was available as an option for those wanting to make more of a visual statement. A further popular option was the

RS package, which included hidden headlamps and revised taillamps. Although the Camaro was offered as both a coupé and a convertible, the Z28 package was only ever made available on the coupé. Despite the very existence of the Z28 options package being hidden way down in the small print, 602 of the 220,000 Camaros sold in 1967 were prime examples of America's latest muscle car. It seems that Chevrolet got round the Trans-Am 1,000 homologation number by homologating the 350 cu in Camaro under FIA Group I rules and then qualifying the base vehicle with Z28 option under Group II rules.

The following year, some changes were made to the specification. These later Z28 cars are recognizable by

their raised cowl induction hoods. Gradually more people got to hear of the availability of the Z28, and 7,199 were sold in 1968 and 20,302 in 1968. Amazingly, GM applied the same warranty to the Z28 as it did to the rest of the Camaro range – two years and 24,000 miles for the car as a whole and five years and 50,000 miles for the powertrain.

On the Trans-Am scene, the Camaro was a near-instant success. GM didn't have an official factory team but instead lent its support to Roger Penske's semi-official team. Driving for Penske, Mark Donohue took the title in both 1968 and 1969 and his successes on the track substantially drove up sales of the Camaro in showrooms right across the USA.

CHEVROLET CAMARO Z28 1967

ENGINE: 4,958 cc V8

MAXIMUM POWER: 290 bhp at 5,800 rpm

MAXIMUM TORQUE: 393 Nm at 4,200 rpm

MAXIMUM SPEED: 140 mph / 241 km/h

0–60 MPH ACCELERATION: 6.9 secs

TRANSMISSION: 4-speed manual

LENGTH: 185 in / 4,700 mm

WIDTH: 72½ in / 1,840 mm

HEIGHT: 51¼ in / 1,300 mm

WHEELBASE: 108 in / 2,746 mm

MANUFACTURE DATE: 1967–69

BRAKES: discs (f), drums (r)

SUSPENSION: independent A-arm (f), semi-elliptic leaf spring (r)

WHEELS: steel, 14 in

TIRES: 7.35x14 (f and r)

Chevrolet Corvette Sting Ray

The first Chevrolet Corvette was launched in 1953 and over the years its combination of style and power ensured that it was not only a very popular element in the General Motors range, but also a very profitable one for the company.

Ten years after its launch, however, it was clear that the Corvette needed attention. By 1962, although it certainly wasn't lacking in terms of power, it struggled to compete with a new generation of European sports cars, which had far more sophisticated chassis and suspension arrangements, and which therefore rode and handled much better than the Corvette.

GM's response was already in preparation: during 1961, GM's styling chief, Bill Mitchell, had created a concept car called the Mako Shark – his own idea of the direction in which Corvette should be heading. It was aggressive in appearance but with smooth, sleek and aerodynamic lines – just like a shark, in fact. It was also a closed-top coupé design, with a split rear window with deeply curved glass panels. Until then, all Corvettes had been convertibles, so the Mako Shark offered the potential for broadening the appeal of the model.

The Mako Shark was accepted as the basis for a new generation of Corvettes, which, to maintain the deep-sea theme, was called the Corvette Sting Ray. Importantly, the Sting Ray wasn't just a smart new body over the old mechanicals. A whole new chassis was designed, with a shorter wheelbase, front suspension of unequal-length upper and lower arms with coil springs, and fully independent rear suspension consisting of control arms, shock absorbers and a transverse leaf spring fitted between the rear differential and each rear wheel.

Buyers could choose between four versions of the 327 cu in, 5,359 cc V8 that had been introduced the year before. The base model produced 250 bhp, while with different carburettors fitted, this output could be boosted to 300 bhp or 340 bhp. The final option was a 360 bhp fuel-injected version, though this was expensive ($480 extra) and needed frequent servicing to keep it in tune. It produced its peak power at 6,000 rpm and also offered a healthy 477 Nm of torque at 4,000 rpm, more than enough to offer 0–60 mph acceleration in 5.9 seconds, 0–100 mph in 14.5 seconds and a top speed of 142 mph / 229 km/h.

Whichever engine option was chosen, it was mated to either a three-speed manual, a four-speed Borg-Warner manual or a three-speed Powerglide auto box.

The Corvette Sting Ray was an instant success: more than 21,000 were sold in 1963 alone, at prices starting at $4,037 for the convertible and $4,257 for the coupé. In many ways this was one of the most technically advanced cars on the American market at the time: it was the first to use fibreglass plastic body panels, its V8 engine provided great levels of performance, and even if its independent suspension wasn't as sophisticated as that fitted to the Jaguar E-Type, it still represented a major step forward.

The Sting Ray stayed in production until 1967 and was developed and improved each year. For example, the split rear glass remained for only one year before being changed for a single glass unit; in 1965, disc brakes were adopted and the 396 cu in 'Big Block' V8 was offered, and this engine was later bored out to 427 cu in in 1966. This 6,974cc version is one of the most collectable today.

Rarest of all the first-generation Sting Rays is the L-88, a version of the 427 aimed at the racing fraternity. Bored out to 6,997 cc, it produced 550 bhp at 6,200 rpm and a stunning 637

Nm or torque at 5,200 rpm. Only 20 of these 170 mph / 274 km/h beasts were sold.

The L-88 may be the most extreme Sting Ray, but any Sting Ray is a highly desirable car. Some will argue that the 1967 models were the best, while others will insist that the 1963 version with the split rear window is the real classic, but every model is a great American sports car.

CHEVROLET CORVETTE STING RAY 1963

ENGINE: 5,359 cc V8

MAXIMUM POWER: 360 bhp at 6,000 rpm

MAXIMUM TORQUE: 477 Nm at 4,000 rpm

MAXIMUM SPEED: 142 mph / 229 km/h

0–60 MPH ACCELERATION: 5.9 secs

TRANSMISSION: 4-speed manual

LENGTH: 175¼ in / 4,453 mm

WIDTH: 69½ in / 1,768 mm

HEIGHT: 50 in / 1,265 mm

WHEELBASE: 98 in / 2,489 mm

MANUFACTURE DATE: 1963–67

BRAKES: drum (f and r)

SUSPENSION: independent wishbone (f), independent trailing arm (r)

WHEELS: alloy, 15 in

TIRES: 6.70x15 (f and r)

Citroën SM

CITROËN SM 1970

ENGINE: 2,670 cc V6

MAXIMUM POWER: 170 bhp at 5,500 rpm

MAXIMUM TORQUE: 233 Nm at 4,000 rpm

MAXIMUM SPEED: 142 mph / 229 km/h

0–60 MPH ACCELERATION: 8.9 secs

TRANSMISSION: 5-speed manual

LENGTH: 192½ in / 4,892 mm

WIDTH: 72¼ in / 1,836 mm

HEIGHT: 52 in / 1,321 mm

WHEELBASE: 117 in / 2,946 mm

MANUFACTURE DATE: 1970–75

BRAKES: disc (f and r)

SUSPENSION: independent wishbone (f), independent trailing arm (r)

WHEELS: steel, 15 in

TIRES: 205/70 VR-15 (f and r)

The French car manufacturer Citroën has never been afraid to innovate. It was the first to volume-produce a front-wheel drive in its incredibly advanced Traction Avant model of 1933. The Traction Avant also saw the first use of monocoque construction (all earlier cars had a body bolted onto a separate chassis). And because some people were nervous about the strength of this new monocoque construction technique, founder Andre Citroën became the very first car maker to conduct any sort of crash testing: he pushed Traction Avant models off a cliff then checked to see how much damage had been caused. Later, in 1955, Citroën launched the futuristic DS model, with a high-pressure hydraulic system that powered both its brakes and its suspension.

So if any manufacturer was going to produce a high-powered sports coupé, it would be Citroën. The problem was that Citroën's own four-cylinder engines, aimed squarely at the mass market, just weren't up to the job. However, when Citroën took over Italian sports car manufacturer Maserati in 1968, the concept suddenly became a reality.

Maserati adapted its existing V8 to create an all-new 170 bhp V6 for the Citroën SM and took the opportunity to create another higher-powered version of this new V6 for its own mid-engined Merak model, which produced 190 bhp (later increasing to 220 bhp). The new V6 was mounted longitudinally and mated to a five-speed manual gearbox in the sleek GT saloon that Citroën designed, styled on similar lines to the DS model but with sharper angles, a lower nose and a sloped roof incorporating a rear

hatchback. The styling was the work of Jacques Charreton and Robert Operon, who between them created a timeless classic.

Uniquely, the SM sported six headlamps at the front, which were not only height adjustable but also swivelling, to 'look round corners' as the steering wheel was turned. The steering wheel itself was typically Citroën: a single-spoke design incorporating column stalks that moved with the wheel as it was adjusted for reach.

Although 170 bhp may not sound much today, it was far more power than most mainstream cars produced in 1970, and it was more than enough to provide a top speed of 142 mph / 229 km/h. Better still, it was performance potential that really could be put to good use because the SM carried over from the DS an all-independent suspension system powered hydraulically by engine-drive pumps, and thanks to this advanced hydropneumatic suspension, the SM soaked up even the roughest of road surfaces. It was truly a revelation.

The SM drove like no other car on the market, thanks to just two turns lock-to-lock in its ultra-quick steering. Its super-sensitive brake pedal operated on four disc brakes and stood the car on its nose if pressed too sharply. Yet this did nothing

to put off a plethora of celebrities – including Soviet premier Leonid Brezhnev, F1 driver Mike Hailwood and Dutch football superstar Johan Cruyff – who queued up to take delivery of the new sensation.

The Citroën SM stayed in production until 1975, during which time various improvements were made. The triple carburettors were replaced by a fuel-injection system that boosted output to 178 bhp, and later, a 3.0-liter 180 bhp version was offered, combined with a three-speed Borg-Warner automatic gearbox.

Sadly the SM's high performance came at the expense of high fuel consumption and the 1973–4 Oil Crisis made it virtually unsellable, though production wasn't actually stopped until 1975, when Citroën was taken over by Peugeot.

Shadows of the SM could still be seen in the design of the later Citroën CX and much of its engineering soldiered on in the Maserati Merak and Khamsin. But Citroën has never attempted such an outrageous car since, and nor has any other mainstream manufacturer. As a combination of space-age styling, state-of-the-art engineering, world-class aerodynamics and stunning performance, the SM was truly unique.

De Lorean DMC-12

The DeLorean DMC-12, designed by Giorgio Giugiaro, was supposedly the recipient of massive engineering development resources and was intended to be modern, radical, technically advanced and premium priced. What it turned out to be was a good-looking sports coupé that was ill-developed, underpowered, poorly built and late coming to market. Given that about the only goal set for it that held good was its high price – and indeed that doubled – it's no wonder that *Time* magazine voted it one of the 50 Worst Cars Of All Time.

The DeLorean project had started off with such high hopes. John Z DeLorean was a sharp-dressing automotive executive with a shining career at GM behind him – he had developed both the Pontiac GTO and the Firebird in his time. He had persuaded the British Government to provide grants for a new factory in Northern Ireland and had commissioned from Giugiaro a derivative of his Tapiro concept car design of 1970. What made the gullwinged two-seater so extraordinary was not just its sharp lines, reminiscent of the Lotus Esprit, but that its body panels were all constructed from unpainted stainless steel. The idea was that it wouldn't need painting and minor scratches and blemishes wouldn't show.

The DMC-12 (DMC was DeLorean Motor Company and the 12 referred to the planned list price of $12,000 in the USA, expected to be its biggest market) was powered by an all-alloy 2,849 cc V6 then in use in Peugeot, Renault and Volvo models.

Either five-speed manual or three-speed automatic transmission was available. DeLorean planned a car with about 200 bhp, but the engine he settled upon was good for only about 170 bhp. Worse, emissions regulations in the USA meant that its output had to be reduced to 130 bhp, and this resulted in woeful performance: 0–60 mph took more than 10 seconds and the top speed was only about 110 mph / 177 km/h. The lack of performance was all the more disappointing because the car had a sophisticated suspension system derived from the Lotus Esprit, with double wishbones at the front and a multi-link arrangement at the rear.

But if the performance was unimpressive, the price of the DMC-12 was a real shock. Despite that target price of $12,000, it came to market, three years late, with a price tag of $25,000, or $25,650 for the automatic version. Even so, the early hype was such that many buyers paid premiums of some $10,000 extra just to get their hands on one of the first cars in 1981. Little did they know that by the end of 1982, DeLorean would be bankrupt, the factory would be closed and thousands of unsold cars would be flooding the market at prices well below list.

The British Government had advanced loans of around £85,000,000 to get production started near Belfast, where unemployment was high. But, fearing there had been some financial mismanagement, it put the plant into administration in October 1982. Just one week earlier, federal drug agents had arrested DeLorean in a Los Angeles motel, where he was allegedly negotiating a drugs deal. Though he was eventually acquitted on the grounds of entrapment, the DeLorean car business was at an end.

John DeLorean's legal problems were not over, however. A Michigan Grand Jury started investigating the whereabouts of $17,650,000 that had disappeared from the company and that was assumed to be in Swiss bank accounts. DeLorean was acquitted for lack of proof, but he didn't pay his $150,000 lawyer's fees and never returned to Michigan state.

Only 8,583 cars had been built by the time the plant was closed, which happened too soon for either the car or the company to benefit from the worldwide publicity the DMC-12 derived from being showcased in the *Back To The Future* movies.

DE LOREAN DMC-12 1981

ENGINE: 2,849 cc V6

MAXIMUM POWER: 130 bhp at 5,500 rpm

MAXIMUM TORQUE: 208 Nm at 2,750 rpm

MAXIMUM SPEED: 110 mph / 177 km/h

0–60 MPH ACCELERATION: 10.5 secs

TRANSMISSION: 5-speed manual or 3-speed automatic

LENGTH: 168 in / 4,267 mm

WIDTH: 78¼ in / 1,990 mm

HEIGHT: 45 in / 1,140 mm

WHEELBASE: 94¾ in / 2,408 mm

MANUFACTURE DATE: 1981–82

BRAKES: disc (f and r)

SUSPENSION: independent coil spring (f), independent trailing arm (r)

WHEELS: alloy, 14 in (f), 15 in (r)

TIRES: 195/60 HR-14 (f), 235/60 HR-15 (r)

Ferrari 246 GT Dino

When first launched at the Turin Motor Show in 1968, the 206GT Dino on Ferrari's stand had neither a Ferrari badge nor the famous Prancing Horse logo. It also lacked the 12-cylinder engine for which Ferrari was famous, and instead had a 2.0-liter V6 mounted behind the driver. But it was still very much a Ferrari, and indeed it bears the name of

Enzo Ferrari's only legitimate son, who had tragically died from kidney disease at the age of just 24. It was also the model that permitted the company to greatly increase its production by offering a new, smaller and lighter car that would widen the marque's appeal without offending the Ferrari purists, who would never consider any model without a V12 under its bonnet.

In fact, the Dino was one of the company's most significant models of all, as not only did it boost production volumes but it also brought Ferrari closer to the giant Fiat conglomerate, which was eventually to take a majority shareholding in the company. Ferrari wanted to race in Formula 2, but new regulations meant that it had to built at least 500 examples of the 1.6-liter V6 engine in order to comply, so a deal was struck with Fiat under which Ferrari would design a V6 engine and Fiat would manufacture it in large enough volumes to homologate the unit for racing, provide engines for a new small Ferrari model and allow Fiat itself to create its own sports car, the front-engined Fiat Dino.

Although the racecars had the 1.6-liter engine, early production cars used a 2.0-liter engine, and these were fitted to the first run of Dino Ferraris, the 206GT. Only around 150 of these were made before the engine was bored out to 2.4 liters, and the classic 246GT starting rolling off the production line in 1969. It differed from the earlier 206 in that, as well as boasting a larger-capacity engine, it now had a steel body instead of an alloy one, its wheelbase was increased slightly and it had a more luxurious cabin.

The four-cam 2,418 cc V6 with triple Weber carburettors was transversely mounted behind the driver and mated to a five-speed manual transmission. Suspension was by double wishbones, coil springs and telescopic dampers. With 195 bhp at 7,600 rpm, the performance of the Dino was never going to match that of the mighty V12 Ferraris, despite its relatively low 2,800 lb / 1,270 kg weight, but it still managed a very respectable top speed of 146 mph / 235 km/h and acceleration from 0 to 60 mph in 7.0 seconds. More to the point, its well-designed chassis produced wonderful handling and beautifully fluid dynamic finesse, which meant that it could be driven faster than many cars with far more power.

Whatever it may have lacked in terms of outright performance, the Dino more than made up for in its appearance. It was one of the most graceful, delicate and elegant cars that Ferrari ever offered, with near-perfect proportions and a clever 'flying-buttress' design around the rear pillars that solved the problem of fitting an engine midships. Pininfarina's design looks stunning from every angle, and this timeless beauty is what makes the 246GT Dino one of Ferrari's most iconic models of all.

FERRARI 246 GT DINO 1968

ENGINE: 2,418 cc V6

MAXIMUM POWER: 195 bhp at 7,600 rpm

MAXIMUM TORQUE: 225.07 Nm at 5,500 rpm

MAXIMUM SPEED: 146 mph / 235 km/h

0–60 MPH ACCELERATION: 7.0 secs

TRANSMISSION: 5-speed manual

LENGTH: 171 in / 4,343 mm

WIDTH: 67 in / 1,702 mm

HEIGHT: 45¼ in / 1,150 mm

WHEELBASE: 92¼ in / 2,340 mm

MANUFACTURE DATE: 1968–74

BRAKES: disc (f and r)

SUSPENSION: unequal wishbone (f and r)

WHEELS: alloy, 14 in

TIRES: 205/70 VR-14 (f and r)

Most of the Dinos sold were GTs, though a 246GTS Spyder version was introduced in 1972, which, instead of being a true convertible, had a lift-off targa panel. Of the total production of just under 4,000, some 1,275 were Spyders. Interestingly, the V6 Dino engine continued to be made long after the Dino went out of production in 1974, to be replaced by the 308 GT4 – most importantly in the Lancia Stratos, which dominated World Rallying in the 1970s.

Ferrari 250 GTO

The iconic Ferrari GTO started life as a development of the 250 GT intended for competition in the World Sportscar Championship. The FIA had declared that the Grand Touring cars that were taking part in competition should be genuinely production cars – in Italian, GTO stands for Gran Turismo Omologato. The 250 GT's aerodynamics prevented it exceeding around 150 mph / 241 km/h, despite the healthy 280 bhp its 3.0-liter V12 was producing. So Ferrari hatched a plan to create a new aerodynamic body and claim it was only a variant of the 250 GT, which would mean the company wouldn't have to build the full 100 GTOs that homologation would normally require.

The styling was entrusted to Giotto Bizzarrini, who would later create his own supercar. He devised a low-nose, high-tail wedge-shape that radically improved airflow over the body without creating excessive lift at high speeds. At the front, the grille was reduced in size and the headlights were faired in, while the rear was shortened and incorporated an integral spoiler. Under the beautiful flowing bodywork was a classic Ferrari chassis, consisting of a hand-welded alloy-tubing frame with double-wishbone and coil-spring front suspension and a live rear axle with semi-elliptical springs, shock absorbers and double Watts linkage. Most Ferrari racing cars had fully independent rear suspension by this time, but Ferrari was forced to stick with this rather agricultural arrangment because of the pretence that the GTO was simply a development of the earlier GT. Disc brakes and Borrani wire wheels completed the package.

At the heart of the GTO was a magnificent aluminium V12 fed by a bank of six twin-barrel Weber carburettors producing 300 bhp at 7,500 rpm and 294 Nm of torque at 5,500 rpm. It was a dry sump design, which meant it could be mounted lower in the car to the benefit of both center of gravity and aerodynamics. Power was fed to the rear wheels via a new five-speed manual transmission. Its performance was sensational: 0–60 mph in 6.1 seconds, 0–100 mph in 13.1 seconds, and, thanks to Bizzarrini's work on the aerodynamics, the top speed was pushed up to 173 mph / 278 km/h.

Because this was primarily a racing car, little attention was paid to either driver comfort or ergonomics in what was, by any standards, an extremely sparse cabin. The driver had to put up with oddly positioned pedals, an over-large steering wheel and an awkward long-throw gearshift. The passenger, meanwhile, had to share space with a frame brace, the battery and the engine-oil tank. Instrumentation was rudimentary – not even a speedometer was fitted, as only a rev counter was considered necessary for racing – and many of the switches were proprietary units lifted off the humble Fiat 500.

But the Ferrari GTO was built for speed, not for comfort. And it certainly made its mark on the racetrack, running away with the 1962 World Sportscar Manufacturers' Championship that year and again in 1963 and 1964. It also won the GT class at Le Mans in 1962 and came a stunning second overall.

Not only was the 250 GTO highly successful, but it is also generally considered to be one of the most elegant and beautiful cars that Ferrari – or any other manufacturer – has ever produced. It is also part of racing history in that it was the very last successful front-engined racing car that Ferrari ever produced. In total, just 39 examples of the 250 GTO were produced, between 1962 and 1964, at a price of around £6,000. Today's supercars may be quicker, but the 250 GTO remains one of a kind, and because of its rarity, it has become one of the most desirable and valuable cars in the world, with one example changing hands at auction in 2008 for $28,500,000.

FERRARI 250 GTO 1964	
ENGINE: 2,953 cc V12	**WIDTH:** 69¼ in / 1,760 mm
MAXIMUM POWER: 300 bhp at 7,500 rpm	**HEIGHT:** 45 in / 1,140 mm
MAXIMUM TORQUE: 294 Nm at 5,500 rpm	**WHEELBASE:** 94½ in / 2,398 mm
MAXIMUM SPEED: 173 mph / 278 km/h	**MANUFACTURE DATE:** 1962–64
0–60 MPH ACCELERATION: 6.1 secs	**BRAKES:** disc (f and r)
TRANSMISSION: 5-speed manual	**SUSPENSION:** independent double wishbone (f), live axle (r)
LENGTH: 169¼ in / 4,300 mm	**WHEELS:** alloy, 15 in
	TIRES: 600lx15 (f and r)

Ferrari 365 GTB/4 Daytona

During the 1960s, Ferrari gained a rival in the supercar stakes. Ferrucio Lamborghini, a wealthy manufacturer of tractors, set up shop at Sant'Agata Bolognese, just a few miles from Ferrari's Modena headquarters, and stunned the automotive world when he revealed his mid-engined Miura in 1966.

Ferrari's response was another traditional front-engined, rear-wheel drive car, but it was one that was destined to become one of the world's all-time classics – the 365GTB/4. The 365 refers to the capacity of each of its 12 cylinders, GTB stands for Grand Turismo Berlinetta, the body is a GT Coupé and the /4 indicates that it had four camshafts in its engine.

Known as the Daytona (because the previous year Ferrari had finished 1-2-3 at Daytona Beach in Florida, America's most prestigious sports car race), it was the most expensive production car Ferrari had ever produced, the most powerful road car of its time, and also the fastest when it was launched in 1968.

Its 4,390 cc V12 engine produced 352 bhp at 7,500 rpm together with 431 Nm of torque at 5,000 rpm. That was enough to provide a top speed of around 175 mph / 282 km/h and acceleration from 0 to 60 mph in just 5.4 seconds and 0–100 mph in 12 seconds. If this wasn't enough, Ferrari offered a handful of its favoured customers a tuning upgrade to some 380 bhp.

But what set the Daytona apart from the rest was not only its powerful speed, but also the way in which it handled. Although steering was heavy at low speeds, it lightened up as speed increased, grip was outstanding for the time, despite the limitations of 1960s tires, and its handling was truly outstanding, thanks in part to the 50/50 weight distribution achieved by mounting the five-speed transaxle at the rear. Disc brakes all round and independent suspension, consisting of unequal-length wishbones and spring/damper units, completed the dynamic package.

On top of all this, the Daytona was, by any standards, one of the most beautiful cars on the road, and it was practical, too. The Daytona was a genuine Grand Tourer, with a relatively spacious and comfortable cabin, with leather bucket seats, optional electric windows and even air conditioning, and a reasonably sized boot.

FERRARI 365 GTB/4 DAYTONA 1970		WIDTH: 69¼ in / 1,760 mm
ENGINE: 4,390 cc V12		HEIGHT: 49 in / 1,245 mm
MAXIMUM POWER: 352 bhp at 7,500 rpm		WHEELBASE: 94½ in / 2,400 mm
MAXIMUM TORQUE: 431 Nm at 5,000 rpm		MANUFACTURE DATE: 1968–74
MAXIMUM SPEED: 175 mph / 282 km/h		BRAKES: disc (f and r)
0–60 MPH ACCELERATION: 5.4 secs		SUSPENSION: double wishbone (f and r)
TRANSMISSION: 5-speed manual		WHEELS: alloy, 15 in
LENGTH: 174¼ in / 4,425 mm		TIRES: 215/70 VR-15 (f and r)

Despite its weight, the Daytona was also reasonably successful on the track. Although Ferrari never officially raced the car, private entrants were encouraged, and, upgraded to 450 bhp, the Daytona managed a creditable fifth place at Le Mans in 1972 and second at Daytona in 1979.

Styling, as so often at Ferrari, was by Pininfarina, though the cars were actually built by Scaglietti. The chassis was constructed from tubular steel, on which a steel body was fixed, though the doors, bonnet and bootlid were constructed from aluminium alloy in order to save weight. The earliest Daytonas had four headlights set behind clear plastic lenses, but these were later changed to retractable pop-up headlights because of US regulations.

The Daytona stayed in production for six years, until 1974, by which time around 1,285 Coupés and 127 softtop Spyders had been built. The convertible Spyder, launched in 1969,

initially generated little interest, but in later years, it became so desirable that a number of Coupés were converted to convertibles by ardent collectors.

After the Daytona went out of production, Ferrari built further front-engined V12 cars, but this was the last front-engined true performance car that Ferrari produced for many years. It was replaced as the flagship of Ferrari's range by the mid-engined Berlinetta Boxer, and a succession of mid-engined Ferrari supercars followed. Yet in the 1990s, the very real packaging benefits of the conventional front-engine, rear-wheel drive layout brought Ferrari's engineers back to the drawing board to produce modern classic such as the 456GT, 550, 575 and 612 Scaglietti.

The Daytona remains as one of its generation's most elegant, luxurious and quick Grand Tourers, which is why values of the few examples that come on the market today are stratospheric.

Ferrari California

Launched in 2008, the Ferrari California was inspired by the legendary 1957 Ferrari 250 California, a model with which it shares much of its essential DNA. Both cars are elegant convertibles designed first and foremost for high-performance track work, and both represent the very pinnacle of speed, exclusivity, craftsmanship and desirability.

Like every recent Ferrari model, the California was styled by Pininfarina. It offers a host of typical Ferrari design cues – it certainly couldn't be mistaken for any other make – yet at the same time, the body has been honed for optimum aerodynamics. It has low drag for higher top speeds and lower fuel consumption, while still producing enough downforce to ensure absolute stability.

The California's all-aluminium V8 engine is positioned at the front – a first for Ferrari, which has only ever placed a V12 up front before. The 4,300 cc powerplant produces 460 bhp at 7,500 rpm and 485 Nm of torque at 5,000 rpm, though 75 per cent of that torque is available as low as 2,250 rpm, which makes this one of the most tractable, as well as one of the most fuel-efficient, Ferraris of modern times. Stunning performance is available thanks to direct fuel injection and variable valve timing – 0–62 mph takes under four seconds and the top speed is 193 mph / 311 km/h.

Power from the engine is directed to the rear transaxle via a new double-clutch seven-speed gearbox that preselects the next gear to allow virtually instant gear changes. It also allows the driver to choose either manual or fully automatic mode.

The California driver can also opt for other settings, not least the 'Manettino', positioned on the steering wheel (just

FERRARI CALIFORNIA 2008

ENGINE: 4,300 cc V8

MAXIMUM POWER: 460 bhp at 7,500 rpm

MAXIMUM TORQUE: 485 Nm at 5,000 rpm

MAXIMUM SPEED: 193 mph / 311 km/h

0–60 MPH ACCELERATION: 3.9 secs

TRANSMISSION: 7-speed semi-automatic

LENGTH: 179¾ in / 4,563 mm

WIDTH: 75 in / 1,902 mm

HEIGHT: 51½ in / 1,308 mm

WHEELBASE: 105 in / 2,670 mm

MANUFACTURE DATE: 2008–present

Brakes: disc (f and r)

SUSPENSION: independent double wishbone (f), independent multi-link (r)

WHEELS: alloy, 19 in

TIRES: 245/40 ZR 19 (f), 285/40 ZR 19 (r)

red, and it's certainly achingly desirable. But it's also usable on an everyday basis, its less demanding to drive fast than most supercars and it's reasonably spacious and practical. It's also easy to get in and out of – something that can't be said for every sports car capable of nearly 200 mph / 322 km/h.

The new California won't be quite as exclusive as the original 250 California, launched some 50 years earlier, of which only 125 were ever made. Production volumes have been set at 2,500 units a year and at launch in 2008, the entire first two years' worth of cars had been pre-ordered. No wonder it's attracted so much interest: the California is a true supercar with fabulous aesthetics that can still be taken to the supermarket to pick up the shopping.

like on a Formula 1 car), which controls the gearbox, stability and traction-control systems and the suspension set-up. Either Comfort or Sport modes can be selected for road use, or, when on a track, the driver can switch off all the electronic aids except ABS braking.

The California's traction-control system, called F1-Trac, is so sophisticated that as well as ensuring maximum grip and stability, it is claimed to produce 20 per cent better acceleration out of corners than can be offered by a traditional system.

But this is not the car's only safety system: it also has an automatic roll bar that rises in milliseconds if the car overturns, as well as front and side airbags. You wouldn't want to crash a California, but if you do, it will mitigate the effects.

Both chassis and bodywork are aluminium to keep weight to a minimum. Also constructed from aluminium is the retractable hardtop that transforms the California from a coupé to a convertible at the touch of a button in just 14 seconds. There is a choice of either rear seats or a bench arrangement, and cleverly, boot space remains generous for a car of this class, whether the top is up or down and with: Ferrari claims it's possible to carry golf clubs or skis.

Any new Ferrari is expected to be sexy, sassy, red and impractical, but this one is different. It's certainly available in

Fisker Karma

The environmental movement is growing and it's not going to go away. Whether or not climate change is taking place as a result of man's activities, it clearly makes sense to reduce as far as possible the levels of carbon dioxide and other greenhouse gases that are being produced. And it's also the case that the world's supply of oil is dwindling, which is why governments and motor manufacturers are devoting increasing attention to these issues.

Some manufacturers, including BMW and Mercedes-Benz, are researching the use of fuel cells, and BMW has already launched a hydrogen-powered 7-Series limousine. Others, notably Honda and Toyota, have taken the hybrid route, combining electric motors with conventional engines to reduce fuel consumption. Yet others are striving to make compact, fully electric cars more user friendly with improved performance and range.

Former BMW and Aston Martin designer Henrik Fisker – he was responsible for the BMW Z8 and the Aston Martin B9 and V8 Vantage – is one of those working on hybrid-electric cars. However, his interest is not in a small, lightweight runabout, and in the Fisker Karma, he is offering a car that is sleek, elegant and supremely comfortable. As he has said: 'There's no rule

written anywhere that says a green car has to be ugly or small or uncomfortable'.

The Fisker Karma was first unveiled at the 2009 Detroit Auto Show, where more than 1,000 orders for the 100 mpg / 42.5 km/l plug-in hybrid were taken. It is powered by two 201 bhp electric motors that are in turn powered from a lithium-ion battery pack that is charged by connecting it directly to the household electricity supply. If driven in purely 'Stealth Mode', it has a range of 50 miles / 80 km, during which it produces no emissions whatsoever. According to Fisker, that will be enough for the majority of drivers, for whom the daily commute or a trip to drop children at school and do the shopping rarely exceeds this distance.

However, if greater range or greater performance is needed, then the driver can switch to 'Sport Mode', in which a 260 bhp turbocharger 2.0-liter Ford Ecotec direct injection petrol engine comes into play. It does not drive the wheels directly, but instead runs a generator that powers the two electric motors on the rear differential. Operating in this way, the Karma produces some 400 bhp and gives 0–60 mph acceleration in under six seconds and

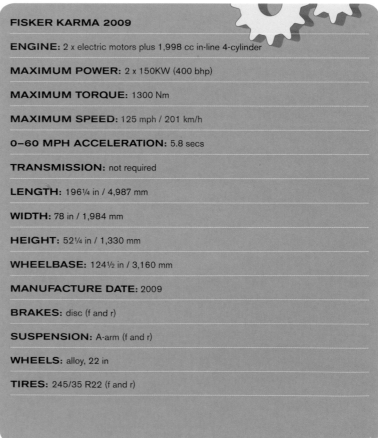

FISKER KARMA 2009

ENGINE: 2 x electric motors plus 1,998 cc in-line 4-cylinder

MAXIMUM POWER: 2 x 150KW (400 bhp)

MAXIMUM TORQUE: 1300 Nm

MAXIMUM SPEED: 125 mph / 201 km/h

0–60 MPH ACCELERATION: 5.8 secs

TRANSMISSION: not required

LENGTH: 196¼ in / 4,987 mm

WIDTH: 78 in / 1,984 mm

HEIGHT: 52¼ in / 1,330 mm

WHEELBASE: 124½ in / 3,160 mm

MANUFACTURE DATE: 2009

BRAKES: disc (f and r)

SUSPENSION: A-arm (f and r)

WHEELS: alloy, 22 in

TIRES: 245/35 R22 (f and r)

a top speed of around 125 mph / 201 km/h. Total range using the engine and the electric motors is around 300 miles / 483 km. What is perhaps even more extraordinary is that a fully charged Karma can achieve an average fuel consumption of around 100 mpg / 42.5 km/l.

And, thanks to its low center of gravity and sports suspension system, its handling and ride is claimed to offer a world-class driving experience.

Importantly, it does all this without sacrificing either style or comfort. The Karma is the height of a Porsche 911, the length of a Mercedes CLS and the width of a BMW 7-Series. Its low, wide body is aerodynamic in shape to keep drag to a minimum, and it has the world's largest continuously formed glass solar-panel roof. This incorporates photovoltaic cells, which generate enough electrical charge to keep the car cool and avoid having to use an energy-sapping air-conditioning unit.

Different trim levels are offered in the cabin, with conventional leather seating if required. However, there's also an Eco-Chic package, which uses no animal products, replacing leather with bamboo viscose, and uses wood trim from fallen trees and interior trim made from fossilized leaves.

Production of the Fisker Karma, which is priced at $87,900, has been contracted to Finnish company Valmet Automotive, which has also made cars for Saab and Porsche.

Ford GT40 Mk I Production

In the early 1960s, Ford decided it should get into GT racing, and in its quest to win the Le Mans 24-Hour race, it entered negotiations to buy Ferrari. At first, Ferrari's owner, Enzo Ferrari, seemed keen, and let the Ford people into his factory to take a complete inventory prior to the sale. But then he changed his mind and showed Ford the door. Henry Ford II, by then chairman of the company that bore his name, was not happy, and vowed to 'kick Ferrari's ass' by beating him at Le Mans.

And so, with the help of race specialists Lola, Ford began development of its own mid-engined Le Mans car, powered by a Ford 4.2-liter V8. It produced 350 bhp and 368 Nm of torque and tests showed it was good for a top speed of 207 mph / 333 km/h, more than enough to make it competitive with the Ferraris of that time. The car was just 40 in / 1,016 mm high, which is how it got its name, GT40.

Ford entered three cars at Le Mans in 1964, but all failed to finish, leaving Ferrari to take the honours. After further development, and with the engine capacity increased to 4.7 liters, the car went into limited production in 1965. Fifty had to be built to qualify for Production Sports Car homologation, and these Mark I GT40s were offered for sale at just £5,900 each! The GT40 was again taken to Le Mans and again failed to win.

As well as better reliability, Ford realized it needed more power, so a 7.0-liter V8 was shoehorned into the car, producing maximum power of 485 bhp and peak torque of 636 Nm. In 1966, it finished first, second and third at the Daytona 24 Hours and the cars then crossed the Atlantic for the Le Mans 24 Hours; here too, the GT40 took first, second and third places. It also became the first car ever to be measured at a speed of over 200 mph / 322 km/h on Le Mans' famous Mulsanne Straight. In 1967, 1968 and 1969, the GT40 again won at Le Mans, making it four in a row – Ford had well and truly 'kicked Ferrari's ass'!

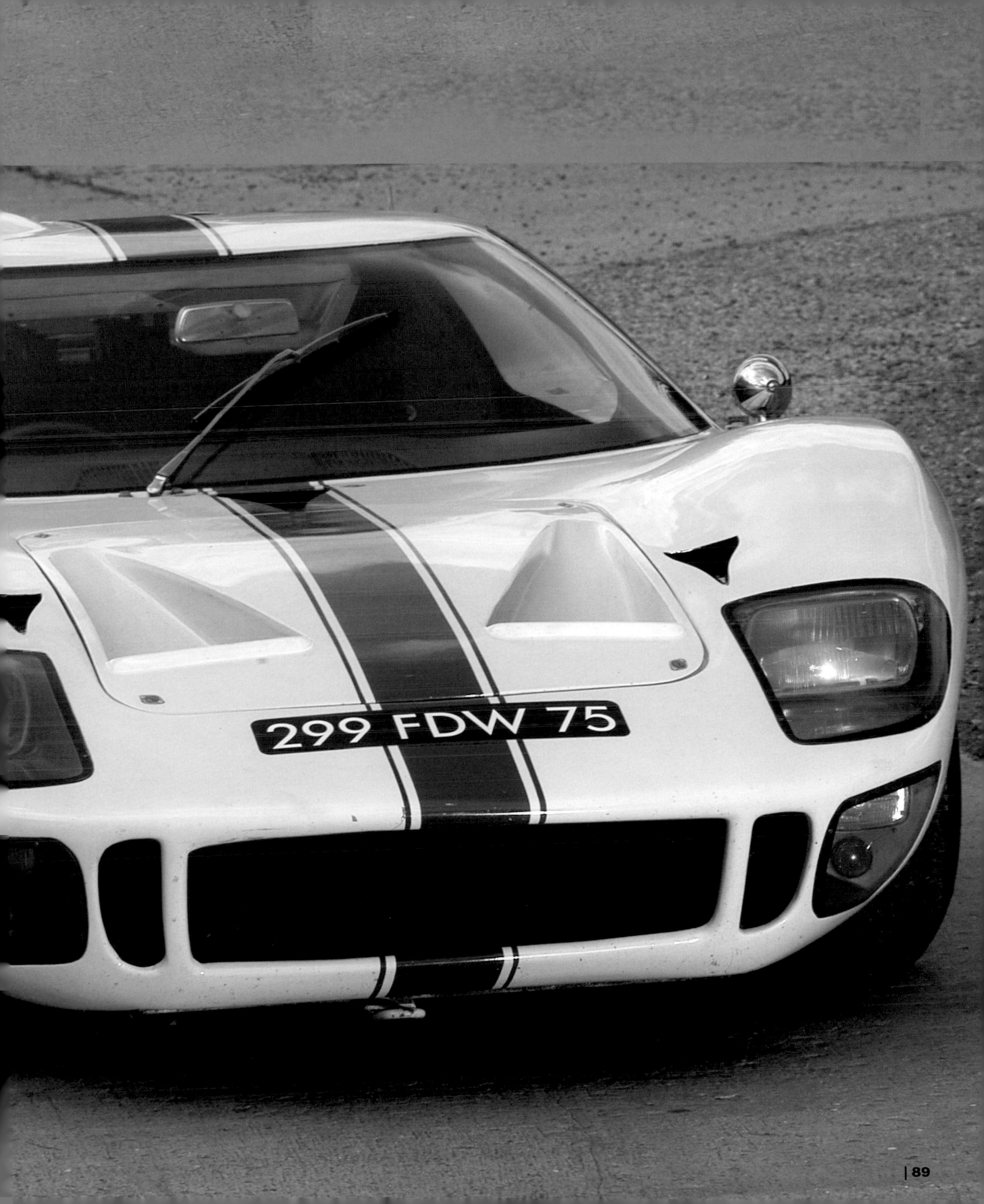
299 FDW 75

FORD GT40 MARK I PRODUCTION 1966		WIDTH: 70 in / 1,778 mm
ENGINE: 4,736 cc V8		HEIGHT: 40 in / 1,016 mm
MAXIMUM POWER: 335 bhp at 6,500 rpm		WHEELBASE: 95 in / 2,413 mm
MAXIMUM TORQUE: 446 Nm at 3,200 rpm		MANUFACTURE DATE: 1966–1972
MAXIMUM SPEED: 164 mph / 264 km/h		BRAKES: disc (f and r)
0–60 MPH ACCELERATION: 5.2 secs		SUSPENSION: unequal wishbone (f), dual trailing arm (r)
TRANSMISSION: 5-speed manual		WHEELS: alloy, 15 in
LENGTH: 158½ in / 4,028 mm		TIRES: 7.00x15

The GT40 had a fibreglass body that was fitted on a sheet-steel semi-monocoque chassis. Its suspension arrangement incorporated wishbones with coil springs and an anti-roll bar at the front, and a transverse top link with a lower wishbone, coil springs and anti-roll bar at the rear. Disc brakes were fitted all round and the Ford V8 drove the rear wheels via a five-speed manual ZF transmission.

In total, 107 GT40 cars were produced at Ford Advanced Vehicles in Slough in England between 1966 and 1972, and of these, 31 were road cars. Rarest of all is the Mk III car, intended to

be the ultimate road car, only seven of which were built, between 1967 and 1969. The engine was detuned to produce 306 bhp at 6,000 rpm and 440 Nm of torque at 4,200 rpm, though this was still plenty to provide 0–60 mph acceleration in 5.2 seconds, 0–100 mph in 12.2 seconds and a top speed of 160 mph / 257 km/h. Since it was intended for road use, the car was fitted with silencers that actually worked, a great deal more interior trim, and even a modicum of luggage space, achieved by extending the body at the rear to make space for a small locker. The Mk III cars look a little different to the racecars, mainly because the headlamps had to be changed to meet traffic regulations. Unlike the earlier cars, this had a central gearshift, which meant left-hand drive was possible. Sadly, the GT40 became uncompetitive at the top end of motorsport and Ford canned the whole project.

Original GT40s are now among the most collectable cars in the world, worth many hundreds of thousands of pounds. But for those of more limited means, there are more replicas of the GT40 on the roads than originals. Copying the classic has become something of an industry in itself.

Ford Mustang

The 1960s was the era of youth, free choice and individualism. It was also the time, especially in the USA, of postwar wealth creation after the austerity years of the 1950s, which gave consumers far greater buying power. This had an effect on the auto industry: families were no longer restricted to one car and younger drivers were starting to clamour to own a car of their own. Ford in general, and its genius marketer Lee Iacocca in particular, saw this trend developing earlier than anyone else. Iacocca argued that if Ford could produce a car that looked good and looked as though it had plenty of performance, it would sell, even if, in truth, it was manufactured from low-cost, standard components.

The stylists at the Ford's headquarters in Dearborn, Michigan, came up with a classic sports car look – two doors, choice of convertible or coupé body styles, a long bonnet and short boot – together with a reasonably practical four-seat cabin. Under that exciting-looking exterior were parts taken from Ford's standard cars, including a rigid rear axle, though the car did have independent front suspension. The engine was lifted from Ford's smallest car, the Falcon. It was a 2.8-liter six-cylinder unit producing just 101 bhp, which meant top speed was under 100 mph / 161 km/h.

The Ford Mustang was launched in April 1964 and was an instant success, partly because it looked great, partly because it was cheap – just $2,320 – and partly because it was perhaps the first car in the world to be offered with a huge range of options and accessories that allowed buyers to customize their own cars. One of those options was a 4.2-liter V8 engine mated to either a three-speed auto or four-speed manual gearbox, which produced 164 bhp and gave the Mustang reasonable performance.

On day one, 22,000 orders were taken, and more than 400,000 cars were sold in the first year, despite Ford having predicted maximum sales of 100,000 a year. With such a huge success on its hands, Ford's biggest problem was finding ways of boosting production to meet demand. It also became clear that real performance was a desire of many buyers, so two more

V8 engine options were offered, including the legendary 4.7-liter V8, which churned out 200 bhp at the time of its launch and 270 bhp in its most powerful variant. Ford also introduced a third body variant, the Fastback, as a 1965 model. But the most visible signs of the Mustang gaining more power and more real sporting ability were the trademark racing stripes on the sills, dual exhaust pipes and GT badges.

As the 1960s progressed, so the Mustang became larger and heavier and needed ever-more powerful engines to maintain its performance potential. By 1968, a 6,997 cc V8 producing 390 bhp was offered, and the same year, a 7,014 cc Cobra Jet variant was made available for racing enthusiasts. In 1969, yet more engine options were offered, along with a range of special editions, such as the Grand Luxury with its vinyl roof, the Mach I, the Boss 302 and 429 and the Shelby GT350 and GT500.

In the early 1970s, the Mustang grew more portly than ever – it now weighed 600 lb / 272 kg more than the original. Worse, the fuel crisis resulted in a rapid growth of demand for more fuel-

FORD MUSTANG 1964	**WIDTH:** 68¼ in / 1,732 mm
ENGINE: 4,727 cc V8	**HEIGHT:** 51¼ in / 1,300 mm
MAXIMUM POWER: 270 bhp at 6,000 rpm	**WHEELBASE:** 108 in / 2,743 mm
MAXIMUM TORQUE: 423 Nm at 3,400 rpm	**MANUFACTURE DATE:** 1964–73
MAXIMUM SPEED: 128 mph / 206 km/h	**BRAKES:** drum (f and r)
0–60 MPH ACCELERATION: 7.3 secs	**SUSPENSION:** independent coil spring (f), live axle (r)
TRANSMISSION: 4-speed manual	**WHEELS:** alloy, 14 in
LENGTH: 181½ in / 4,613 mm	**TIRES:** 7.00x14

efficient vehicles, and the 'dinosaur' muscle cars fell out of favour. The last of the first-generation Mustangs went out of production in 1973, but not before Ford's first 'pony car' had prompted other manufacturers to respond, with models such as the Chrysler Barracuda and Chevrolet Camaro. The Mustang is still in production today, though it's a very different car to the original. The truly great Mustangs were the light and compact early cars, which still have a true magic about them.

Ford Thunderbird

Is it possible that Ford could have sold more than three million examples of a car named the Whizzer? It seems unlikely, and yet that was one of the front runners as Ford marketing executives pondered a name for their new two-seater before they eventually plumped for Thunderbird. There were two catalysts in Ford's decision to design this supercar. Firstly, thousands of American servicemen had spent time in Europe during World War II, where they had seen the small, nimble and elegant sports cars that were available there from manufacturers such as MG, Jaguar and Mercedes-Benz. Secondly, Ford's arch-rival GM had just launched the Corvette.

Ford needed to respond, and it did so with a concept at the Detroit Auto Show in January 1954 that was put into production later that same year. The original Thunderbird was not a straight copy of the Corvette, and in fact Ford was at pains to differentiate their model. It was not a sports car as such, but what they described as a 'personal luxury car', an elegantly styled, well-appointed and powerful convertible with

a speedometer that read speeds up to a dizzying 150 mph / 241 km/h. It was both a very clever design – it raided the parts bins of many other Ford models so production and development costs were kept to a minimum – and a very simple one, with sheet-metal body panels and a large V8 driving the rear wheels through either a manual or automatic transmission.

The Thunderbird sold solidly, though it quickly became clear that the lack of rear seats was adversely affecting sales. The second-generation Thunderbird – usually called the 'Squarebird' because of its strongly angular design – rectified this problem. This later car also developed the simple chassis and body-on-frame construction of the original to a more modern monocoque design, and for the first time, both hardtop and convertible options were available. Interestingly, the hardtop was much more popular: of a total of around 38,000 Thunderbirds sold per year, only some 2,000 were soft tops.

In 1961, the Thunderbird underwent a total restyle, becoming longer, wider and lower. This sleeker, more aerodynamic design

resembled a bullet, and thus these third-generation Thunderbirds, which were produced until 1964, were commonly known as 'Bullet Birds' or 'Projectile Birds'. Reflecting the general interest of the time in flying and jet planes, impressive fins and taillights were adopted at the back. The sleek modern design was extended to the interior too, where the ends of the wraparound fascia curved into the door panels. Another new feature on the 1961 Thunderbird was a steering wheel that could be swung away to make getting in and out of the car a little easier.

If the design changed, however, the basic structure did not. The Bullet Bird retained the monocoque structure of the Squarebird, though the suspension was revised to give a more comfortable and compliant ride. Power came from a 300 bhp 6,391 cc V8, which provided some true sporting flavour, especially in the rare Sports Roadster, whose power was increased to 340 bhp with the adoption of a Holley two-barrel carburettor. Even so, the Thunderbird, which tipped the scales at close to two tonnes, could never be described as outstandingly

FORD THUNDERBIRD 1963

ENGINE: 5,768 cc 352 cu.in

MAXIMUM POWER: 300 bhp at 4,400 rpm

MAXIMUM TORQUE: 535 Nm at 2,800rpm

MAXIMUM SPEED: 120 mph / 193 km/h

0–60 MPH ACCELERATION: 10.5 secs

TRANSMISSION: 3-speed automatic

LENGTH: 205.3 in / 5,164 cm

WIDTH: 77 in / 1,956 cm

HEIGHT: 52.5 in / 1,333 cm

WHEELBASE: 119 in. / 3,022 cm

MANUFACTURE DATE: 1954–64

BRAKES: drum (f and r)

SUSPENSION: independent coil spring (f), live axle (r)

WHEELS: alloy, 14 in

TIRES: 8.00x14

quick. It took a leisurely 10.5 seconds to reach 60 mph from a standstill, and its owners could only ever dream of attaining the 150 mph / 241 km/h the speedometer promised.

When the Bullet Birds went out of production in 1964, they were followed by the sharper, more angular 'Jet Birds'. Next came the 'Big Birds' of 1972–76, the 'Torino Birds' of 1977–79 and the thoroughly mediocre 'Fairmont Birds' of 1980–82. Not until the 1983–86 'Aero Birds' did Ford recapture a hint of the true sporting nature of the 1963 Thunderbird. However, although the Aero Birds remain highly sought after today, the true classic, iconic Thunderbird remains the 1961–63 Bullet Bird.

Infiniti FX50

Infiniti is to Nissan as Lexus is to Toyota and Acura is to Honda. All three Japanese manufacturers realized many years ago that if they were to achieve their ambition of moving upmarket into the premium sector, it would have to be with a separate brand, sold from separate, smarter showrooms. The Infiniti brand was introduced into the US market in 1989, and the following year, it launched the Q45 saloon, a powerful, elegant car with active suspension and a truly luxurious cabin. Later, it launched the QX4, a premium luxury SUV, and in 2003, the G35, a sports coupé based on the Nissan Skyline, which became an instant hit thanks to its outstanding performance and fine handling.

Then in 2003, came the FX, one of the first examples of the 'cross-over' vehicle, in which the lower part of the vehicle is a chunky SUV while the upper part is sleeker and smarter – a body more likely to be found on a sports car. The car thus provides both the high performance of a GV and the functionality of an SUV. At launch, two versions were offered: the FX35, fitted with a 280 bhp 3.5-liter V6, and the FX45, which has a 320 bhp V8 under its bonnet. In keeping with the Infiniti image, both models were very highly specified. After a facelift in 2006, a totally redesigned model was introduced at the Geneva Motor Show in 2008 to coincide with the Infiniti brand's launch in Europe. Although their proportions are very similar to those of the earlier FX, the new FX35 and FX50 have what some commentators have

described as 'challenging' styling. Others have dismissed the cars as just plain ugly.

However, there's no doubting the dynamic abilities of the FX50, in particular. Its 5,026 cc V8 produces 390 bhp at 6,500 rpm and 500 Nm of torque at 4,400 rpm. That's enough to provide 0–62 mph acceleration in 5.8 seconds and a top speed of 155 mph / 249 km/h. Power is transmitted mainly to the rear wheels via a seven-speed automatic transmission operated by paddles on the steering wheel, though when extra traction is required, the electronically controlled all-wheel-drive system comes into play. The smaller engined FX35, incidentally, can be specified either as a two-wheel-drive or an all-wheel-drive vehicle. Suspension is by double wishbones and electronically controlled dampers at the front, and multi-link with the same electronically adjustable dampers at the rear. Four piston discs at the front and two piston discs at the rear ensure adequate stopping power.

The basic dynamic set-up of the FX50 is backed up by a whole army of electronic aids, including Lane Departure Prevention, which uses the brakes to ensure the vehicle does not drift out of its lane; Intelligent Cruise Control with Distance Control Assist, which uses a forward radar to ensure a constant distance is kept from the car in front; and Intelligent Brake Assist, which can bring the FX50 to a complete stop and then resume the selected speed. It raises the theoretical possibility of the car being driven for miles on a highway without the driver ever having to touch the brake, accelerator or even the steering wheel. The awesome specification continues in the cabin, which is equipped with a hard-drive navigation system with more than 9GB of digital music storage, tire-pressure monitoring, diamond quilted leather front seats that can be heated and cooled, and even an ionizing air-purification system.

The FX50 is, in many ways, a quite remarkable vehicle, offering performance and luxury in equal measures. And there's no doubt that the best place to view the FX50 is from inside the cabin, as only from there is the unfortunate exterior styling invisible.

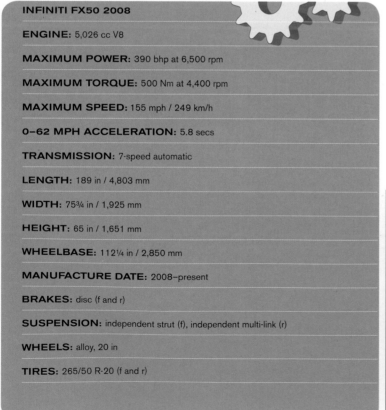

INFINITI FX50 2008

ENGINE: 5,026 cc V8

MAXIMUM POWER: 390 bhp at 6,500 rpm

MAXIMUM TORQUE: 500 Nm at 4,400 rpm

MAXIMUM SPEED: 155 mph / 249 km/h

0–62 MPH ACCELERATION: 5.8 secs

TRANSMISSION: 7-speed automatic

LENGTH: 189 in / 4,803 mm

WIDTH: 75¾ in / 1,925 mm

HEIGHT: 65 in / 1,651 mm

WHEELBASE: 112¼ in / 2,850 mm

MANUFACTURE DATE: 2008–present

BRAKES: disc (f and r)

SUSPENSION: independent strut (f), independent multi-link (r)

WHEELS: alloy, 20 in

TIRES: 265/50 R-20 (f and r)

Iso Grifo

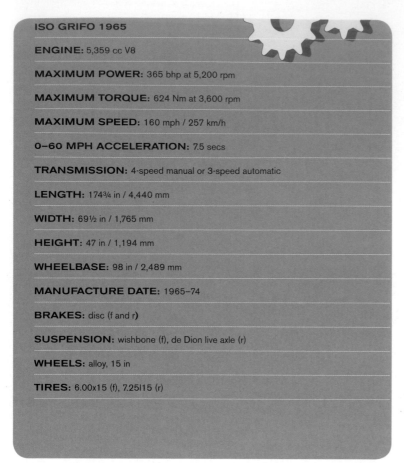

ISO GRIFO 1965

ENGINE: 5,359 cc V8

MAXIMUM POWER: 365 bhp at 5,200 rpm

MAXIMUM TORQUE: 624 Nm at 3,600 rpm

MAXIMUM SPEED: 160 mph / 257 km/h

0–60 MPH ACCELERATION: 7.5 secs

TRANSMISSION: 4-speed manual or 3-speed automatic

LENGTH: 174¾ in / 4,440 mm

WIDTH: 69½ in / 1,765 mm

HEIGHT: 47 in / 1,194 mm

WHEELBASE: 98 in / 2,489 mm

MANUFACTURE DATE: 1965–74

BRAKES: disc (f and r)

SUSPENSION: wishbone (f), de Dion live axle (r)

WHEELS: alloy, 15 in

TIRES: 6.00x15 (f), 7.25l15 (r)

Who would have believed that the manufacturer of the Isetta bubble car would later build a supercar capable of outperforming just about any other car on the road? The Italian Iso company started out building refrigeration units, then diversified into scooters in the 1950s before designing the Isetta bubble car, which was built in Germany under licence by BMW. But by 1962, Iso's founder, Renzo Rivolta, had decided to create a high-speed luxury car, and duly produced a svelte 2+2 coupé styled by Bertone called the Iso Rivolta, which was based upon a Chevrolet Corvette powertrain.

The following year saw the launch of a new model, the Iso Grifo. For this new car, Rivolta employed Giotto Bizzarrini, creator of the Ferrari GTO, as chief engineer and Giorgio Giugiaro as chief designer. Though based on the Rivolta chassis, the Grifo was shorter and was a true two-seater, aimed firmly at Ferrari's market. Even the name was intended to put the wind up Ferrari – Grifo (Griffin) is a mythical creature that consumed horses for breakfast, and Ferrari's logo was, and still is, a prancing horse!

To ensure plenty of performance, a Chevrolet 5,359 cc V8 was fitted up front, producing either 300 or 365 bhp, mated either to a five-speed ZF or a Borg-Warner four-speed manual gearbox from the Corvette or even a GM three-speed automatic. The chassis was fairly conventional, with wishbones and coil springs at the front and a de Dion live axle with coil springs, radius arms and a Watt linkage at the rear. Disc brakes were fitted all round to improve stopping power, but the steering was a rather agricultural recirculating-ball unit.

Even if the chassis wasn't state of the art, the performance of the Iso Grifo was impressive: early versions were said to accelerate from 0 to 60 mph in 7.5 seconds, would reach nearly 70 mph / 113 km/h in first gear, top 100 mph / 161 km/h in

13.5 seconds and had a maximum speed of at least 160 mph / 257 km/h given an open road – which made it just as fast as any other Italian supercar of its day – while the later seven-liter models could reach 190 mph / 306 km/h.

And it wasn't just the Iso's performance that turned heads. Its steel bodywork, with a curved fastback design, long and low bonnet, massive cooling vents in the front bumpers and wide grille, made quite an impression. Even today, the Iso Grifo looks sensuously beautiful, with its swooping curves and elegant Kamm tail. Another outstanding feature of the car was its luxurious cockpit, which was considerably more comfortable than that of many of its direct competitors. It also boasted air conditioning, electric windows and a wood-rimmed steering wheel.

Despite all these advantages, the Iso Grifo wasn't a huge commercial success, partly because, for whatever reason, its American V8 engine was considered somehow less appealing than a 'proper' Italian V8, even though the Chevvy V8 was a far more dependable unit. And so, because the Iso Grifo never attracted the sort of prestige that Ferraris so effortlessly displayed, only around 470 examples were built between 1965 and 1974, when production finally ended.

Later during its production lifetime, further engine options were made available, with a 6,998 cc Chevrolet 427 Big Block V8 coming on line in 1968, which was later still bored out to 7,443 cc. Because of the height of this engine, a bonnet air scoop had to be incorporated into the design, and this makes the

later '7 Litri' cars instantly recognizable. The very last few cars, built from 1972, were fitted with a Ford Boss 5,752 cc V8, which required an even bigger bonnet air scoop, giving these cars an even more aggressive look. Also built were the very rare Targa Top models – there were just 14 of them – which had a stainless steel removable roof and a rear window that could be zipped out. Rarer still is the Grifo Spyder convertible: it was displayed at the Geneva Motor Show but never put into production.

Jaguar D-Type

The Jaguar D-Type was conceived with just one aim in mind: to win at Le Mans. The earlier C-Type had won in 1951 and 1953 and the D-Type's job was to go out and do it again.

The D-Type was a radically different car from its predecessor. Although it used the same six-cylinder XK engine, the D-Type had a monocoque chassis welded to a subframe. This was a radical departure, as it was the first time that aircraft engineering techniques had been applied to a racing car. The same techniques were also employed in the design of the bodywork. The highly aerodynamic shape was created by Malcolm Sayer, who had a background in aircraft engineering and who also designed the earlier C-Type and later E-Type.

To increase stability on the long Mulsanne straight at Le Mans, where the highest speeds were routinely reached, Sayer specified a large vertical fin behind the driver, and it is this feature that made the D-Type instantly recognizable.

The engine was developed from Jaguar's 3,442 cc straight-six design, but was fitted with a dry-sump lubrication system that both lowered the height of the engine (allowing for a more aerodynamic profile) and also reduced the risk of oil surge under severe cornering. The engine produced 250 bhp at 6,000 rpm and 325 Nm of torque at 4,000 rpm, which gave the car acceleration from 0 to 60 mph in around seven seconds and a top speed of 170 mph / 274 km/h. The close-ratio four-speed manual gearbox and Salisbury rear axle were lifted directly from the production XK, though the ratios were changed for ultimate performance rather than long-legged cruising.

First time out, at the 1954 Le Mans 24-Hour race, the D-Type came a creditable second, just one lap behind a victorious Ferrari. The following year, a longer nose was fitted to improve aerodynamics still further and permit a faster top speed. The D-Type of Mike Hawthorn and Ivor Bueb took the chequered flag, though the victory was overshadowed by one of motor racing's worst accidents, when the Mercedes-Benz SLR of Pierre Levegh crashed into the crowd, killing 80 people. The D-Type won Le Mans again in 1956, thanks to the efforts of the privately entered

Ecurie Ecosse team. Jaguar withdrew from racing at the end of 1956 and it was once again left to Ecurie Ecosse to take first and second place in 1957.

In all, 68 Jaguar D-Types were built, but after the company's withdrawal from motor racing, 25 were left over. These were converted to road-going cars, known as the Jaguar XKSS. Bumpers and faired-in headlights were added to make the car road legal, the rear fin was removed, and a passenger-side door was installed. The cockpit remained fully exposed to the elements, alhough a rather rudimentary canvas hood was added to the specification, along with leather seats and a full range of instrumentation.

The mechanical specification of the XKSS was virtually identical to that of the racing D-Type and the car offered scintillating performance – 0–60 mph acceleration in 5.2 seconds and a top speed of 144 mph / 232 km/h with a standard 3.54:1 ratio axle. Customers could, however, opt for a higher ratio axle that gave a top speed of nearly 160 mph / 257 km/h.

Sadly, however, only 16 XKSS cars were completed before a massive factory fire at Jaguar's Browns Lane plant in Coventry, England, halted all production for six weeks. After that, it seemed much more important to increase production of the 3.4 Jaguar saloon, and the XKSS was consigned to history.

The XKSS went on sale at the 1957 New York Auto Show and one of the earliest customers was film star Steve McQueen. Of the 16 XKSS cars built, 12 were sold in the USA, two in Canada and one each in the UK and Hong Kong.

JAGUAR D-TYPE 1954

ENGINE: 3,442 cc inline 6-cylinder

MAXIMUM POWER: 250 bhp at 6,000 rpm

MAXIMUM TORQUE: 325 Nm at 4,000 rpm

MAXIMUM SPEED: 170 mph / 274 km/h

0–60 MPH ACCELERATION: 7.0 secs

TRANSMISSION: 4-speed manual

LENGTH: 154 in / 3,912 mm

WIDTH: 65½ in / 1,664 mm

HEIGHT: 54 in / 1,372 mm

WHEELBASE: 90½ in / 2,300 mm

MANUFACTURE DATE: 1954–56

BRAKES: disc (f and r)

SUSPENSION: double wishbone (f), solid axle (r)

WHEELS: steel, 16 in

TIRES: 6.5x16

Jaguar E-Type

When the Jaguar E-Type was first revealed at the Geneva Motor Show in 1961, it wasn't its sleek and elegant proportions that caused the most wonder, nor was it the claimed 150 mph / 241 km/h top speed; it was the fact that its list price was just £1,500. That was still a lot of money at a time when small runabouts could be had for a few hundred pounds, but it was far less than a Ferrari or Mercedes sports car cost back then.

The E-Type's construction was relatively simple, with a cockpit comprised of welded-steel pressings with independent coil-spring rear suspension carried on a sub-frame beneath. At the front, square-section steel tubing supported the engine, and torsion-bar front suspension and a smaller tubular-steel subframe supported the radiator and the forward-hinged bonnet.

Under that massively long bonnet was Jaguar's 3,781 cc straight-six engine producing 265 bhp at 5,500 rpm and 352 Nm of torque at 4,000 rpm. Drive was directed to the rear wheels via a four-speed manual gearbox.

At the time, Jaguar claimed that the top speed of the fixed head coupé (FHC) was 150 mph / 241 km/h, that of the slightly less aerodynamic roadster was 149 mph / 240 km/h, and both

JAGUAR E-TYPE 1970

ENGINE: 4,235 in-line six cylinder

MAXIMUM POWER: 265 bhp at 5,400 rpm

MAXIMUM TORQUE: 380 Nm at 4,000 rpm

MAXIMUM SPEED: 150 mph / 241 km/h (claimed)

0-60 MPH ACCELERATION: 7.1 secs

TRANSMISSION: 4-speed manual

LENGTH: 175¼ in / 4,450 mm

WIDTH: 65¼ in / 1,650 mm

HEIGHT: 48 in / 1,220 mm

WHEELBASE: 96 in / 2,440 mm

MANUFACTURE DATE: 1961–75

BRAKES: disc (f and r)

SUSPENSION: independent wishbone (f), independent lower wishbone (r)

WHEELS: alloy, 15 in

TIRES: ER70 VR-15

1963 to compete with the likes of the Ferrari 250GT and Aston Martin DB4GT. But it was on the road that the E-Type made the biggest impression: its combination of massive performance potential and head-turning good looks made it the sports car that every enthusiastic driver ached to own.

Over the years, the E-Type was continually improved. In 1964, just three years after the launch of the Series I cars – recognizable by their glass-covered headlights and smaller air intake at the front – it gained a larger 4.2-liter engine and a decent gearbox. This car version of the E-Type became known as the Series 1½. The 1966 Series II cars included a larger cabin option, with two small rear seats in the form of the 2+2. Finally, the Series III cars had a 5,343 cc V12 engine shoehorned under the bonnet in 1971.

By the time the E-Type finally went out of production in 1975, 70,000 had been sold. Not surprisingly, given that even archrival Enzo Ferrari, when he first saw the E-Type, described it as 'the most beautiful car ever made'.

versions of the E-type could reach 60 mph in seven seconds. It seems that Jaguar was guilty of gilding the lily somewhat: when specialist motoring magazines got their hands on cars for testing, the magic 150 mph / 241 km/h was never attainable. But that didn't mean the E-Type was not incredibly quick for its time and nor did it stop those early testers from raving about this wonderful new and graceful Jaguar.

In particular, its ride and handling set new standards that would not be surpassed for years. The E-Type was not perfect – its inboard disc brakes suffered from overheating and its clunky Moss gearbox was hardly state of the art – yet it very quickly established itself as the quintessential sports car and a vibrant symbol of the Swinging Sixties.

It was called E-Type to link the car to Jaguar's Le Mans winning C-Type and D-Type racers. All three cars had bodies designed by Malcolm Sayer, whose background was in the aircraft industry. His smooth and efficient designs gave these Jaguars an aerodynamic advantage over their rivals that to a large degree accounted for their success on the racetrack.

Like its predecessors, the E-type was given a smooth and rounded shape that aided airflow over the body. It also had the same low build and long bonnet that emphasized a racing heritage. No surprise then, that the E-Type, too, soon found itself out on the track, in the form of a lightweight racer, developed in

Jaguar XFR

For decades, Jaguar has been building upmarket saloons and sports cars. Its reputation as a sportscar manufacturer really started in 1948, when the XK120 appeared. It was dazzlingly beautiful and offered performance that was as good as that of any of its competitors. It started a heritage that ran through various other XK derivatives, the C-, D- and E-Type Jaguars, and, more recently, to the XKR high-performance two-seater roadster and coupé. But Jaguar has a heritage of building fast, comfortable saloons too, so much so that the company's motto for a while was 'Grace, Pace and Space' – the three key ingredients that made a Jaguar car unique.

When it was launched in 2008, the Jaguar XF was radically different in design terms from its predecessor, the S-Type, but there was no doubt that it encapsulated each of those virtues. Its bold modern design was certainly graceful; 0–62 mph in 5.7 seconds and a top speed of 155 mph / 249 km/h most definitely gave it pace; and although it was designed to look like a coupé, the XF's four-door body provided plenty of space for four passengers and their luggage.

The flagship derivative of the XF range takes the Jaguar experience to all-new levels, retaining the grace and the space but shifting the emphasis towards the sort of pace normally associated with supercars.

At the very core of the Jaguar XFR is a new 5.0-liter direct-injection supercharged V8 that produces 510 bhp at 6,000 rpm and 625 Nm of torque at 2,500 rpm. Driving the rear wheels via a six-speed automatic transmission, the XFR accelerates from 0 to 62 mph in 4.9 seconds and on to an electronically limited top speed of 155 mph / 249 km/h. Perhaps more relevantly on today's congested roads, the car accelerates from 50 to 70 mph in just 1.9 seconds, which gives it XFR Ferrari or Lamborghini standards of overtaking.

It's an engine that not only provides outstanding performance but also manages to be more fuel efficient and produces fewer emissions than the 4.2-liter V8 found in other XF models, conforming both to the European EU5 and the American ULEV2 emissions regulations. It achieves this partly thanks to a high-efficiency twin-vortex supercharger and partly to a world first – central spray-guided direct injection, delivering fuel at a pressure of 150 bar directly into the cylinders to maximize air-fuel mixing, improve combustion control and thereby increase both efficiency and torque.

On paper, the performance looks outstanding; on the road, it's even better. That's because instead of wasting all that horsepower on spinning the wheels, the XFR is fitted with Active Differential Control and Adaptive Dynamics – new technologies that involve the electronically controlled differential and the suspension system working in tandem to optimize traction in both acceleration and cornering. The differential automatically varies the torque directed to each of the rear wheels depending on the surface condition and the amount of power applied, and so it differs fundamentally from a conventional traction-control system, which relies on the brakes to counteract wheelspin after it has occurred. The Adaptive Dynamics suspension is also a major development, automatically adjusting the damper settings to suit the road conditions and the way in which the car is being driven. So instead of a choice between 'Comfort' and 'Sport' modes, as in many other systems, it offers a fully progressive variable damping strategy to provide comfort and pin-sharp handling in all conditions.

Visually, the XFR is distinguishable by its unique bonnet louvres and grille, its four exhausts, boot spoiler and its special 20-inch alloy wheels. In fact, it has all that's needed – performance, luxury, style and desirability – to justify its position as the definitive Jaguar sports saloon.

JAGUAR XFR 2009

ENGINE: 5,000 cc V8

MAXIMUM POWER: 510 bhp at 6,000 rpm

MAXIMUM TORQUE: 625 Nm at 2,500 rpm

MAXIMUM SPEED: 155 mph / 249 km/h

0–62 MPH ACCELERATION: 4.9 secs

TRANSMISSION: 6-speed automatic

LENGTH: 195¼ in / 4,961 mm

WIDTH: 74 in / 1,877 mm

HEIGHT: 57½ in / 1,460 mm

WHEELBASE: 114½ in / 2,909 mm

MANUFACTURE DATE: 2009–present

BRAKES: disc (f and r)

SUSPENSION: double wishbone (f and r)

WHEELS: alloy, 20 in

TIRES: 245/35 R20 (f and r)

Jensen FF

To introduce one world first in a new car is quite something, but in 1966, the small British firm Jensen managed two firsts with the launch of the Jensen FF, the world's first production car not only with four-wheel drive but also with ABS brakes.

The idea of a four-wheel drive road car was not new, and Jensen had shown a CV-8 concept in 1965 that was fitted with the Dunlop Maxaret system that would find its way onto the FF. The problem with the CV-8 was that it was an old design, and Jensen realized that such a radical technological concept would require a radical new car, too.

And so, in 1966, Jensen launched not one but two new models – the two-wheel drive Jensen Interceptor and the four-wheel drive Jensen FF (for Ferguson Formula, as the system had been designed by the Ferguson tractor company).

Both models shared a similar bodyshell, designed and manufactured by Vignale in Italy, and both shared a Chrysler 'Big Block' 6,276 cc V8, which produced 330 bhp – an enormous output for a European car in those days, and more than enough to give the FF a top speed of 130 mph / 209 km/h.

The ultramodern-looking coupé, with its massive wraparound rear window, attracted loads of attention, but it was the FF, with its four-wheel drive and anti-lock braking, that caused the biggest stir. The anti-lock braking worked by splitting the drive behind the Torqueflite three-speed automatic gearbox and taking drive to the front wheels via a second propshaft to a new front axle. Torque was split 37 per cent to the front and 63 per cent to the rear wheels. To fit the axle in front of the engine, the FF's wheelbase was lengthened by around 4 in / 10 cm. Other changes included fitting constant velocity joints to the front drive shafts and adopting a bespoke front suspension system with double wishbones on either side of coil springs.

The Maxaret anti-lock braking system, which was developed from an aircraft system, was crude by today's standards, but it's difficult to underestimate just how massive Jensen's

technological breakthrough was at the time. It was incorporated into the master differential, where it sensed any differences between the relative speeds of the front and rear wheels and electrically released brake servo assistance to the slower (locked-up) wheels. As soon as the wheel speeds equalized, brake pressure was re-applied.

At the time of its launch, the Jensen FF was the safest, most stable car on the roads. It was a genuine Grand Tourer, with a large and airy cabin, plenty of luggage space and the ability to be driven quickly and effortlessly. Some even argued that it was, by some margin, the best car in the world.

All that technology cost money, of course, and there was a huge premium to be paid for an FF over the standard Interceptor model. While the two-wheel drive Interceptor cost £3,743 in 1966, the FF was £5,340 – a huge amount of money at a time when a Rolls-Royce cost £6,670. Obviously, the FF was never going to be a massive seller, but 320 were sold before production

was finally brought to an end in 1971. The Interceptor continued in production until 1976, by which time a convertible had been added to the range and around 6,300 examples had been sold.

Nevertheless, despite its far smaller sales volumes, it's the Jensen FF that is guaranteed the bigger place in history.

JENSEN FF 1966	
ENGINE:	6,276 cc inline 8-cylinder
MAXIMUM POWER:	330 bhp at 4,600 rpm
MAXIMUM TORQUE:	587 Nm at 2,800 rpm
MAXIMUM SPEED:	130 mph / 209 km/h
0–60 MPH ACCELERATION:	8.4 secs
TRANSMISSION:	3-speed automatic
LENGTH:	191 in / 4,851 mm
WIDTH:	70 in / 1,778 mm
HEIGHT:	52¾ in / 1,340 mm
WHEELBASE:	109 in / 2,769 mm
MANUFACTURE DATE:	1966–71
BRAKES:	disc (f and r)
SUSPENSION:	independent wishbone (f), live axle (r)
WHEELS:	alloy, 15 in
TIRES:	6.70x15

Lamborghini Miura P400

There's no doubt which was the most important model to grace the 1966 Geneva Motor Show: the Lamborghini Miura was a sleek mid-engined design with ultra-modern bodywork, designed by Bertone, that covered a technically extremely advanced chassis, engine and transmission.

Ferrucio Lamborghini manufactured agricultural machinery and had bought a number of Ferraris as his personal cars. But he was dissatisfied with the quality of the cars, and even more dissatisfied with the way he felt he was treated at the Ferrari factory. His response was to finance, build and market his own supercar in Ferrari's backyard. Appropriately, Lamborghini, who was also a lover of fine livestock, chose a raging bull as the logo for the supercar company he founded, and named his first car, the Miura, after one of the finest breeds of fighting bull.

Lamborghini recruited some of the best people in the business to create the Miura, including Giotto Bizzarini to build the engine, Gianpaolo Dallara to hone the chassis and Bertone to design the bodywork. Marcello Gandini, who was then employed at Bertone, is usually credited with the styling, but Giorgetto Giugiaro, who had earlier worked at Bertone, claimed that 70 per cent of the design work was his. The team created a cutting-edge new car that took the motor industry by storm.

Not only was it one of the most rakishly beautiful supercars of its time, but it had the performance to match. In addition, it was one of the very first successful mid-engined designs, thanks to Bizzarini's ingenious work. He managed to fit the V12 transversely within the Miura's monocoque and take the drive to the rear wheels via a five-speed transaxle fitted within the crankcase – the same solution that Alec Issigonis had come up with for the original Mini.

One interesting aspect of the Miura's design was that the fuel tank was positioned at the front of the car, which meant that as fuel was burnt, the front became lighter, which resulted in difficult handling at very high speeds.

The original plan was to build a limited run of just 50 cars, but the Miura was so successful that 762 cars were delivered in all. The earliest Miura models were known as P400 and boasted 350 bhp; the P400S, which appeared in 1968, offered a little more power, together with more creature comforts in the cabin, including electric windows.

Finally, in 1971, the P400SV was launched, the best – and the most sought-after – Miura. The SV had revised cam timing and different carburettors that boosted power to 385 bhp at 7,000 rpm, more than enough to provide a top speed of 170 mph / 274 km/h and acceleration from 0 to 60 mph in 6.2 seconds. It had wider tires, revised suspension geometry and its chassis was built from heavier gauge steel, which helped improve the handling. The SV (which stands for Spinto Veloce or pushed fast) also had a limited slip differential fitted to further improve both handling and outright grip.

The Miura became an icon of the 1960s that was driven by such celebrities as Frank Sinatra and Michael Caine, who drove one in the opening sequences of the *The Italian Job* (1969). A Miura roadster prototype was revealed at the 1968 Brussels Motor Show but it never went into production as Lamborghini decided, probably wisely, to avoid the distraction of producing another model and concentrate instead on delivering cars to customers.

However, the next model was already in the wings: at the 1971 Geneva Motor Show, Lamborghini not only launched the Miura SV, but also presented another prototype, the LP500 Countach.

LAMBORGHINI MIURA P400 1971

ENGINE: 3,929 cc V12

MAXIMUM POWER: 350 bhp at 7,000 rpm

MAXIMUM TORQUE: 400 Nm at 5,750 rpm

MAXIMUM SPEED: 170 mph / 274 km/h

0–60 MPH ACCELERATION: 6.2 secs

TRANSMISSION: 5-speed manual

LENGTH: 172¾ in / 4,390 mm

WIDTH: 70 in / 1,780 mm

HEIGHT: 43¼ in / 1,100 mm

WHEELBASE: 98½ in / 2,504 mm

MANUFACTURE DATE: 1966–72

BRAKES: disc (f and r)

SUSPENSION: independent double wishbone (f and r)

WHEELS: alloy, 15 in

TIRES: 205/70 VR-15 (f and r)

Land Rover Range Rover

Only one vehicle has won the Paris/Dakar Rally, completed an East to West crossing of the Sahara Desert and been exhibited at Louvre Museum in Paris. The same vehicle was as likely to be seen on the King's Road in London or 5th Avenue in New York as it was to be found mud-plugging on a farm or dragging a horse-box to the local gymkhana. That vehicle was the original Range Rover, a truly unique vehicle when it was launched in 1970. It was the first ever 4x4 vehicle that was also luxurious, offering high levels both of performance and of style and presence. It started a trend that spread worldwide, because now the 'Chelsea Tractor' or 'Sport Utility Vehicle' comprises one of the largest and most valuable sectors of the car market. Where the Range Rover lead the way, virtually every other car manufacturer in the world has followed.

The 1970 Range Rover was a very different machine to the Range Rover of the 21st century. Though the interior was far more comfortable than that of the standard utilitarian Land Rover, it was still workmanlike – indeed, it had no carpets, so that the footwells could be hosed out when muddy! But what the original did have in common with today's Range Rover was its permanent four-wheel-drive system, powerful V8 engine under the bonnet and a high, dominant driving position. And like its more contemporary versions, it was a vehicle that was just as at home on a trip to the theatre or to a Board meeting as it was at a horse show or pheasant shoot.

The difference is that today's flagship Range Rover is as plush and opulent as any premium saloon. Indeed, in price and in market positioning, it competes directly with top-end Jaguars, BMWs and Mercedes-Benzes. Now the cabin is awash with leather, wood and every conceivable extra, including a massive stereo system and satellite navigation. It even has seats that are heated in cold weather and cooled in hot climates.

Mechanically, the Range Rover has grown up over the years, too. Now it's powered either by a supercharged petrol V8 or a twin-turbocharged V8 diesel, mated to a six-speed automatic transmission. Its performance on the road is effortless – the 4,197cc V8 supercharged produces 396 bhp at 5,750 rpm and an enormous 550 Nm of torque, making it the most powerful Range Rover ever, capable of accelerating from 0 to 62 mph in 7.5 seconds and giving a top speed of 130 mph / 209 km/h.

But it's the way in which the Range Rover delivers its performance that is so astonishing. Normally a heavy car weighing some two tons could not be expected to handle well, nor should it be possible to hustle a vehicle with a relatively high center of gravity swiftly and safely on bendy roads. But thanks to its wealth of electronic trickery, the Range Rover does just that. It has a refined electronically controlled air-suspension system that allows the ride height to be altered, an electronic differential to allocate just the right amount of torque to the front and rear wheels, Electronic Traction Control, ABS brakes and Dynamic Stability Control, all under the watchful eye of a powerful central computer. That computing power is also put to use in the Terrain Response system, which allows the driver to dial in the surface – sand, snow, rocks, gravel, grass or normal road – so that the system can instantly reconfigure the engine, transmission, suspension and traction settings to ensure optimum performance.

But in essence the Range Rover has not changed since 1970. Then it was advertised as a luxury car, a performance car, an estate car and an off-road car all in one. Today, it's just the same.

LAND ROVER RANGE ROVER 2009	
ENGINE: 4,197 cc V8	
MAXIMUM POWER: 396 bhp at 5,750 rpm	
MAXIMUM TORQUE: 550 Nm at 3,500 rpm	
MAXIMUM SPEED: 130 mph / 209 km/h	
0–62 MPH ACCELERATION: 7.5 secs	
TRANSMISSION: 6-speed automatic	
LENGTH: 195¾ in / 4,972 mm	
WIDTH: 77 in / 1,956 mm	
HEIGHT: 75 in / 1,903 mm	
WHEELBASE: 113½ in / 2,880 mm	
MANUFACTURE DATE: 1970–present	
BRAKES: disc (f and r)	
SUSPENSION: MacPherson strut (f), double wishbone (r)	
WHEELS: alloy, 19 in	
TIRES: 255/55 R-19 (f and r)	

Lexus LS460

LEXUS LS460 2006

ENGINE: 4,608 cc V8

MAXIMUM POWER: 375 bhp at 6,400 rpm

MAXIMUM TORQUE: 498 at 4,100 rpm

MAXIMUM SPEED: 155 mph / 249 km/h

0–62 MPH ACCELERATION: 6.5 secs

TRANSMISSION: 8-speed sequential automatic

LENGTH: 198 in / 5,029 mm

WIDTH: 73¾ in / 1,875 mm

HEIGHT: 58 in / 1,476 mm

WHEELBASE: 117 in / 2,969 mm

MANUFACTURE DATE: 2006–present

BRAKES: disc (f and r)

SUSPENSION: independent multi-link (f and r)

WHEELS: alloy, 18 in

TIRES: 235/50 R-18 (f and r)

When Toyota decided to expand out of volume car production and into the luxury end of the market, it brooked no compromise: its intention, plain and simple, was to produce the best car in the world. In the boardrooms of Jaguar, Mercedes-Benz and BMW, little concern was shown. Surely it was inconceivable that a maker of small cars – albeit very good small cars – could produce anything to match the XJ6, the S-Class or the 7-Series.

But Toyota was serious, and it directed massive resources at the project. A team of nearly 4,000 started by evaluating the existing competition, buying cars like the XJ6, the S-Class and the 7-Series, stripping them down and analyzing every part in minute detail, looking for ways to improve quality at every turn.

After having built 1,000 prototype engines and 450 prototype cars, Toyota eventually came up with its first large luxury car, which was fitted with a brand new V8 engine. But still, the motor industry's establishment remained unconcerned, especially when the car was first presented. Its exterior styling was unexceptional: it was workmanlike and rather bland, and it didn't make a strong statement about the new brand – Lexus. In fact, it had no readily identifiable design cues to differentiate it from other cars.

However, when those same executives from Europe's premium brands first got the opportunity to drive the new Lexus LS 400, they were terrified. Against all the odds, Lexus really had got it right first time. The new car's 3,969 cc V8 produced

294 bhp at 6,000 rpm, more than enough to provide a top speed of 155 mph / 249 km/h, the speed to which most cars of that time were electronically limited. The V8 was mated to a brand new four-speed automatic transmission, driving the rear wheels in a conventional manner. The end result was far from conventional – it was truly impressive. The Lexus was quieter, smoother and more refined than any of its competitors. Its ride was effortless and compliant, yet at higher speeds, its handling was as good as that of any other large saloon.

As with its exterior styling, the cabin was understated, perhaps even rather dull. But there was no denying the sheer levels of comfort and luxury – the development teams had spent two years selecting exactly the right leather for the seats and had assessed no fewer than 24 different woods for the trim. Its cabin was filled with every conceivable luxury and gadget, which matched anything the opposition could muster.

The LS 400 was actually launched, in 1989, not in Japan but in the USA, which was always going to be its biggest market.

It was an instant success, partly because its price, $38,000, represented remarkable value, partly because the Americans recognized true quality when they saw it, and partly because, in true Toyota fashion, the Lexus was far more reliable and far better built than any of its competitors.

Since 1989, the Lexus brand has expanded to a full range of cars, but the LS remains the flagship. The most recent LS incarnation, the LS 460, has a larger 4,608 cc engine and its power is up to 375 bhp. Equally as interesting is the LS 600h, which has the same V8 engine but adds electric motors, thus improving fuel consumption in this hybrid model by 20 per cent.

What has not changed in the intervening years is the ethos of the company. When Toyota began the Lexus project in the early 1980s, the corporation's chairman, Eiji Toyoda, told his people to build 'the world's finest luxury performance saloon'. There will always be arguments about what is actually the best car in the world at any given time, but surely the Lexus flagship comes very, very close.

Lincoln Continental Mark IV

When the Mark IV Lincoln Continental was launched in 1972, it didn't appear to be dramatically different to the Mark III it had superseded, yet it was a fresher, more modern design that was destined to become an all-time classic. Many at the time considered it to be the best-looking car on the road in the USA, a car that simply oozed class and elegance. In fact, it was an all-new design that was longer, lower and slightly wider than its predecessor, and in which only the engine and transmission had been carried over from the Mark III.

It was quiet, smooth and refined, and while its soft suspension soaked up all the bumps in the road, it still managed to handle pretty respectably for such a massive car. The oil crisis had to put paid to the horsepower race of the 1960s, and emission controls were also having a serious effect on performance levels, yet the Lincoln Continental, with its big, lazy V8 engine, still provided highly respectable turn of speed and acceleration.

It had a Rolls-Royce-inspired prominent upright grille, with concealed headlamps on either side and front indicator lamps set into the wings. At the back, the rear boot lid was humped, as it had been in earlier Continentals, and the rear lights were set into the bumper, which served to emphasize the boot lid hump above

it. The two-door Continental Mark IV coupé was a little shorter, a little more powerful, and considerably more expensive than the four-door Continental sedan. (In 1972, the sedan cost $7,302 while the Mark IV was listed at $8,640.)

Under the massively long bonnet of the Mark IV was Ford's cast-iron 460 V8. The 7,538 cc unit produced 220 bhp at 4,000 rpm and 482 Nm of torque at 2,200 rpm. For such a large and heavy machine, 10.4 seconds to accelerate from 0 to 60 mph through its three-speed automatic transmission was quite respectable, and its 118 mph / 190 km/h top speed was on a par with that of its major competitors such as the Cadillac Eldorado.

But, like the Eldorado, its focus wasn't really on performance, but on luxury and comfort. The Mark IV cosseted its occupants not only with deep, soft seating but also with power windows, a powered moonroof and even illuminated vanity mirrors.

Owners were also given enormous amounts of choice in personalizing their cars, being offered, for example, a choice of 23 different paint colours, along with nine stripe colours. For the interior, options included four colours of velour trim and 13 of leather. In addition, there were Silver and Gold Luxury Groups, which offered metallic Silver or Gold paintwork, a

special colour-vinyl roof and an even more luxurious interior, with deeper carpets and special seat-cover designs. These packages did not come cheap: the Silver Luxury Group was an additional $400 and Gold, $438.

That this was just the sort of choice and opulence that Continental Mark IV customers wanted became clear when 1974 sales figures were announced: 57,316 units were sold that year, compared to 40,412 Cadillac Eldorados. This was the first time that the Continental had beaten its rival.

The Mark IV stayed in production until 1977, when it was replaced by the Mark V. Before that, though, a number of special editions were launched, called the Designer Series Marks, in which Lincoln collaborated with companies such as Givenchy, Cartier and Bill Blass to create specially coloured cars with unique interiors. This innovation was so successful that it was continued in the Mark V series of cars.

The Lincoln Continental Mark IV was a true classic of its time – a large, luxurious and prestigious limousine with style and elegance to match its performance. It was instantly recognizable on the road in its heyday and, indeed, it is still seen as one of the all-time greats.

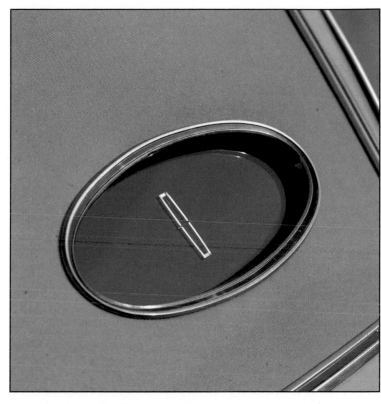

LINCOLN CONTINENTAL MARK IV 2-DR COUPÉ 1974

ENGINE: 7,538 cc V8

MAXIMUM POWER: 220 bhp at 4,000 rpm

MAXIMUM TORQUE: 482 Nm at 2,200 rpm

MAXIMUM SPEED: 118 mph / 190 km/h

0–60 MPH ACCELERATION: 10.4 secs

TRANSMISSION: 3-speed automatic

LENGTH: 228½ in / 5,801 mm

WIDTH: 79¾ in / 2,027 mm

HEIGHT: 53½ in / 1,359 mm

WHEELBASE: 120½ in / 3,058 mm

MANUFACTURE DATE: 1972–77

BRAKES: disc (f), drum (r)

SUSPENSION: independent coil spring (f), live axle (r)

WHEELS: alloy, 15 in

TIRES: 235/75 H-15 (f and r)

Maserati GranTurismo S

Maserati was bought by Fiat in 1993 after years of decline at the once-great Italian carmaker. Investment in a new model to re-establish Maserati's reputation was the first priority for the new owners, and with Fiat's help, the Maserati 3200GT duly appeared in 1999. It was an elegant coupé, styled by Giugiaro's ItalDesign and powered by a 3.2-liter turbocharged V8. It looked good, it performed well and it put Maserati back on the road to full recovery. During 1999, control of Maserati was passed to Ferrari (which was also owned by Fiat), with the idea that Maserati would become Ferrari's luxury-car division, while Ferrari itself continued to concentrate on supercars. With Ferrari's input, the Maserati Coupé and the convertible Maserati Spyder superseded the 3200GT in 2004.

Three years later, these models, in turn, were superseded by the Maserati GranTurismo. Maserati chose the same designer, Pininfarina, that it had used for its Quattroporte, and the GranTurismo shares its platform, suspension and engine with this earlier model. The GranTurismo's stylist, Jason Castriota, created a classic Maserati, with an eggshell grille that harks back to earlier models set into an aggressive but flowing 'coke-bottle' body shape that does more than hint at the car's performance potential. It's one of the most beautiful cars on the road today, effortlessly attracting attention wherever it goes.

Its 4,244 cc V8 produced 400 bhp at 7,100 rpm and 460 Nm of torque at 4,750 rpm and provided effortless performance: 0–62 mph in 5.2 seconds and a top speed of 177 mph / 285 km/h. That was more than enough to provide serious competition for the likes of the Aston Martin V8 Vantage or even the Porsche 911. Because Maserati viewed the GranTurismo as a grand tourer – hence its name – it was available only with automatic transmission, though it could be manually controlled via steering-wheel paddleshifters.

Then in 2008, Maserati introduced the GranTurismo S, fitted with a bigger and more powerful engine, uprated 'Skyhook' suspension, Brembo brakes and a sequential robotized manual transmission capable of changing gear in 100 milliseconds. Power from the V8, now bored out to 4,691 cc, was increased to 440 bhp at 7,000 rpm and maximum torque to 490 Nm at 4,750 rpm, which resulted in the 0–62 mph time coming down to 4.9 seconds and the top speed going up to 183 mph / 295 km/h. It shares the same engine, incidentally, with the Alfa Romeo 8C Competizione, though it has been tuned slightly differently here to suit the Maserati's greater weight and grand tourer character.

On the road, the GranTurismo S is one of the best-handling Maseratis of recent times. With the transmission incorporated in the rear transaxle, weight is 47:53 front to rear for good traction and reasonable balance, and thanks to the innovative Skyhook system's Sport mode, the dampers in the adaptive suspension system are sharpened up, the throttle response is quickened and the upshift points in the six-speed auto gearbox are raised when the car is being driven vigorously. Inside, the cabin is luxuriously tailored with fine Poltrona Frau leather upholstery and refined wood trims. It's a sophisticated, elegant and mature sort of environment with touches of Italian flair.

Soon after, a fully automatic GranTurismo S was launched, and in many ways, this became the perfect grand tourer. In place of the rear transaxle, the gearbox is fitted to the rear of the engine, and this improves the balance of the car to a near-perfect 49:51 front to rear. It can still be brutally fast when speed is required, but when driven more sedately, it provides the most comfortable and elegant means possible to transport four people and their luggage.

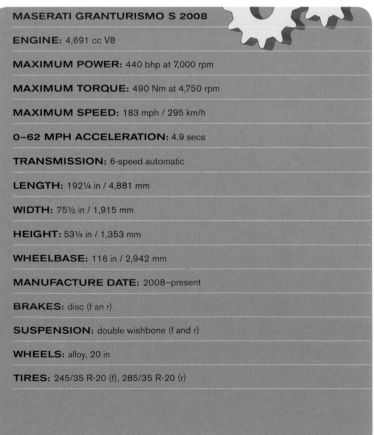

MASERATI GRANTURISMO S 2008

ENGINE: 4,691 cc V8

MAXIMUM POWER: 440 bhp at 7,000 rpm

MAXIMUM TORQUE: 490 Nm at 4,750 rpm

MAXIMUM SPEED: 183 mph / 295 km/h

0–62 MPH ACCELERATION: 4.9 secs

TRANSMISSION: 6-speed automatic

LENGTH: 192¼ in / 4,881 mm

WIDTH: 75½ in / 1,915 mm

HEIGHT: 53¼ in / 1,353 mm

WHEELBASE: 116 in / 2,942 mm

MANUFACTURE DATE: 2008–present

BRAKES: disc (f an r)

SUSPENSION: double wishbone (f and r)

WHEELS: alloy, 20 in

TIRES: 245/35 R-20 (f), 285/35 R-20 (r)

Maserati Quattroporte

MASERATI QUATTROPORTE 2004

ENGINE: 4,244 cc V8

MAXIMUM POWER: 400 bhp at 7,000 rpm

MAXIMUM TORQUE: 451 Nm at 4,500 rpm

MAXIMUM SPEED: 171 mph / 275 km/h

0–62 MPH ACCELERATION: 5.6 secs

TRANSMISSION: 6-speed automatic

LENGTH: 199 in / 5,052 mm

WIDTH: 74½ in / 1,895 mm

HEIGHT: 56½ in / 1,438 mm

WHEELBASE: 120¾ in / 3,064 mm

MANUFACTURE DATE: 2004–present

BRAKES: disc (f and r)

SUSPENSION: independent double wishbone (f and r)

WHEELS: alloy, 18 in

TIRES: 245/45 ZR-18 (f), 285/40 ZR-18 (r)

Maserati Quattroporte: it's a name that sounds exotic, as befits a car that is one of the world's fastest and most luxurious saloons, but in Italian, the word means simply 'four doors'. The first Quattroporte was launched as long ago as 1963 and since then there have been five other Quattroporte models – almost as many as the famous Italian manufacturer has had owners during those years.

That 1963 original was an exceptional car, powered by a 256 bhp V8 that gave it a top speed of 143 mph / 230 km/h. It had competitors at the time – the French Facel Vega and the British Lagonda Rapide were also spacious saloons capable of transporting four passengers in great luxury at high speeds – but the Quattroporte, designed by Frua, added great elegance to the mix. Subsequent, less memorable, Quattroportes included the Biturbo model produced from 1994 to 2000, which, despite being styled by Marcello Gandini of Lamborghini Countach fame, was an unremarkable, albeit impressively aerodynamic, design.

By the time the sixth generation of Quattroporte was launched in 2004, Maserati had become part of the giant Fiat empire and its operations had been moved alongside those of Ferrari. Pininfarina was commissioned to design the car, which was powered by the same dry-sump V8 engine fitted to the Maserati Coupé and Spyder, tuned to produce 400 bhp. Like the 1963 Frua original, this latest Quattroporte is sophisticated, luxurious and immensely comfortable, while at the same time offering its occupants plenty of space and high performance.

It's a genuine Grand Tourer in the real sense of the words. The interior is an object lesson in sheer craftsmanship. Owners can choose from six different wood veneers and numerous leather colours. The beautiful Poltrona Frau leather that's used on the seats and door panels has been subjected to a special tanning treatment, which results in ultra-soft but extremely hard-wearing leather. And to ensure that all occupants are aware of the model in which they are traveling, each headrest proudly boasts the famous Maserati Trident emblem.

Suspension is by double wishbones with coil springs over electronically controlled dampers and an anti-roll bar at both the front and the back. In normal circumstances, the ride is fairly soft and compliant, as befits a luxury saloon. But if the driver wants to press on, he or she can switch to Sport mode, which will firm up the dampers and virtually eliminate body roll in bends. It's a relatively simple system, but one that works very well.

The Quattroporte's 4,244 cc engine is set as far back as possible behind the front axle, and the automatic transmission is housed in the rear transaxle to provide a front:rear weight balance of 47:53 with the semi-automatic DuoSelect gearbox and 49:51 with the automatic. The result is excellent traction and well-balanced handling. With 400 bhp at 7,000 rpm and 451 Nm of torque on tap, it's good for 0–62 mph acceleration in 5.6 seconds and a top speed of 171 mph / 275 km/h.

And if that's not quite enough performance, owners can opt for the Maserati Quattroporte S. The same burbling V8 is used, but bored out to 4.7 liters to boost the peak power output to 433 bhp at 7,000 rpm and peak torque to 489 Nm at 4,750 rpm. It shares the standard Quattroporte's six-speed semi-automatic transmission and accelerates from 0 to 62 mph in 5.1 seconds and races on to a top speed of 177 mph / 285 km/h.

There are numerous alternatives to the Maserati Quattroporte, most notably from BMW, Audi and Mercedes-Benz. Volkswagen's Phaeton might also be considered. But one thing the Maserati has in its favour is its badge. There are not that many Maseratis around – only about 15,000 Quattroportes have been sold between 2004 and 2009 – and the Quattroporte has massive presence on the road. It's a car guaranteed to be noticed.

Maybach 62

When DaimlerChrysler decided in the late 1990s to develop the ultimate luxury car – one that would compete with, and even surpass, Bentley and Rolls-Royce – their research indicated that the world contained some 8,000 potential customers in the high-end luxury class. The same research also suggested that there were clear signs that this ultra-luxury market would actually grow over the coming years, so they felt comfortable predicting sales volumes of around 1,000 a year. The green light was pressed and Mercedes-Benz engineers and designers started work on developing a limousine that would embody the very highest standards of technology, design and quality.

The car would be called Maybach, which, until 1941, had been the name of a German luxury car brand. Mercedes decision to revive the name was a good one in many ways: the 1930s Maybach DS8, also known as the Zeppelin, had been the most prestigious German car of its day, and the founder of the brand, Wilhelm Maybach, was the engineering genius who worked with Gottlieb Daimler to produce the world's first cars. In 1901, he had designed the very first Simplex Mercedes, which is generally considered to be the world's first modern car.

For the latter-day Maybach, no stone was left unturned in the search for the ultimate in size, luxury and technical specification. The exterior styling is traditional, classic and even a little staid, but there is no denying that the Maybach has enormous presence on the road – literally, because the longer wheelbase Maybach 62 is nearly 20 ft 4 in / 6.2 m in length, and even the smaller Maybach 57, at 18 ft 8 in / 5.7 m, is enormous by normal standards. But in developing the Maybach, normal standards were never expected to apply. Instead, the idea was to recreate the space and luxury of a first-class aircraft cabin in a road car. And so the 62 is long enough to provide room for a pair of fully reclining rear seats, above which is a huge roof skylight – a laminated glass pane with a layer of liquid crystal foil that becomes more or less transparent as an electric charge is fed through it. So passengers can choose between a fully opaque, slightly frosted or totally clear roof. And that's just the start of the luxuries: ambient lighting, TV and DVD system, surround-sound stereo, rear curtains, folding tables, refrigerator, telephones, solar panels and acres of leather and deep pile carpeting are all part of the specification.

Despite its size and weight, the Maybach has astonishing performance on the road. Acceleration of the Maybach 62 from 0 to 62 mph takes just 5.4 seconds, and it has an electronically limited top speed of 155 mph / 249 km/h. It can achieve such performance thanks to its new 5.5-liter twin turbocharged V12 engine, which develops 550 bhp at 5,250 rpm and maximum torque of 900 Nm at 2,300 rpm. At the time the Maybach was launched, that gave it a higher output and more torque than any other standard production saloon-car engine in the world.

The car was launched in 2002 in one of the automotive industry's most lavish events: a Maybach 62 was transported to New York on board the QE2, then air lifted by helicopter to New York's Wall Street before being driven past the Stock Exchange. Despite this, the über rich failed to write the 622,748 cheques in the numbers Maybach had expected. Far from reaching 1,000 a year, sales volumes have been between 250 and 400 most years since the car's launch. To increase interest, sportier Maybach 52S and 62S models were introduced, followed by an armoured version, and finally, in 2007, by the ultimate Maybach 62 Landaulet, a semi-convertible model intended to be sold in small numbers. And it did sell in very small numbers, perhaps because of its 713,058 euro price tag.

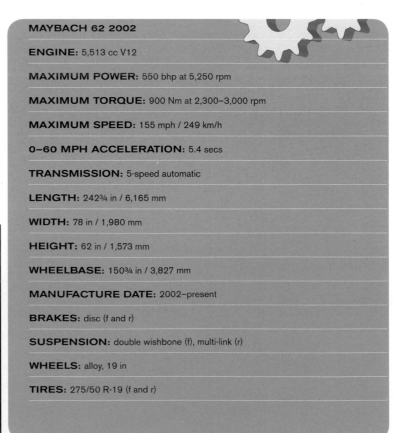

MAYBACH 62 2002

ENGINE: 5,513 cc V12

MAXIMUM POWER: 550 bhp at 5,250 rpm

MAXIMUM TORQUE: 900 Nm at 2,300–3,000 rpm

MAXIMUM SPEED: 155 mph / 249 km/h

0–60 MPH ACCELERATION: 5.4 secs

TRANSMISSION: 5-speed automatic

LENGTH: 242¾ in / 6,165 mm

WIDTH: 78 in / 1,980 mm

HEIGHT: 62 in / 1,573 mm

WHEELBASE: 150¾ in / 3,827 mm

MANUFACTURE DATE: 2002–present

BRAKES: disc (f and r)

SUSPENSION: double wishbone (f), multi-link (r)

WHEELS: alloy, 19 in

TIRES: 275/50 R-19 (f and r)

Mercedes-Benz 300 SL

When the aluminium-bodied Mercedes-Benz 300 SL was first revealed at the International Motor Sports Show in New York in February 1954, it was immediately clear that this was something truly special. Not only did it have eye-catching gullwing doors, but it was also claimed to be the fastest production car in the world, with a top speed of 165 mph / 266 km/h.

The 300 SL was originally conceived as a racing car, and it certainly proved its worth in 1952, winning at Le Mans, the Nürburgring and the Carrera Panamericana in Mexico. There were no plans to put it into production until Maxi Hoffman, the US importer of Mercedes cars, begged for a sports car to offer his wealthy customers. The 300 SL and the smaller 190 SL were duly signed off for limited production, though Mercedes-Benz never expected to sell very many, pricing the 300 SL at 29,000 Marks at a time when a standard Mercedes 170 saloon cost 7,900 Marks.

It wasn't just the gullwing doors that set the 300 SL apart. Its highly aerodynamic bodywork is beautifully proportioned and supremely elegant – and it's to the credit of its designers that it still looks fresh even today, more than half a century later. The aluminium body panels are fitted to a tubular frame, and it's that frame that dictated the choice of gullwing doors – because the frame extends so far up the side of the car, it would have been impossible to fit conventional doors.

The engine of the 300 SL was a six-cylinder 2,995 cc unit that was tilted to one side to fit it under the bonnet. This reduced space in the passenger's footwell, but helped keep the center of gravity as low as possible, as well as right in the center of the car. One of the 300 SL's innovations was the adoption of fuel injection, which raised the power output to 215 bhp, enough to provide a top speed of 146 mph / 235 km/h and 0–60 mph acceleration in 8.8 seconds with the standard set of gear ratios. Other ratios were offered, which either improved the acceleration or boosted the top speed to a maximum of 165 mph / 266 km/h.

With its 215 bhp on tap and a total weight of 2,855 lb / 1,295 kg, the 300 SL was extremely rapid for its time, though

34

customers wanting yet more performance could opt for a model constructed entirely from light-alloy aluminium, which reduced the total weight by 176 lb / 80 kg. Only 29 SL customers opted for this model, which is why these all-aluminium cars are so highly sought-after today.

Inside the 300 SL's cockpit, fabric seat material was standard, though most customers upgraded to a leather option. Getting in and out over the high sills was not easy, though facilitated thanks to a folding steering wheel. What all 300 SL models benefitted from was secure handling, impressive roadholding, accurate and precise steering, and performance that put most of its contemporaries in the shade. Its dynamic abilities alone were enough to ensure the 300 SL's place in history. But the addition of those gullwing doors established its destiny as one of the all-time classics. It was even voted 'Sports Car of the Century' in a poll held at the end of the 20th century.

Incredibly, only 1,400 of these 300 SL Coupés were built between 1954 and 1957. Of these, 1,100 were sold in the USA, which indicated that Hoffman knew his market well. He also quickly recognized, however, that demand was growing for a slightly larger, more comfortable and convertible sports car. He conveyed this message to Mercedes-Benz management, which first listened, then responded, with the more practical, open-topped 300 SL Roadster that first appeared in 1957.

MERCEDES-BENZ 300 SL 1954

ENGINE: 2,995 cc inline 6-cylinder

MAXIMUM POWER: 215 bhp at 5,800 rpm

MAXIMUM TORQUE: 275 Nm at 4,600 rpm

MAXIMUM SPEED: 146 mph / 235 km/h

0–60 MPH ACCELERATION: 8.8 secs

TRANSMISSION: 4-speed manual

LENGTH: 178 in / 4,520 mm

WIDTH: 70 in / 1,778 mm

HEIGHT: 51¼ in / 1,302 mm

WHEELBASE: 94½ in / 2,400 mm

MANUFACTURE DATE: 1954–57

BRAKES: drum (f and r)

SUSPENSION: independent coil spring (f and r)

WHEELS: steel, 15 in

TIRES: 6.70x15

Mercedes-Benz S65 AMG

MERCEDES-BENZ S65 AMG 2008

ENGINE: 5,980 cc V12

MAXIMUM POWER: 603 bhp at 4,800 rpm

MAXIMUM TORQUE: 1,000 Nm at 2,000 rpm

MAXIMUM SPEED: 155 mph / 249 km/h

0–62 MPH ACCELERATION: 4.4 secs

TRANSMISSION: 5-speed automatic

LENGTH: 199¾ in / 5,075 mm

WIDTH: 73½ in / 1,870 mm

HEIGHT: 58 in / 1,475 mm

WHEELBASE: 119½ in / 3,035 mm

MANUFACTURE DATE: 2008–present

BRAKES: ventilated disc (f and r)

SUSPENSION: active suspension (f and r)

WHEELS: alloy, 19 in

TIRES: 255/40 R-19 (f), 275/40 R-19 (r)

Most Mercedes-Benz S-Class customers are likely to be looking for a blend of high quality, refinement and luxury when making their choice of car. Certainly, a reasonable turn of performance is important, but it's unlikely to be the primary reason for signing on the dotted line in a dealership. But not all customers are looking for the same thing, and that's why there's room in the range for an out-and-out performance car, the S65 AMG. AMG is the performance arm of Mercedes-Benz, so it's not surprising to discover a faster car after AMG has breathed its magic on the S-Class flagship. What is amazing is that the S65 AMG is as actually as quick as many two-seater supercars.

The S65 AMG is claimed to be the world's most powerful production saloon, thanks to its hand-built 5,980 cc 36-valve twin-turbo V12 that pushes out a tarmac-blistering 603 bhp at 4,800 rpm and 1,000 Nm of torque. That's enough, despite the car's two-tonne weight, to accelerate from 0 to 62 mph in 4.4 seconds and on to an electronically limited top speed of 155 mph / 249 km/h. (Who knows what the maximum would be without that limiter?) Because of the massive torque, the whole of the drivetrain has had to be strengthened, so the five-speed automatic transmission, the driveshafts and the hub carriers have all been uprated, while the auto box has been reprogrammed to cope with the awesome output.

Normally, high performance and high weight are not a good combination, but the S-Class chassis, which was good at the outset, now becomes even better, as the Mercedes Active Body Control (ABC) system prevents roll in cornering, pitch under harsh acceleration and dive under braking. The driver can choose between Comfort, Sport and Manual modes for the dampers and leave the electronics to do the rest. The most recent incarnation of the ABS system even includes crosswind stabilization: influences caused by crosswinds are automatically compensated for, or in the case of strong gusts, reduced to a minimum. The system works by adjusting the wheel load distribution almost instantaneously whenever the yaw-rate and lateral acceleration sensors of the Electronic Stability Programme (ESP) detect the effect of crosswinds. Another piece of electronic wizardry is the Torque Vectoring system, which brakes the inside

rear wheel in a corner to assist handling and allow even swifter progress through the bends.

Inside the car, the driver is left in no doubt that this is a serious performance car. An AMG V12 Biturbo logo in the instrument cluster's central display is something of a giveaway, and it's confirmed by the main on-board computer menu that shows engine oil temperature, current gear range, battery voltage, and even lap times when on the race track.

But the S65 AMG is certainly not a stripped-out racer. Quite apart from a full leather and burr-walnut interior, there are all the comforts of a luxury saloon, including front seats with integral climate control and even a massage function. From the outside, the S65 AMG is distinguished by its flared wheelarches and unique five-spoke alloy wheels, and by more aggressive-looking air intakes, front spoiler and side-skirts. Front wing badges bearing the 'V12 Biturbo' logo simply confirm its identity.

In many ways, this is a completely mad car, not least because of its £145,000 price tag – very nearly three times that of the entry-level S-Class saloon. It's hard to rationalize why there should be a market for a super-luxury, super-performance saloon of this sheer size and weight. For some, the mere fact that it's the world's most powerful production saloon is reason enough. For others, the combination of fantastic performance with the ultimate in luxury means they can enjoy the best of both worlds.

Plymouth Superbird

To race in the NASCAR series in 1970, it wasn't enough for a manufacturer to build a certain number of standard road cars for homologation purposes – they also had to sell road cars that looked the same, aerodynamic add-ons and all. And that is how the Plymouth Superbird came to be one of the most outlandish, extragavent muscle cars of them all.

It had a long, bullet-shaped nose cone fitted at the front, a lengthened bonnet, a modified flush-fitting rear window and a massive rear aerofoil. In truth, the rear wing had virtually no aerodynamic effect at under 90 mph / 145 km/h and the reason it was set so high was mundane – it allowed the rear boot to be opened. Though the angle was fixed on road cars, in NASCAR racing, its angle was carefully adjusted to suit the characteristics of each different track.

All the 1,935 Plymouth Superbirds that were sold to the public also sported a vinyl roof, necessary to conceal the welding marks incurred during installation of that modified rear window. And if that wasn't enough to grab attention, the Superbird also came as standard with huge 'Plymouth' decals on the rear wings.

The standard Superbird engine was GM's 7,210 cc, fitted with a four-barrel carburettor and mated to a three-speed TorqueFlite automatic gearbox. It produced 375 bhp at 4,600 rpm and a healthy 650 Nm of torque at 3,200 rpm. An uprated 390 bhp version of the same engine with three dual-barrel carbs could be opted for and a four-speed manual transmission was also an option. Finally, owners looking for the optimum in performance could opt for the 6,981 cc Hemi engine, with its dual four-barrel carbs that churned out 425 bhp at 5,000 rpm and a tire-

smoking 664 Nm of torque at 4,000 rpm. The Hemi may have been the ultimate Superbird, but performance was outstanding whatever engine was fitted. Even the base Superbird was good for 0–60 mph acceleration in under six seconds, while the Hemi-engined versions shaved that time to 4.8 seconds. Top speed was between 130 and 160 mph / 209 and 257 km/h depending on the model.

The Plymouth Superbird was closely related to the Dodge Charger Daytona and it shared its torsion bar and heavy-duty hydraulic shock absorbers, front suspension and rear leaf semi-elliptical springs and heavy-duty shocks. It wasn't a sophisticated set-up, but then this was not a sophisticated car. Its sole aim was to extract maximum performance from its massive V8 engine. Vented disc brakes were fitted at the front, while self-adjusting rear drums were specified at the back. Inside, black or white vinyl bench seats were standard, though front bucket seats could be ordered. The carpets, instrument panel, rear shelf panel, steering wheel and headlining were black in all versions.

The Superbird remained in production for only one year, because NASCAR officials changed the regulations and decreed that any car running these aerodynamic modifications would be restricted to 4,998 cc engines, which would have made them uncompetitive. Though it seems strange today, Plymouth dealers struggled to find homes for all the Superbirds that had been produced, and some were even converted back to standard Road Runner specification just to get rid of them. Maybe it was because this supercar's appearance was just a little too extreme. Maybe it was because its extra 19 in / 483 mm

PLYMOUTH SUPERBIRD 1970	
ENGINE: 6,981cc V8	**WIDTH:** 76½ in / 1,941 mm
MAXIMUM POWER: 425 bhp at 5,000 rpm	**HEIGHT:** 61½ in / 1,560 mm
MAXIMUM TORQUE: 664 Nm at 4,000 rpm	**WHEELBASE:** 115¾ in / 2,941 mm
MAXIMUM SPEED: 160 mph / 257 km/h	**MANUFACTURE DATE:** 1970
0–60 MPH ACCELERATION: 4.8 secs	**BRAKES:** disc (f), drum (r)
TRANSMISSION: 3-speed auto or 4-speed manual	**SUSPENSION:** torsion bars (f), live axle (r)
LENGTH: 220 in / 5,588 mm	**WHEELS:** steel, 15 in
	TIRES: F60x15 (f and r)

in length meant it wouldn't fit in a standard garage. Or maybe it was because the standard colours – Lemon Twist Yellow, Limelight Green and Vitamin C Orange, for example – had rather too much visual impact.

Since then, however, it has become one of the most desirable and valuable muscle cars of all, with auction values for good examples reaching as high as $200,000 – not bad for a model that was difficult to sell for $4,298 in 1970!

Porsche Panamera

For the first time in its history, Porsche has announced a four-door Gran Turismo car – the Panamera. In another first, the car was initially unveiled at the 2009 Shanghai Motor Show, an indication of the growing importance of the Chinese market to prestige car manufacturers like Porsche.

A choice of two engines is available – a normally aspirated 395 bhp V8 petrol or a twin-turbocharged 493 bhp V8 petrol. Both rear-wheel- and all-wheel-drive chassis configurations are available, with the option of either a six-speed manual or a seven-speed double-clutch PDK transmission on the rear-wheel driver models. All-wheel-drive cars have a multi-plate clutch that adjusts the engine torque between the front and rear wheels according to need, and are fitted only with the double-clutch transmission.

There's also some choice in the suspension system: either steel springs or adaptive air suspension with a fully controlled damper system. The latter allows the driver to choose at the touch of a button how hard the suspension system should be set, allowing leisurely comfort in traffic but a more sporting set up on the open road. In this sense, the Panamera is trying to be two things at once: a luxurious limousine but also a thoroughbred Porsche sports car. It achieves this through some very clever technology, including the first engine Start-Stop system in conjunction with automatic transmission in the luxury-car sector, air suspension with additional air volume available on demand in each spring, and an active aerodynamics package that includes adjustable and extending rear spoiler on the flagship Panamera Turbo.

The specification list is astounding. Standard equipment includes a full leather interior, Porsche Active Suspension Management (PASM), Bi-Xenon headlights, rear ParkAssist, tire-pressure monitoring, automatically dimming rear-view mirrors, Porsche Communication Management with touch-screen satellite navigation and audio controls, and a Bluetooth telephone module – complete with cordless handset for use by rear seat passengers. An interesting feature of the Panamera is its 'Sport' button, which increases throttle pedal responsive, switches to harder suspension settings and adapts the shift patterns of the PDK transmission for quicker acceleration. And models equipped the PDK transmission also feature the Porsche Auto Start/Stop function. This automatically switches off the engine to reduce fuel consumption and emissions whenever the car comes to a halt in traffic or at traffic lights and then restarts the engine automatically when required.

The normally aspirated 395 bhp V8 provides 0–62 mph acceleration in 5.4 seconds and a top speed of 176 mph / 283 km/h, while thanks to its improved traction, the 0–62 mph acceleration time of the all-wheel-drive Panamera 4S is five seconds. There is a small payback in terms of top speed due to the slightly increased weight of this model, which can only achieve 175 mph / 282 km/h. As for the flagship twin-turbo 500 bhp V8, 0–62 mph time is reduced to 4.2 seconds and the top speed is 188 mph / 303 km/h.

Of course, that's just the sort of performance to be expected of a Porsche, but what is astonishing is that the Panamera also offers four well-appointed seats and plenty of luggage space. In this sense, it takes Porsche into a totally new market segment, combining a uniquely luxurious interior within a high-technology environment that's cloaked in a supremely elegant bodywork. It's clearly a Porsche – it couldn't be anything else – but it has the presence of a limousine rather than the raw aggressive power of a sports car.

Maserati, with its Quattroporte, has already demonstrated that there is a market for a seriously fast and seriously good-looking four-door limousine. Porsche faces further competition in the form of the Aston Martin Rapide, but its range of prices, from just over £72,000 to a little over £95,000, look competitive.

PORSCHE PANAMERA 2009

ENGINE: 4,806 cc V8

MAXIMUM POWER: 493 bhp at 6,000 rpm

MAXIMUM TORQUE: 700 Nm at 2,250 rpm

MAXIMUM SPEED: 188 mph / 303 km/h

0–62 MPH ACCELERATION: 4.2 secs

TRANSMISSION: 6-speed manual or 7-speed sequential

LENGTH: 195¾ in / 4,970 mm

WIDTH: 76 in / 1,931 mm

HEIGHT: 55¾ in / 1,418 mm

WHEELBASE: 115 in / 2,920 mm

MANUFACTURE DATE: 2009–present

BRAKES: disc (f and r)

SUSPENSION: double wishbone (f and r)

WHEELS: alloy, 19 in (f) 20 in (r)

TIRES: 265/35 ZR19 (f) 335/30 ZR 20 (r)

Rolls Royce Phantom Drophead Coupé

To celebrate its 100th anniversary in 2004, Rolls-Royce created the 100EX concept, a stunning drophead coupé that, in typical Rolls-Royce style, effortlessly combines elegance and engineering. It was displayed at various motor shows around the world and was so well received that work on a production version started almost immediately.

By the time of the 2006 Detroit Motor Show, the 100EX had been transformed into the Rolls-Royce Phantom Drophead Coupé, a two-door four-seater convertible that combines an ultra-modern aluminium spaceframe chassis with traditional craftsmanship – wood, leather, chrome and brushed steel are all part of the mix.

Thanks in no small measure to its hand-welded spaceframe chassis, the Drophead is not just one of the most rigid convertibles in the world but also one of the safest. The body uses both aluminium and brushed steel in the construction of the bonnet, grille and A-frame around the windscreen. (To solve the problem of corrosion, which is usually inevitable when these two metals are brought together, the Rolls-Royce engineers studied 20-year old stainless-steel-bodied DeLorean cars to assess long-term durability.)

The car features double-wishbone suspension at the front incorporating a hydraulic mount to reduce vibration. The multi-link rear suspension employs anti-lift and anti-dive technology to maximize comfort levels and ensure a smooth ride. To improve handling, the engine, gearbox and propshaft are sited as low as possible within the chassis to ensure a low center of gravity, and the lack of a roof helps in this respect, too.

The Drophead Coupé is powered by Rolls-Royce's 6,749 cc naturally aspirated V12, which produces 453 bhp at 5,350 rpm and 720 Nm of torque at 3,500 rpm. The company describes the output of the direct injection and variable valve timing engine, which is mated to a six-speed automatic shift-by-wire gearbox, as 'ample'. In this instance, 'ample' means 0–60 mph acceleration in 5.7 seconds and an electronically limited top speed of 149 mph / 240 km/h. Stopping power is provided by massive ventilated disc brakes as part of a sophisticated braking system that incorporates a four-channel anti-lock system, and Emergency Brake Assist in case of an emergency. This braking system operates in conjunction with an advanced dynamic stability control system that gives outstanding car control on the ragged edge.

So the Drophead Coupé is clearly no slouch on the open road, but most customers are not going to choose this car because of its performance, but because of its elegance, its luxurious cabin and its sheer beauty. The successfully achieved aim of the designers was to provide a practical all-weather

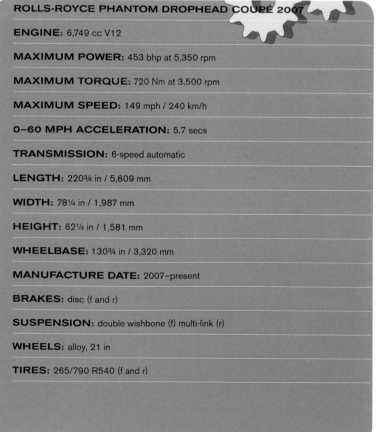

ROLLS-ROYCE PHANTOM DROPHEAD COUPÉ 2007

ENGINE: 6,749 cc V12

MAXIMUM POWER: 453 bhp at 5,350 rpm

MAXIMUM TORQUE: 720 Nm at 3,500 rpm

MAXIMUM SPEED: 149 mph / 240 km/h

0–60 MPH ACCELERATION: 5.7 secs

TRANSMISSION: 6-speed automatic

LENGTH: 220¾ in / 5,609 mm

WIDTH: 78¼ in / 1,987 mm

HEIGHT: 62¼ in / 1,581 mm

WHEELBASE: 130¾ in / 3,320 mm

MANUFACTURE DATE: 2007–present

BRAKES: disc (f and r)

SUSPENSION: double wishbone (f) multi-link (r)

WHEELS: alloy, 21 in

TIRES: 265/790 R540 (f and r)

convertible passenger compartment with the style and luxury expected of a Rolls-Royce. Inspiration came from the purposeful elegance of the 1930s America's Cup J-class yachts and, like a yacht, the Phantom Drophead Coupé was designed to be used in all weathers. In case of a sudden downpour, the seats have a smooth surface so moisture can be wiped off, and ultra-practical sisal mats are fitted. To ensure the car's suitability to all environments, hot-weather tests were held in Death Valley, USA, and the Namib Desert, while cold-weather testing was undertaken in the harsh winter conditions of Scandinavia. Of course, it's doubtful whether owners will drive in the rain with

the five-layer hood down, but the nautical theme is continued at the rear, where teak decking is used instead of conventional metals for the area under which the convertible roof is stored. Incidentally, according to Rolls-Royce, even with the roof down, there's still enough luggage space for three golf bags.

Those fortunate enough to be able to afford the Phantom Drophead Coupé are given a choice of nine unique exterior colours, six hood colours, 10 interior leather colours and six different wood veneers. Given that only a few hundred examples are made each year, this means that the chances are high that each one truly is unique.

Rolls-Royce Phantom

The German BMW Group took full control of the famous British Rolls-Royce Motor Cars Limited in July 1998 after a tussle with Volkswagen Group, which thought it had bought both Bentley and Rolls-Royce from the Vickers Group. It transpired that the rights to the Rolls-Royce remained with a different company, aero-engine maker Rolls-Royce Aerospace, so VW was left with Bentley and all the joint company's production facilities, while BMW owned the rights to use the Rolls-Royce name and little else.

BMW therefore got to work designing a new car from the ground up and building a brand new factory at Goodwood in southern England. By 2002, the first pre-production prototypes were completed, and the all-new Phantom was launched at the Detroit Motor Show in early 2003.

The design harked back to famous Rolls-Royce cars of the past, in particular the Phantom I and II models of the 1930s, the Silver Cloud of the 1950s and the Silver Shadow of the 1960s. All these earlier cars shared an extended wheelbase, a short front overhang, a prominent C-pillar, an enormous bonnet and an almost crouching stance, which gave the car the appearance of acceleration even when parked. These fundamental Rolls-Royce

design elements were all incorporated into the new Phantom, which of course also boasted the famous front grille and The Spirit of Ecstasy mascot.

Inside, the cabin is trimmed with the very finest leathers, cashmere trim and intricate cabinetwork. The rear doors open backwards in a feature that is not only another reminder of classic Rolls-Royce models of the past, but also allows easier access to the rear passenger compartment with its curved rear seat.

If the design and appearance of the Phantom looks to the past for inspiration, however, the car is as modern as it could be in technical terms. It has a lightweight aluminium spaceframe body, a bespoke V12 engine producing massive power and torque, self-levelling air springs and electronic dampers, which combine with the multi-link rear suspension, long wheelbase and high-profile tires to give both a wonderfully smooth ride and surprisingly good handling for such a large car.

One of the most astonishing features of the Phantom is that it is genuinely a driver's car. Its 6,749 cc direct-injection V12 produces 453 bhp at 5,350 rpm and 720 Nm of torque at 3,500 rpm. Despite its massive 5,478 lb / 2,485 kg total weight, it accelerates from 0 to 60 mph in 5.8 seconds and from 0 to 100 mph in 15.2 seconds and has an electronically limited top speed of 149 mph / 240 km/h. Yet despite its performance potential, the latest in combustion technology – which includes variable valve lift, variable valve timing and direct injection – gives the Phantom exceptional fuel economy for a super-luxury car of this size and weight. On the EU extra urban cycle it returns 25.7 mpg / 10.9 km/l and a combined figure of 17.8 mpg / 7.6 km/l.

When the new Rolls-Royce Phantom was launched, a number of unique detail touches ensured that no-one was left in any doubt that this is a truly special motor car. For example, the Spirit of Ecstasy mascot is electrically retractable, so it can be lowered

out of sight whenever the car is parked; the interlinked double-R logo at the center of each freely revolving wheel hub remains upright at all times; and an umbrella is stored in each rear door.

Developed from scratch, the Roll-Royce Phantom is a triumph of design and engineering. It oozes quality, luxury and distinction, while employing the best of modern technology. It's a truly worthy latest addition to one of the world's most famous brands.

ROLLS-ROYCE PHANTOM 2008

ENGINE: 6,749 cc V12

MAXIMUM POWER: 453 bhp at 5,350 rpm

MAXIMUM TORQUE: 720 Nm at 3,500 rpm

MAXIMUM SPEED: 149 mph / 240 km/h

0–62 MPH ACCELERATION: 5.8 secs

TRANSMISSION: 6-speed automatic

LENGTH: 229¾ in / 5,834 mm

WIDTH: 78¼ in / 1,990 mm

HEIGHT: 64¼ in / 1,630 mm

WHEELBASE: 140½ in / 3,570 mm

MANUFACTURE DATE: 2003–present

BRAKES: disc (f and r)

SUSPENSION: double wishbone (f), multi-link (r)

WHEELS: alloy, 21 in

TIRES: 255/50 R-21 (f), 285/45 R-21 (r)

Spyker C8 Laviolette

'Nulla tenaci invia est via' is the Dutch Spyker company's motto, which, translated from the Latin, reads 'For the tenacious, no road is impassable'. The company started as long ago as 1880, building the Golden Carriage in 1889 that is still used by the Dutch Royal Family, as well as a range of road and race cars – and also aeroplanes and aero engines during World War I – until it went bankrupt in 1926.

Then, in 1999, Victor Muller, a wealthy Dutch businessman, acquired the rights to the brand name. Within a very short period of time, the company has made a big impact, launching a series of high-performance supercars and creating the Spyker Squadron factory racing team to compete in endurance events such as the 24 Hours of Le Mans and the 12 Hours of Sebring. It even bought the Midland (formerly Jordan) Formula 1 team in 2006, racing under the Spyker name until selling it on to Force India in 2008.

Spyker's first car was unveiled at the Amsterdam Motor Show in 2001, and it was clear from the very outset that this was a different kind of supercar. As Victor Muller acknowledged, no one needs this sort of car, any more than anyone needs a Louis Vuitton handbag, but people still want to buy them.

The Spyker C8 Laviolette represents the extremes of both luxury and performance. Huge scissors doors that open upwards and a plush quilted-leather interior combine with gimmicks such as an engine starter button concealed by a red safety toggle (as found in jet fighters) to produce a car that's unashamedly like no other and that's done well in the Middle East as well as with Hollywood rappers and actors.

Whether you love or hate the car's 'in-your-face' style, there's no denying that its engineering is exemplary. It has an aluminium space frame, to which aluminium panels are mounted, and fully adjustable F1-style suspension with Koni in-board shock absorbers and massive ventilated disc brakes. The mid-mounted 4.2-liter V8 engine is fitted with stainless-steel four-into-one high-performance exhausts on either side. It drives the rear wheels through a sequential or manual six-speed gearbox via an optional limited slip differential. ABS is standard, as is switchable ASR traction control. Performance is sparkling: the car accelerates from 0 to 62 mph in 4.5 seconds and can reach a top speed of 187 mph / 301 km/h.

Many companies are set up to produce supercars – usually the dream of one man. But Spyker is different in that in a very short period of time it has created a range of supercars. Just eight years on from that initial launch in 2001, Spyker is offering, in addition to the 'normal' C8 Laviolette, a short wheelbase C8 Laviolette SWB, a convertible C8 Spyder, an extraordinary D8 Peking-to-Paris SUV and, most extraordinary of all, a C12 Zagato, of which only 24 will be built at a cost of £334,000 each. The latter's Audi-powered V8 is boosted to 5,998 cc and its power output to 500 bhp with 610 Nm of torque – more than enough to provide 0–62 mph acceleration in 3.8 seconds and a top speed of 195 mph / 314 km/h.

One thing is certain about the Spyker Laviolette – it is aimed at the very wealthiest car enthusiasts in the world. Having placed their £210,000 order, they can watch their very own car being built via a personal web cam installed at the workstation in the factory at Zeewolde in Holland. And while watching the aluminium panels being lovingly positioned, they can consider which options to add: perhaps a Chronoswiss Spyker watch with their own chassis number engraved for £24,000, a set of bespoke luggage for £12,350, or even a Louis Vuitton tool kit at £2,500.

SPYKER C8 LAVIOLETTE 2001

ENGINE: 4,172 cc V8

MAXIMUM POWER: 400 bhp at 7,000 rpm

MAXIMUM TORQUE: 480 Nm at 7,500 rpm

MAXIMUM SPEED: 187 mph / 301 km/h

0–60 MPH ACCELERATION: 4.5 secs

TRANSMISSION: 6-speed sequential or manual

LENGTH: 159½ in / 4,050 mm

WIDTH: 74 in / 1,880 mm

HEIGHT: 49 in / 1,245 mm

WHEELBASE: 100½ in / 2,550 mm

MANUFACTURE DATE: 2001–present

BRAKES: disc (f and r)

SUSPENSION: double wishbone (f and r)

WHEELS: alloy, 18 in

TIRES: 225/40 ZR-18 (f), 255/35 ZR-18 (r)

Volkswagen Phaeton W12 4 Motion

The Phaeton, Volkswagen's flagship saloon, is available with a V6 petrol or diesel engine, a 4.2-liter V8, or a diesel V10, but the really special model is the range-topping W12, with its 6.0-liter 426 bhp powerplant. The new luxury saloon was first revealed at the 2002 Geneva Motor Show and it went on sale in Europe that same year. It was an overt attempt by VW to upstage its German rivals BMW and Mercedes-Benz by producing a prestige car that would surpass the 7-Series and the S-Class.

A new steel platform was created, to be used for both the Phaeton and VW Group's Bentley Continental GT. And a radical new engine was also designed, a 5,998 cc W12, comprised of three banks of four cylinders to reduce weight and create a very compact unit. It's mated to a five-speed automatic transmission that allows the driver to shift gears via paddles mounted on the steering column. Air-sprung suspension allows the ride to be adjusted for normal or sportier driving and the ride height to be changed. VW's '4motion' four-wheel drive is standard on all Phaetons.

In keeping with VW's desire to create the very best, the huge cabin is sculpted in leather and wood, with every conceivable 'extra' provided as standard, including four-zone air conditioning, satellite navigation, rain-sensitive wipers and a magnificent stereo system. Build quality, too, is second to none: the cars are hand-assembled at a new high-tech and eco-friendly facility in Dresden.

On the road, the Phaeton is impressively quick. Its W12 engine produces its peak power of 426 bhp at 6,000 rpm and maximum torque of 550 Nm at just 3,000 rpm. That huge amount of torque at low engine revs produces speedy and effortless performance for such a large and weighty saloon – it accelerates from 0 to 62 mph in 7.7 seconds, while its maximum speed, like that of the majority of modern German cars, is electronically limited to 155 mph / 249 km/h.

The level of refinement is also superb. With its double-glazed windows, the Phaeton is virtually silent at tickover, and even when travelling at speed, noise from the engine, tires and wind is almost imperceptible. The Phaeton is an astonishingly comfortable, quick, spacious and refined luxury car, and VW's engineers are to be congratulated on their undoubted achievement.

There are just two problems. The first is its rather anodyne appearance: the Phaeton looks like a slightly larger VW Passat and has no real presence on the road. Like the Lexus LS range, its styling is bland and rather disappointing in that it fails to make any real statement. The second is its badge. Volkswagen started making small cars – in fact, the very name 'Volkswagen' means 'people's car' – and it is still one of the world's leading manufacturers of high-quality, high-volume production cars. And so, however good the Phaeton might be, it was always going to

struggle to match the prestige of its German competitors BMW and Mercedes-Benz, and even of that other VW marque, Audi. As a result, sales volumes were never as high as VW had hoped, and residual values of second-hand Phaetons suffered too.

Whether the Phaeton will be replaced in due course by a new VW flagship saloon remains to be seen. The company might decide it's enough to have one prestige luxury saloon in its range-topping Audi A8. But even if the Phaeton is considered to have been a commercial failure, it's been a glorious one, because in terms of quality, performance and comfort, the W12 is right up there with the very best in the world.

VOLKSWAGEN PHAETON W12 4 MOTION 2002

ENGINE: 5,998 cc W12

MAXIMUM POWER: 426 bhp at 6,000 rpm

MAXIMUM TORQUE: 550 Nm at 3,000 rpm

MAXIMUM SPEED: 155 mph / 249 km/h

0–62 MPH ACCELERATION: 7.7 secs

TRANSMISSION: 5-speed automatic

LENGTH: 199 in / 5,055 mm

WIDTH: 75 in / 1,903 mm

HEIGHT: 57 in / 1,450 mm

WHEELBASE: 113½ in / 2,881 mm

MANUFACTURE DATE: 2002–present

BRAKES: disc (f and r)

SUSPENSION: independent 4 link (f), independent trapezoidal link (r)

WHEELS: alloy, 18 in

TIRES: 235-50 R-18 (f and r)

FAST CARS

J222 MPH

AC Cobra 427

In 1961, AC Cars was an old-established British car company that had been manufacturing cars since 1904 and had been building the Ace sports car at its Thames Ditton factory in Surrey since 1953. The Ace, an elegant two-seater, was fitted with a Bristol 2.0-liter straight-six engine, a pre-World War II BMW engine whose performance was no longer really up to par. However, the chassis of the Ace was an excellent design. Consisting of a rigid ladder-frame construction with fully independent suspension all round, it was capable of handling far more power than the aged Bristol/BMW engine could offer.

American racing driver Carroll Shelby had raced in Europe and had noticed the Ace's potential – given a great deal more horsepower. He reckoned that a large V8 engine would transform the car, and asked AC if it could create a car modified to take just such an engine. He approached General Motors to see if they would provide the V8, then powering the Corvette, but was rebuffed, as the company at that time had a policy against racing. Ford, however, greeted Shelby with open arms, and offered him its recently developed 3.6-liter small-block V8.

Back at Thames Ditton, AC's engineers fitted the new V8 with little difficulty and, to cope with the added torque, mated it to a stronger Salisbury rear differential. With its disc brakes mounted inboard, this was the same unit used on the Jaguar E-Type. The first prototypes were ready in 1962 and so impressed Shelby and Ford that Shelby pressed AC to put thee cars into immediate production and Ford offered the even more powerful 4.2-liter V8 it had recently developed for the Fairline saloon.

Production duly started in 1962, AC building the cars and then shipping them to the US, where Shelby completed the fitting out in Los Angeles. Seventy-five of these Mark I AC Cobras were built before Ford uprated the Fairline engine to 4,736 cc, and these were then fitted from 1963 to the Cobra Mk II, of which around 500 examples were built. It was this engine that powered the Cobra to countless racing victories in the US and around the world.

A couple of years later, Shelby reckoned he needed even more power if he was to remain competitive. Thankfully, in 1965, Ford introduced a massive new seven-liter V8 for its Galaxy saloon, and this soon found its way under the bonnet of the AC Cobra. This Mark III Cobra – then called the 427 (the capacity of the 6,997 cc engine in cubic inches) – produced 425 bhp at 6,000 rpm and 490 bhp at 6,500 rpm in racing versions. All that extra power required some major modifications to the chassis, 4-speed manual transmission, and even the wheels and tires. All had to be strengthened and upgraded. What had started as an elegant and relatively understated sports car now had something of the appearance of a hotrod. The 427 was a nakedly aggressive beast whose appearance screamed raw power, and nothing demonstrated that potential more than the massive wheels and the widely splayed wheel arches that accommodated them.

And it wasn't all for show. The Mk III Cobra had a top speed of 180 mph and 0–60 mph acceleration in 4.5 seconds and 0–100 mph in 10.3 seconds. More radically, a special closed-top coupé, produced to compete at Le Mans, was clocked at 196 mph on the M1 motorway in England. Around 300 Mk III Cobras were despatched from England to Shelby in the US, including 31 cars intended for racing that were detuned and modified for the road. These S/C cars are among the rarest Cobras of all.

The final AC Cobras were made in 1967. Although since then, various similar models have been produced by AC and AutoKraft in the UK, and even by Shelby himself in the US, the real thing was made only in the 1960s, when the AC Cobra became a living embodiment of the American saying 'there's no substitute for cubic inches'.

AC SHELBY COBRA 427 1965

ENGINE: 6,997 cc V8

MAXIMUM POWER: 410 bhp at 5,600 rpm

MAXIMUM TORQUE: 626 Nm at 2,800 rpm

MAXIMUM SPEED: 165 mph / 266 km/h

0–60 MPH ACCELERATION: 4.5 secs

TRANSMISSION: 4-speed manual

LENGTH: 156 in / 3,962 mm

WIDTH: 68 in / 1,727 mm

HEIGHT: 49 in / 1,245 mm

WHEELBASE: 90 in / 2,286 mm

MANUFACTURE DATE: 1965–67

BRAKES: disc (f and r)

SUSPENSION: unequal wishbone (f and r)

WHEELS: alloy, 15 in

TIRES: 185x15 (f), 195x15 (r)

Ascari KZ1

Ascari Cars was established in Dorset, England, in 1995 to build a new supercar. This was the Ascari Ecosse, designed by Lee Noble (who later left to set up his own car company). With a BMW V8 engine in a light body, the Ecosse offered 200 mph / 322 km/h performance. Although only 17 were sold, the car caught the eye of wealthy industrialist Klaas Zwart, who bought the company and moved it to brand new premises in Banbury, Oxfordshire. Here, a new supercar was developed – the KZ1, which was first produced in 2003.

The KZ1 was developed from Ascari's racing activities, with the aim of creating a road car based on serious racing technology. Like the earlier Ecosse, the KZ1 used a BMW V8, borrowed from the 400 bhp M5 saloon, which but that was then tuned by Ascari to produce 500 bhp at 7,000 rpm and 550 Nm of torque at 4,500 rpm. The V8 was set behind the driver in a classic mid-engined layout, driving the rear wheels through the same CIMA six-speed manual transmission that is specified for the Pagani Zonda.

Interestingly, the proportions of the KZ1 are very similar to those of the McLaren F1. It has the same 169¼ in / 4,300 mm length and 44¾ in / 1,138 mm height as the latter and is just slightly wider at 73 in / 1,852 mm. Like the F1, it also has a carbon-fibre tub for strength and lightness with carbon-fibre body panels on top. In the KZ1's design, much attention was paid to aerodynamics. With a fixed front spoiler and extending

ASCARI KZ1 2003

ENGINE: 4,491 cc V8

MAXIMUM POWER: 500 bhp at 7,000 rpm

MAXIMUM TORQUE: 550 Nm at 4,500 rpm

MAXIMUM SPEED: 200 mph / 322 km/h

0–60 MPH ACCELERATION: 3.8 secs

TRANSMISSION: 6-speed manual

LENGTH: 169¼ in / 4,300 mm

WIDTH: 73 in / 1,852 mm

HEIGHT: 44¾ in / 1,138 mm

WHEELBASE: 103¾ in / 2,636 mm

MANUFACTURE DATE: 2003–present

BRAKES: disc (f and r)

SUSPENSION: double wishbone (f and r)

WHEELS: alloy, 19 in

TIRES: 235/35 X-19 (f), 305/30 X-19 (r)

rear spoiler, the KZ1 achieves both a relatively low drag coefficient of 0.35 and good stability.

The chassis, which was tuned by former Lotus engineers, uses unequal length wishbones, anti-roll bar and coil-over dampers at the front, with double unequal-length wishbones and coil-over dampers at the rear in a race-bred set-up, which results in pinpoint handling. Above all, the KZ1 was designed to be used by ordinary drivers, and although a pared-down track version is available – the KZ1-R – the standard car is intended to be malleable at low speeds and focused at higher speeds. Cross-drilled and ventilated discs ensure that the KZ1 stops as well as it goes.

Its performance is stunning: 0–60 mph takes 3.8 seconds and 0–100 mph only 8.3 seconds, while its top speed is more than 200 mph / 322 km/h. The Ascari KZ1 is more than a match for the Ferraris and Lamborghinis with which it competes. The difference is one of exclusivity. Only 50 KZ1 cars are to be built, each one by hand, taking 340 hours.
The KZ1 is beautifully crafted, in terms of both its aerodynamic

body panels and the cosseting interior, with its deep leather seats, leather-trimmed fascia and back-lit gauges, polished-aluminium controls and climate-controlled air conditioning. Above all, the KZ1 is a luxury GT – as befits its £235,000 price tag.

The car was first launched at Race Resort Ascari in Southern Spain, a private racetrack that Ascari owner Zwart developed near the town of Ronda, and whose corners are modelled on some of the most famous bends of racetracks around the world. There, KZ1 owners can explore the outer edges of their car's performance as part of a special package that gives them membership privileges at the resort.

In 2006, a revised Ascari model, the A10, was launched, based on the KZ1-R GT, which competed in the Spanish GT Championship. Even more power has been squeezed out of the BMW V8, whose output was boosted to 625 bhp, top speed raised to 220 mph / 354 km/h, and 0–60 mph acceleration time lowered to 2.8 seconds. The price too was raised – to a cool £350,000 for each of the 50 examples that Ascari plans to build.

Aston Martin DB5

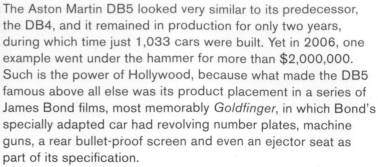

ASTON MARTIN DB5 1963

ENGINE: 3,995 cc inline 6-cylinder

MAXIMUM POWER: 282 bhp at 5,500 rpm

MAXIMUM TORQUE: 380 Nm at 4,500 rpm

MAXIMUM SPEED: 135 mph / 217 km/h

0–60 MPH ACCELERATION: 8.6 secs

TRANSMISSION: 5-speed manual

LENGTH: 180 in / 4,572 mm

WIDTH: 66 in / 1,676 mm

HEIGHT: 52 in / 1,321 mm

WHEELBASE: 98 in / 2,489 mm

MANUFACTURE DATE: 1963–65

BRAKES: disc (f and r)

SUSPENSION: wishbone (f), live axle (r)

WHEELS: alloy, 15 in

TIRES: 6.70x15

The Aston Martin DB5 looked very similar to its predecessor, the DB4, and it remained in production for only two years, during which time just 1,033 cars were built. Yet in 2006, one example went under the hammer for more than $2,000,000. Such is the power of Hollywood, because what made the DB5 famous above all else was its product placement in a series of James Bond films, most memorably *Goldfinger*, in which Bond's specially adapted car had revolving number plates, machine guns, a rear bullet-proof screen and even an ejector seat as part of its specification.

That $2,000,000 was for one of the four cars that had been specially adapted for the *Goldfinger* film, but even standard DB5s now attract astronomical values – not bad for a car that could be driven out of the showroom in 1963 for £4,175, or £4,490 for the convertible. Getting the DB5 into *Goldfinger* was brilliant timing for Aston Martin, even though its owner David Brown (the car took his initials) was apparently rather doubtful about loaning cars to the filmmakers. Aston had pulled out of motor racing, and the DB5 represented a heaven-sent opportunity to establish Aston Martin as a prestige road car marque.

In real life, the DB5 was closely based on the DB4, sharing its pressed-steel platform and wheelbase and its six-cylinder DOHC engine, though the capacity was increased from 3,670 cc to 3,995 cc. Maximum power was upped to 282 bhp at 5,500 rpm and peak torque now reached 380 Nm at 4,500 rpm. Other improvements over the DB4 included the adoption of an alternator, better Girling disc brakes in place of Dunlops, Sundym glass, electric windows and an oil pressure gauge as standard equipment. Performance was good for its time, though not outstanding: 0–60 mph acceleration in 8.6 seconds and a top speed of 135 mph / 217 km/h.

At the car's launch in 1963, buyers could choose between a four-speed manual gearbox (with electric overdrive as an added-cost option) and a three-speed Borg Warner automatic. A further option was a new all-synchromesh five-speed ZF manual. This became a standard fitment the following year and the old four-speed unit was dropped. In 1964, too, the Vantage model was introduced, with significantly more power, thanks to the fitment of triple twin-choke Weber carburettors, boosting maximum power output to 325 bhp at 5,500 rpm and maximum torque to 390 Nm at 3,850 rpm.

Both saloon and convertible bodies were available, with a detachable steel hardtop available for the convertible as an on-cost option. Although the bodies were made in England at Aston Martin's factory in Newport Pagnell in Buckinghamshire, they were constructed under licence from Touring of Italy, whose Superleggera – or Super Light – method involved fitting aluminium body panels over a lightweight tubular structure. The result is one of the most effortlessly elegant coupés ever built. Not surprisingly, the DB5 is regularly voted the most iconic and the most beautiful British car ever made.

In typical Aston Martin fashion, the cockpit features plenty of wood, pile carpets and leather – as all traditional British sports cars should. It's the sort of décor found in London gentlemen's clubs and it gives the car a homely yet luxurious feel. Suspension was by double wishbones at the front and a live rear axle, rack and pinion steering and disc brakes all round completed the specification.

For all its charm, the DB5 was beginning to show its age by 1964. Air conditioning was available only as a rather clunky add-on costing £320 and driving the car was a real effort, as both steering and the clutch pedal required considerable strength to operate. The car had also put on a great deal of weight, which meant it was out-performed by the Jaguar E-Type, which cost half as much to buy. These and other issues would be addressed in the later DB6 (1965–70), but not before 898 coupés, 123 convertibles and 12 very rare Shooting Breaks had been built.

Aston Martin V8 Vantage

The Aston Martin V8 Vantage was first shown as a concept car at the Geneva Motor Show in 2003 and was so well received that it was little surprise when a full production version was unveiled at the same show two years later. Like all Astons bearing the Vantage name, this is a serious performance car. At its heart is a newly developed, all-aluminium-alloy V8 tuned for both high power – 380 bhp – and low emissions. Each of the 4.3-liter engines is meticulously hand-assembled at Aston Martin's engine plant in Cologne, Germany.

Before the V8 Vantage was released for sale, 78 prototypes were relentlessly tested over a total of more than a million miles. High-speed testing was conducted at the Nardo test track in Italy and extensive testing was also carried out at Nurburgring's Nordschleife in Germany. Performance is superb, with 0–60 mph acceleration in 4.7 seconds and a maximum speed of 175 mph / 282 km/h. Its price was exceptional, too: at £79,000 in 2006, it cost considerably less than the DB9 and the flagship Aston Martin Vanquish. At the car's launch, the company said that it expected to sell around 3,000 a year, but response to the car was so good that within two years, more than 10,000 had been sold.

The engine of the V8 Vantage is front mid-mounted and connected to the rear transaxle and its six-speed manual transmission by a cast-aluminium torque tube and carbon-fibre prop shaft. This results in 49:51 weight distribution. The reduction of weight is almost an obsession in the design of the V8 Vantage. Its chassis is constructed from lightweight aluminium extrusions, precision castings and pressings, and the underframe is bonded with aerospace adhesives and mechanically fixed with self-piercing rivets. This unique VH (Vertical Horizontal) architecture provides a strong backbone, while the use of materials such as lightweight alloys, magnesium and advanced composites for the body further contributes to the car's low weight and high rigidity.

Unlike other Aston Martins, the V8 Vantage has a large luggage area behind the driver and passenger seats, accessed by a hatchback for practicality. But as with all Astons, owners have immense choice in the customization of the interior, with literally thousands of colour and trim options.

ASTON MARTIN V8 VANTAGE 2005		WIDTH: 73½ in / 1,866 mm
ENGINE: 4,280 cc V8		HEIGHT: 49½ in / 1,255 mm
MAXIMUM POWER: 380 bhp at 7,000 rpm		WHEELBASE: 102¼ in / 2,600 mm
MAXIMUM TORQUE: 410 Nm at 5,000 rpm		MANUFACTURE DATE: 2005–present
MAXIMUM SPEED: 175 mph / 282 km/h		BRAKES: disc (f and r)
0–60 MPH ACCELERATION: 4.7 secs		SUSPENSION: double wishbone (f and R)
TRANSMISSION: 6-speed manual		WHEELS: alloy, 18 in
LENGTH: 184¼ in / 4,683 mm		TIRES: 235/45 ZR-18 (f), 275/40 ZR-18 (r)

Soon after the V8 Vantage Coupé was launched, a convertible Roadster was introduced. A new cross-member was added to the chassis to compensate for the rigidity lost with the removal of the roof, but even the additional 200 lb / 91 kg of weight did little to affect the performance – it had the same 175 mph / 282 km/h top speed as the Coupé and only marginally slower acceleration (0–60 mph in 4.9 seconds). But Aston Martin looked after those owners wanting even more performance, offering various packages that increased the engine output, uprated the suspension and improved the aerodynamics. Then in 2007, a special N400 edition was announced to celebrate Aston's racing successes. It produced 400 bhp, had graphite wheels and upgraded suspension and was available in just three colours – black, silver and orange.

The whole range was updated in 2008, with the engine bored out to 4,700 cc to increase the power output to 420 bhp and peak torque to 470 Nm. In addition, a 'Sportshift' semi-automatic gearbox was offered as an alternative to the manual unit, the suspension was stiffened, and new 20-spoke alloy wheels were specified. The result was a higher top speed of 180 mph / 290 km/h and marginally improved acceleration, but more importantly, it benefited from a healthy increase in mid-range torque, making it even easier to drive quickly on winding roads.

But there's more to the Aston Martin V8 Vantage than mere performance. The reason why Aston had a three-year waiting list for this car is simply that it looks and sounds absolutely fantastic. Rivals such as the Porsche 911 and Audi R8 might beat the Vantage in terms of outright speed, but neither can touch the Aston for sheer elegance and beauty.

Audi Quattro

'Win on Sunday and sell on Monday' is a phrase often used to justify a highly expensive motorsport programme. The belief is that a car or brand that is successful on the track will create a halo effect that will benefit all the models in the same company's showrooms, thereby increasing sales. Another justification given for motor sport is that the technological lessons learnt in designing track cars benefit and speed up the development of the models that ordinary people can buy.

There's some truth in both arguments, and both are especially true of the Audi quattro (always spelt with a lower case 'q'), which was developed to take advantage of new regulations in world rallying that would allow four-wheel drive for the first time in 1980.

The development brief was handed to Ferdinand Piech (the great-nephew of Ferdinand Porsche), who moved to Audi after designing the legendary Porsche 917 racing car. Piech's genius was shown in his creation of a world-beating car at relatively low cost using components that already existed within the Audi range.

The starting point was the Audi 80 Coupé, which provided some of the bodywork, interior, and the front suspension, while the Audi 200 5T saloon shared its 2,144 cc five-cylinder turbo-charged engine, which produced 200 bhp at 5,500 rpm. Piech brought these parts together and created an elegant coupé that attracted much interest at the 1980 Geneva Motor Show.

That interest was directed underneath the car. The four-wheel-drive system was again lifted from the existing Volkswagen company parts bin, in this case from an off-road vehicle, called the Iltis, that VW had built for the German army. The system was a permanent four-wheel-drive arrangement, under which, depending on the conditions, either the front and rear differentials, or the rear differential alone, could be locked.

The new car was a revelation in the 1980 World Rally Championship, winning races in its first season, and attracted even more attention when Michele Mouton became the world's first female ever to win a World Rally Championship. With a little development it did even better: Audi won the World Rally

AUDI QUATTRO 1980		WIDTH: 67¾ in / 1,722 mm
ENGINE: 2,144 cc in-line 5-cylinder		HEIGHT: 53 in / 1,346 mm
MAXIMUM POWER: 200 bhp at 5,500 rpm		WHEELBASE: 99¼ in / 2,522 mm
MAXIMUM TORQUE: 285 Nm at 3,500 rpm		MANUFACTURE DATE: 1980–91
MAXIMUM SPEED: 137 mph / 220 km/h		BRAKES: disc (f and r)
0–62 MPH ACCELERATION: 7.1 secs		SUSPENSION: independent MacPherson strut (f and r)
TRANSMISSION: 5-speed manual		WHEELS: alloy, 15 in
LENGTH: 173½ in / 4,404 mm		TIRES: 205/60 VR-15 (f and r)

Constructors' Championship in 1982 and 1984, while the quattro took Hannu Mikkola and Stig Blomqvist to the World Rally Champions' title in 1983 and 1984 respectively.

On the road, the quattro made an equally impressive statement. On paper, its performance wasn't in the supercar league – it accelerated from 0 to 60 mph in 7.1 seconds and had a top speed of 137 mph / 220 km/h – but it had so much traction, particularly in poor weather conditions, that it could be hustled along swiftly and safely even by less experienced drivers.

The quattro remained in production until 1991, by which time 11,452 examples had been built. Over those 11 years, the body remained largely unchanged, though the engine was boosted to 2,200 cc in 1987, increasing power to 2,220 bhp and top speed to 143 mph / 230 km/h. At the same time, the manual center differential was changed to an automatic Torsen unit. On the rally circuit, the quattro clocked up 21 World Championship wins and then proceded to dominate other events, including the Pike's Peak International Hill Climb in 1986 and 1987.

The ultimate incarnation was the Sport quattro, developed on a shorter wheelbase for Group B rallying in 1984. Just a handful

of these carbon–Kevlar-bodied rockets were offered as road cars, producing 306 bhp and offering 0–60 mph in five seconds and a top speed of 150 mph / 241 km/h.

So successful was the original quattro that every four-wheel drive Audi since has been dubbed 'quattro' (the word, of course, means 'four' in Italian). As to Ferdinand Piech, the quattro's development chief, he went on to become the chief executive of the whole Volkswagen Group, which he expanded by buying Lamborghini, Bentley and Bugatti.

Audi R8

The centerpiece of Audi's stand at the 2003 Frankfurt Motor Show was the Le Mans concept, a two-seater sports car that paid homage to Audi's recent successes in the world-famous 24-hour race. Three years later, the concept became a reality when the Audi R8 was finally unveiled at the 2006 Paris Motor Show. But there was no doubting the heritage of this new supercar and, pointedly, it was officially revealed by Le Mans winners Tom Kristensen and Jacky Ickx.

Audi's audacious plan for the R8 was that, from day one, it should compete on an equal footing with the likes of the Porsche 911 and Aston Martin V8 Vantage. It was a tall order, but Audi is a company that thrives on competition. It put all the knowledge learnt from endurance racing, and particularly Le Mans, into the R8. The new car had a lightweight aluminium spaceframe chassis, a dry-sump aluminium V8 engine, with direct fuel injection and permanent four-wheel drive. Transmission is either a six-speed manual or a shift-by-wire R-Tronic semi-automatic controlled by paddles mounted on the steering wheel, which, in true motorsport tradition, has a flattened bottom.

Power comes from what is essentially the same engine as fitted to the Audi RS4, though adapted for dry-sump lubrication to allow the unit to be placed lower in the spaceframe to keep the center of gravity as low as possible. The 32-valve V8 produces 414 bhp at 7,800 rpm and 430 Nm of torque at 3,500 rpm. That translates into 0–62 mph acceleration in

AUDI R8 2006	
ENGINE:	4,163 cc V8
MAXIMUM POWER:	414 bhp at 7,800 rpm
MAXIMUM TORQUE:	430 Nm at 3,500 rpm
MAXIMUM SPEED:	187 mph / 301 km/h
0–60 MPH ACCELERATION:	4.6 secs
TRANSMISSION:	6-speed manual or semi-automatic
LENGTH:	174½ in / 4,431 mm
WIDTH:	75 in / 1,904 mm
HEIGHT:	49¼ in / 1,249 mm
WHEELBASE:	104¼ in / 2,650 mm
MANUFACTURE DATE:	2006–present
BRAKES:	disc (f and r)
SUSPENSION:	double wishbone (f and r)
WHEELS:	alloy, 19 in
TIRES:	235/35 ZR-19 (f), 295/30 ZR-19 (r)

commercial success, Audi refused to rest on its laurels and continued to develop the car still further. First came a V10-engined version with even greater power and performance. The engine – a development of the Lamborghini Gallardo V10 – has a capacity of 5,204 cc and produces 525 bhp at 8,000 rpm and 530 Nm of torque. Its 0–62 mph acceleration drops to only 3.9 seconds and the top speed is a whisker under 200 mph / 322 km/h.

If that weren't enough, at the 2008 Detroit Show, Audi showed an R8 TDI Le Mans concept, which had a 6.0-liter V12 diesel engine producing 493 bhp and a staggering 1,000 Nm of torque. The car looked even more aggressive than the standard R8, because the extra cooling requirements of the engine required a NACA duct on the roof. Sadly, however, the company believed that the cost of re-engineering the car to accommodate the longer V12 engine would be too high for them ever to make a return on their investment, and so what might have been the world's ultimate diesel-powered supercar never made it to market.

4.6 seconds and a top speed of 187 mph / 301 km/h, which, as Audi planned all along, makes it a genuine alternative to either the Porsche 911 or Aston V8 Vantage.

With a list price of £76,725 at the time of its launch in summer 2007, the Audi R8 cost a little more than the 911 at £71,980 and a little less than the Aston at £82,800. But it has some advantages over both its rivals. For a start, it shares much of its chassis and floorpan with that of the Lamborghini Gallardo, so there's no doubting its serious provenance. The Audi also scores in having permanent four-wheel drive for optimum traction and grip. And it's fitted with optional Magnetic Ride dampers, which can be changed from comfort to sport in an instant to improve handling still further at higher speeds. It's a system that's also used in the Chevrolet Corvette and the Ferrari 599.

The Audi's bodywork is distinctively low, wide and long. Its style has been dictated by the demands of aerodynamics, so it has large and distinctive air apertures under the front light, on the rear flanks and under the rear lights, too. Large diffuser openings and a small pop-up rear spoiler provide extra rear downforce at high speeds.

As soon as the Audi R8 went on sale, demand was such that buyers were willing to pay substantial premiums over the list price to get their hands on an early example. But despite this enormous

Bentley Continental Supersports

Bentley's current factory in Crewe has seen many changes since it started life building Merlin aero-engines for the Spitfire during World War II. After the war, crafting of luxury cars recommenced, but because of the high degree of craftsmanship involved in the woodwork, the leather interior, and even in the manufacture of its bespoke V8 engine, production numbers remained low for decades. As the new millennium came in, barely 1,000 Bentleys were being made per year: by 2008, just over 10,000 were assembled on the site.

The model that instigated this success story was the Continental GT, launched in 2003, which was smaller, lighter and significantly cheaper than other Bentleys. It also relied rather heavily on the Volkswagen Group parts bin, and, specifically, on the floorpan and engine of the VW Phaeton. But in terms of its style, its exclusivity and its effortless power delivery, it was a true Bentley. It is no exaggeration to say that the Continental GT transformed Bentley's fortunes. Unlike the traditional Bentley V8, the engine of the Continental GT was a 6.0-litre twin-turbocharged W12 design, producing 560 bhp at 6,100 rpm and 650 Nm of torque at only 1,500 rpm. It gave a top speed of 317 km/h / 197 mph and 0–62 mph acceleration in 4.7 seconds. Also new for Bentley was the Continental's permanent four-wheel drive system and electronically controlled six-speed automatic transmission. The GT's unique styling was the work of Bentley's Belgian design chief Dirk van Braeckel.

The Continental GT was an immediate sales success right around the world. But instead of resting on its laurels after the launch of the new car, Bentley immediately embarked upon a development programme, launching the four-door Flying Spur in 2005, the convertible GTC in 2006, and a more powerful GT Speed in 2007. For the latter, power was upped to 603 bhp, top speed to 325 km/h / 202 mph (incidentally, this was the first production Bentley capable of exceeding 322 km/h / 200 mph) and 0–62 acceleration in 4.3 seconds. But there was yet more to come. In early 2009, Bentley announced the Continental Supersports, the

BENTLEY CONTINENTAL GT SUPERSPORTS 2009

ENGINE: 5,998 cc W12

MAXIMUM POWER: 621 bhp at 6,000 rpm

MAXIMUM TORQUE: 800 Nm at 1,700 rpm

MAXIMUM SPEED: 204 mph / 328 km/h

0–62 MPH ACCELERATION: 3.9 secs

TRANSMISSION: 6-speed automatic

LENGTH: 189¼ in / 4,804 mm

WIDTH: 86½ in / 2,194 mm

HEIGHT: 54¼ in / 1,380 mm

WHEELBASE: 108 in / 2,745 mm

MANUFACTURE DATE: 2009–present

BRAKES: disc (f and r)

SUSPENSION: double wishbone (f), multi-link (r)

WHEELS: alloy, 20 in

TIRES: 275/35 X-20 (f and r)

fastest and most powerful production Bentley ever. It's also the first Bentley capable of running on either petrol or biofuel. The Supersports started as a project exploring the possibilities of weight reduction on the GT, but it soon blossomed into an official new car programme, with dramatic results. With output from the W12 raised yet again, this time to 621 bhp, and a new 'Quickshift' transmission that halves shift times, the Supersports sets new performance benchmarks, with acceleration from 0–62mph in 3.9 seconds and a top speed of 328 km/h / 204 mph.

To justify its 'Supersports' name, the latest Continental GT incarnation has a significantly uprated chassis and suspension, including retuned steering, and firmer shock absorbers and anti-roll bars. The rear track has been widened (so the rear wings are more flared), and the package is completed with new lightweight 20-inch alloy wheels and a unique electronic stability programme. Carbon ceramic brakes are a standard fitment – just one of the areas in which the engineering team managed to shave 110 kg / 242 lb off the car's weight. The body has a more extreme appearance, with new vertical air intakes at the side, and twin bonnet vents. The exterior grills, light bezels and window surrounds have been given a unique smoked-steel finish. And the changes continue in the cockpit, where carbon fibre and Alcantara trim are used to convey sporting intent and also to save weight. It is styling that underlines the Continental GT Supersports' supercar character – and that signal that this is the fastest, most extreme Bentley ever.

The 'Supersports' name is inspired by the original two-seater, three-litre Bentley Supersports model introduced in 1925, itself an evolution of the three-litre Speed. The lightweight, 85 bhp Supersports was the first production Bentley to reach 161 km/h / 100 mph and was also renowned for the application of Le Mans-winning race technology.

BMW M1

BMW's epic mid-engined M1 supercar was conceived in the mid-1970s as a homologation special: to race in Group 4 and Group 5, at least 400 production cars had to be built within a two-year period, and this was the design that BMW created. It was destined to become the very first of BMW's famous 'M' performance cars, and the first ever mid-engined BMW.

Yet, perversely, the performance potential of the car was never truly tested on the racetracks because BMW switched its attention to Formula 1 before the M1 was ever given a real chance to get into its stride. During 1979–80, a Procar series was instituted, which saw F1 drivers competing in identical M1 cars at each Grand Prix meeting of the season, but apart from that, the factory showed very little interest in the car. As a result, of the 455 M1s that were built between 1978 and 1981, only 56 were racecars; the rest were road cars.

The M1 was a truly radical leap of faith for BMW, which traditionally built front-engined, rear-wheel-drive cars, though it had produced a mid-engined concept in 1972 called the BMW Turbo. In fact, though the M1 is badged a BMW, the Bavarian company contributed only the engine initially – a modified 3,453 cc, six-cylinder inline unit producing 277 bhp at 6,500 rpm and 329 Nm of torque at 5,000 rpm. The design was by Giugiaro at Ital Design and the chassis engineering and manufacture was initially contracted out to Lamborghini, but the Italian company's financial problems meant that BMW had to switch final assembly to German coachbuilder Baur. The engine was mounted behind the driver and drove the rear wheels via a five-speed transaxle incorporating a limited slip differential. The all-independent suspension incorporated coil springs and wishbones front and rear, while massive disc brakes were fitted all round.

Performance was outstanding, with 0–62 mph acceleration in 5.6 seconds and a maximum speed of 162 mph / 261 km/h – figures that matched the performance of rivals such as the Ferrari Boxer or Lamborghini Countach. More importantly, the chassis that Lamborghini originally designed did a great job: the M1 enjoyed high levels of grip, neutral handling and great stopping power. In short, it had superb racetrack ability, and this pedigree was evident in the road cars too.

In fact, the customer cars were well equipped, with plush supportive seats, full carpeting, electric windows and even air conditioning. The engine was unstressed at 277 bhp output (the same unit produced 470 bhp in the Group 4 racers and was later modified, turbocharged and bored out to produce 850 bhp in Group 5 trim), and the M1 was tractable, easy to drive, reliable and reasonably practical. When the engine was revved freely, a cacophony of sound made its way into the cockpit from the

engine positioned just behind the driver, but when driven gently, the M1 was both civilized and even refined. In addition, in true BMW tradition, it was beautifully built – not something that could be said of many Italian supercars of that era. Not until Honda launched its NSX would there be another supercar that was so user-friendly.

Some observers at the time suggested that the M1 was not Giugiaro's finest example of design, and the car is certainly not as extreme as contemporaries such as the Lamborghini Countach, but the fact is that BMW imposed certain restraints, not least that the car had to have its trademark duel-kidney grille and had to use stock taillights. Nevertheless, its clean, elegant design has stood the test of time.

BMW M1 1978

ENGINE: 3,453 cc inline 6-cylinder

MAXIMUM POWER: 277 bhp at 6,500 rpm

MAXIMUM TORQUE: 329 Nm at 5,000 rpm

MAXIMUM SPEED: 162 mph / 261 km/h

0–60 MPH ACCELERATION: 5.6 secs

TRANSMISSION: 5-speed manual

LENGTH: 171¾ in / 4,360 mm

WIDTH: 71¾ in / 1,824 mm

HEIGHT: 45 in / 1,140 mm

WHEELBASE: 100¾ in / 2,560 mm

MANUFACTURE DATE: 1978–81

BRAKES: disc (f and r)

SUSPENSION: wishbone (f and r)

WHEELS: steel, 16 in

TIRES: 205/55 VR-16 (f), 205/50 VR-16 (r)

BMW M3 CSL

BMW M3 CSL 2003

ENGINE: 3,246 cc inline 6-cylinder

MAXIMUM POWER: 360 bhp at 7,900 rpm

MAXIMUM TORQUE: 370 Nm at 4,900 rpm

MAXIMUM SPEED: 155 mph / 249 km/h

0–60 MPH ACCELERATION: 4.9 secs

TRANSMISSION: 6-speed manual

LENGTH: 176¾ in / 4,492 mm

WIDTH: 70 in / 1,780 mm

HEIGHT: 53¾ in / 1,365 mm

WHEELBASE: 107½ in / 2,729 mm

MANUFACTURE DATE: 2003–present

BRAKES: disc (f and r)

SUSPENSION: strut (f), multi-link (r)

WHEELS: alloy, 19 in

TIRES: 235/35 ZR-19 (f), 265/30 ZR-19 (r)

At BMW, the letters 'CSL' are given only to very special models. The first CSL (it stands for Coupé, Sports and Lightweight) appeared in 1938 in the guise of the aluminium-bodied 328 Mille Miglia Coupé. In the 1970s, a further CSL appeared, derived from the 3,000 cc Coupé. Most recently, in 2001, a CSL made its appearance in the form of the BMW M3 concept car, which was followed two years later by a limited run of production cars.

The task faced by BMW engineers was how to improve on the BMW M3 model, which was already one of the fastest and best-handling compact saloons on the market. The starting point was to reduce the car's weight, and so wherever possible, sheet steel was replaced by carbon-fibre-reinforced plastic, as used in Formula 1 cars of that time. It's found in the roof, front bumper and air diffuser. The boot is made of sheet moulding compound (SMC) and incorporates an integral spoiler.

The engine is the straight six used in the M3, but modified with a new carbon-fibre air intake, larger inlet manifolds, revised camshaft profiles and modified exhaust valves to improve the flow of exhaust gases through a lighter thinwall exhaust system. The bald figures are 360 bhp at 7,900 rpm and 370 Nm of torque at 4,900 rpm. This engine is mated to a unique sequential M gearbox with Drivelogic, which again derives from F1 technology and which allows gearshifting in just 0.08 seconds. It can be driven in automatic mode or in manual mode using paddles on the steering wheel. The transmission also contains a sort of 'launch control', which guarantees maximum acceleration as the Drivelogic system shifts the six gears at exactly the optimum point shortly before the engine reaches the rev limit. Other modifications include revised suspension, uprated vented and cross-drilled brakes, a quicker steering rack and new 19-inch lightweight alloy wheels to further reduce unsprung weight.

On paper, the end result of all this development work appears to be not very much: 243 lb / 110 kg of weight have been removed, which is significant, if not life-changing; power is up from 343 bhp on the standard M3 to 360 bhp, and the 0–62 mph acceleration time is slightly quicker, at 4.9 seconds. The top speed, as in most BMW's, is electronically limited to 155 mph / 249 km/h and so

remains the same as that of the M3. But one hint of the M3 CSL's capabilities is shown by the fact that on production of a racing licence, BMW would remove that maximum speed limiter.

Settle into the racing seat that keeps the driver in place, despite 1.5G of lateral acceleration, and it becomes clear that the M3 CSL is indeed a very special car, and one of the very fastest that BMW has ever offered to the public. The first job is to use the many buttons to select the speed of the gearchange, the sharpness of the throttle response and perhaps to turn off the stability control system. There's another button to programme the car for a racetrack because, quite frankly, the outer limits of the CSL's potential could never be found on public roads, not least because the suspension is set so rock hard that it tends to bounce over bumps rather than soak them up.

But on a track, the CSL can truly come alive, and despite that relatively small increase in power and relatively small decrease in weight, it is radically, unbelievably quicker than the standard M3. BMW claim that when it ran the CSL around the north circuit of the Nurburgring, its lap time was a full 30 seconds less than that of the standard M3. And it's able to do this, quite simply because the M3 CSL accelerates and can be cornered faster and comes to a standstill more quickly when the driver applies the brakes. This is the basic difference between the standard M3 and the M3 CSL: the former is a civilized and versatile road car and the

latter is a wholly uncompromising road-legal racing car. One other difference is that, at £58,455, the M3 CSL, cost £18,720 more than the standard M3 when it went on sale in 2003.

BMW M5

The first BMW M5 appeared as long ago as 1984. It was virtually built by hand, with specialists in BMW's Munich factory marrying a 535i chassis with the engine from the M1 racer, and it created an instant sensation. At the time, it was the fastest saloon car in the world. Never before had genuinely supercar performance been available with four seats, and yet BMW actually downplayed the car's performance, quoting 6.2 seconds from 0 to 60 mph and a top speed of 153 mph / 246 km/h.

Since that time, each new generation of 5-Series BMW has had its M5 derivative. The E34 M5, which was launched in 1989, produced 315 bhp and offered 0–62 mph in 6.3 seconds and an electronically limited top speed of 155 mph / 249 km/h. Then in 1998, the E39 M5 was released, with 394 bhp and 0–62 mph acceleration in 5.3 seconds.

Finally, the 2005 E60 M5 was launched, and this raised the game once again. At its heart is a 4,999 cc V10 engine producing 507 bhp at 7,750 rpm and 520 Nm of torque at 6,100 rpm. This was the most powerful engine in BMW's line-up at that time, and it was also the first time BMW had fitted a V10 to one of its saloons. In the M5, it was mated to a seven-speed SMG sequential transmission, driving the rear wheels in true BMW tradition.

The M5's suspension is carried over from the all-aluminium suspension of the standard 5-Series, though uprated to cope with the additional power, and treated to a flurry of additional

BMW M5 2005

ENGINE: 4,999 cc V10

MAXIMUM POWER: 507 bhp at 7,750 rpm

MAXIMUM TORQUE: 520 Nm at 6,100 rpm

MAXIMUM SPEED: 155 mph / 249 km/h

0–60 MPH ACCELERATION: 4.7 secs

TRANSMISSION: 7-speed automatic

LENGTH: 191½ in / 4,864 mm

WIDTH: 72¾ in / 1,847 mm

HEIGHT: 57¾ in / 1,468 mm

WHEELBASE: 113¾ in / 2,889 mm

MANUFACTURE DATE: 2005–present

BRAKES: disc (f and r)

SUSPENSION: MacPherson strut (f), multi-link (r)

WHEELS: alloy, 19 in

TIRES: 255/40 ZR-19 (f), 285/35 ZR 19 (r)

electronic aids. These include Electronic Damper Control (EDC), which allows the driver to adjust the suspension's characteristics from sporty to comfortable by utilizing a choice of three different modes – comfort, normal and sport. The M5's suspension also features Driving Stability Control (DSC), though enthusiastic drivers can deactivate this at the push of a button.

In addition, the M5 is fitted with M Dynamic Mode (MDM), a subfunction of Dynamic Stability Control that allows the M5 driver to push the car to the absolute limit of longitudinal and lateral acceleration at the touch of a button located on the steering wheel. In this mode, DSC is not activated until the absolute limits have been reached, thereby permitting a sideslip angle the driver can just about cope with by means of moderate countersteering.

All those electronic aids are perhaps essential considering the performance of the M5. It accelerates from 0 to 62 mph in 4.7 seconds and from 0 to 125 mph in 15 seconds. Its top speed is limited to 155 mph / 249 km/h, but according to BMW sources, if the limiter were to be removed, the maximum would be around 205 mph / 330 km/h – some speed for a four-seater saloon costing £61,775.

The car looks like any other BMW 5-Series at first glance, though for the cognoscenti, the signs are all there. There's a modified front spoiler and rear apron that can't be found on standard cars, the side sills are modified, and the M5's wheel arches are noticeably wider to accommodate the massively wide Continental SportContact 2 19-inch tires. And for good

measure, the M5 has more aerodynamic exterior mirrors, four tailpipes and exclusive wheels. The exclusive leather interior features sports seats. Other styling touches, from the instrument cluster to the center console and the steering wheel, are all unique to the M5. There's even a head-up display for the driver to keep track of progress when the V10 engine is hurling the car towards the horizon.

When the first BMW M5 was introduced in the mid-1980s, it could fairly claim to be the best performance saloon in the world. Now, four generations of M5 later, BWM can still safely make that claim.

Caterham Superlight R300

The Lotus 7 was one of the works of genius of Colin Chapman, founder of the Lotus car company. His mantra was to always seek the simplest solutions to engineering problems and to strive to keep weight to an absolute minimum. If that could be achieved, he believed, then performance would look after itself.

The Lotus 7 went into production in 1957 and was sold to enthusiasts in kit form because British tax laws at that time exempted kit cars from purchase tax. This cosy arrangement came to an end when Britain joined the EEC in 1993 and introduced VAT in place of purchase tax. With the Lotus 7 now looking more expensive, Chapman decided to cease production and he sold the rights to one of the Lotus dealers, Caterham Cars. At that time, few would have believed that what is essentially the same car would still be in production more than 50 years after its initial launch.

Like the Lotus 7, the Caterham 7 delivers fairly modest power, but thanks to its extremely lightweight construction, it offers acceleration figures that supercars costing ten times

as much struggle to match. Even the most basic Caterham, powered by Rover's 1.4-liter K Series engine producing 105 bhp, is good for 0–60 mph acceleration in 6.5 seconds and a top speed of 110 mph / 177 km/h, thanks to its 200 bhp per tonne power-to-weight ratio. Three Caterham 7 Roadsport models are also available, all Ford-powered, with outputs of 125, 150 and 175 bhp and 0–60 mph times of 5.9, 5.0 and 4.8 seconds respectively.

Next up come the Caterham Superlight cars, which focus on lightweight performance on the road and track. All unnecessary comforts are removed to save weight and reduce mass, and the result is a car that delivers driving thrills at their purest, and quite staggering performance.

The 'basic' Superlight's 1600 Ford Sigma engine produces 150 bhp at 6,900 rpm and offers 0–60 mph acceleration in 4.7 seconds and a top speed of 125 mph / 201 km/h. The Superlight R300 was first launched in 2002, when it was powered by a Rover 1.8-liter K-Series engine producing 160 bhp

CATERHAM SUPERLIGHT 2002		WIDTH: 62 in / 1,575 mm
ENGINE: 1,795 cc inline 4-cylinder		HEIGHT: 31½ in / 800 mm
MAXIMUM POWER: 160 bhp at 7,000 rpm		WHEELBASE: 87¾ in / 2,230 mm
MAXIMUM TORQUE: 176 Nm at 5,000 rpm		MANUFACTURE DATE: 2002–05
MAXIMUM SPEED: 129 mph / 208 km/h		BRAKES: disc (f and r)
0–60 MPH ACCELERATION: 4.9 secs		SUSPENSION: double wishbone (f), de Dion tube (r)
TRANSMISSION: 6-speed		WHEELS: alloy, 15 in
LENGTH: 122 in / 3,100 mm		TIRES: 195/45 R-15

and boasted 0–60 mph acceleration in 4.9 seconds. It was Caterham's best-selling model until it went out of production in 2005, to be replaced by the Ford-powered Duratec powertrain.

This new Superlight R300 produces 160 bhp at 7,000 rpm. With the whole car weighing just 1,135 lb / 515 kg, it has a power-to-weight ratio of 339 bhp per tonne and performance to match – 0–60 mph in 4.9 seconds and a top speed of 129 mph / 208 km/h.

(To put that power-to-weight figure into some sort of perspective, the Porsche 911 Carrrera S boasts only 270 bhp per tonne.)

Standard equipment includes a six-speed close-ratio gearbox, wide-track Superlight suspension, four-caliper disc brakes, slender lightweight composite seats with four-point racing harnesses, and front wings, nosecone and dashboard constructed from carbon fibre. The cost of all this is £24,995 for those willing to build the car from a kit, or £38,445 delivered direct from Caterham ready to drive.

For most drivers, the Superlight R300's performance is more than adequate, but for the most hardcore supercar enthusiasts, Caterham offers two additional options – the R400 and R500. The Superlight R400 weighs the same as the R300 but is more powerful, producing 210 bhp from its 2.0-liter Duratec engine, and its 0–60 mph acceleration time is reduced to a mere 3.8 seconds. (The maximum speed remains at 140 mph / 225 km/h.)

The Superlight R500 produces even more power from the Ford Duratec 2.0-liter unit. It pushes out 263 bhp and, thanks to even more weight saving – the total weight has been reduced to 1,116 lb / 506 kg – it reaches 60 mph from rest in just 2.88 seconds and races on to a top speed of 150 mph / 241 km/h. This is a true record breaker: not only is its power-to-weight ratio an unbelievable 520 bhp per tonne, but its acceleration figures make it the world's fastest to 60 mph – and all for £37,995.

Chevrolet Camaro SS

CHEVROLET CAMARO SS 2009

ENGINE: 6,162 cc V8

MAXIMUM POWER: 422 bhp at 5,000 rpm

MAXIMUM TORQUE: 553 Nm at 4,500 rpm

MAXIMUM SPEED: 155 mph / 249 km/h

0–60 MPH ACCELERATION: 4.7 secs

TRANSMISSION: 6-speed manual

LENGTH: 190½ in / 4,836 mm

WIDTH: 75½ in / 1,918 mm

HEIGHT: 54¼ in / 1,377 mm

WHEELBASE: 112¼ in / 2,852 mm

MANUFACTURE DATE: 2007–present

BRAKES: disc (f and r)

SUSPENSION: multi-link strut (f), 4.5-link (r)

WHEELS: alloy, 20 in (f), 23 in (r)

TIRES: 245/45 ZR-20 (f), 275/40 ZR-23

The original 1967 Chevrolet Camaro and its sister car the Pontiac Firebird were rushed out by GM in direct response to the overwhelming positive public reaction to the Ford Mustang. The Camaro was based on the Chevy Nova, and even if the base model's six-cylinder engine produced only 140 bhp and had only a three-speed manual transmission, it certainly looked the part. Its $2,466 sticker price helped too.

From the earliest days of the Camaro, buyers could choose from a bewildering range of options, including the RS (Rally Sport) and the Super Sport (SS) package, which included an aggressively domed bonnet and a 5,735 cc V8 producing 295 bhp or even a 6,489 cc V8 pushing out 375 bhp. A second-generation Camaro was launched in 1970, a third in 1982, and a fourth in 1993. Some 4.8 million Camaros were sold between 1967 and 2002, when the fourth-generation model went out of production. Part of this massive sales success was due to the fact that each generation of Camaros included an SS version with higher power and unique styling.

After a gap of some five years, a new Camaro was unveiled at the 2007 Detroit Auto Show, and unlike many show cars, this one went into production in virtually identical form. It's built on GM's immensely rigid Zeta platform, which also provides the underpinnings for the Australian-built Holden Commodore and the US-built Pontiac GTO. It is currently available only as a coupé, though a convertible is due to go on sale during 2010.

The new Camaro has plenty of performance to back up its rather aggressive retro appearance. The base LS and intermediate LT models are powered by a 3,564 cc V6, which has variable valve timing to reduce emissions and increase power to 300 bhp at 6,000 rpm, with a healthy 370 Nm of torque available at 5,200 pm.

But, like previous Camaro SS models, the SS version of this latest Camaro has something rather special under the bonnet. Those fitted with the six-speed manual transmission have a 6,162 cc V8 with multiport indirect injection producing 422 bhp at 5,000 rpm and 553 Nm of torque at 4,500 rpm.

The automatic, meanwhile, is equipped with Active Fuel Management, which switches the engine to run on only four cylinders while the car is being driven gently. This reduces fuel consumption and emissions,

and peak power is reduced also, to 400 bhp at 5,000 rpm and 535 Nm at 4,500 rpm.

As for performance, Chevrolet has released no data, but it's reckoned the manual Camaro SS takes 4.7 seconds to accelerate from 0 to 62 mph while the smaller engined LS takes 6.1 seconds. Top speed will probably be electronically restricted to 155 mph / 249 km/h. The auto is unlikely to be quite as brisk, but the Camaro's power-to-weight ratio of 242 bhp per tonne should work very much in its favour.

So the Camaro certainly goes, and it stops quickly too, courtesy of four-piston Brembo disc brakes and standard ABS. And to keep the Camaro on the straight and narrow, it has a sophisticated multi-link strut front suspension and 4.5-link independent rear suspension. The multi-link rear suspension is a major step up from the live rear axle still used in the Ford Mustang. The Chevrolet Camaro's suspension provides secure and agile handling and plenty of grip with little body roll. The steering is communicative and responsive. All round, it's an impressive dynamic package as befits a modern-day muscle car.

At $22,995 for the Camaro LS and $30,995 for the SS, Chevy is offering a lot of car for the money. It's come rather late to

the muscle car revival in the USA, with Ford's Mustang GT and Dodge's Challenger SRT8 both getting to market earlier, but the Camaro is faster than the Mustang and $8,000 cheaper than the Challenger. The Camaro is well and truly back.

Chevrolet Corvette ZR-1

The Corvette is a living legend in American automotive history. Marketed as an affordable sports car for young adults, the first plastic-bodied Corvette was launched in 1953, and there's been a Corvette in production ever since. ZR1 is also a famous name in Corvette history, the first high-powered ZR1 joining the Corvette line-up in 1990. The latest Corvette, the Z06, went on sale in the summer of 2004 and the ZR1 was released as a 2009 model. For sportscar enthusiasts, it was well worth the wait, because it is a quite extraordinary beast.

For a start, its 6,162 cc supercharged V8 produces 638 bhp at 6,500 rpm and 819 Nm of torque at 3,800 rpm. That alone makes it the most powerful Corvette model ever produced. For good measure, it's also the most expensive, with a $105,000 list price at launch. But the cost is perhaps justified by the fact that the Corvette ZR1's performance and specification is the sort of thing that might be expected of an exotic supercar costing two or three times as much as this Corvette.

The supercharged V8 is hand-assembled at GM's Performance Build Center in Wixom, Michigan, using heavy-duty yet lightweight reciprocating components for optimum performance. It is then mated to a new, stronger six-speed manual transmission and a twin-disc clutch. ZR1-specific gearing in the transmission provides a steep first-gear ratio that boosts initial acceleration, and top speed is achieved in sixth gear – a change from the fifth-gear top-speed run-outs in the manual-transmission 'standard' Corvette.

The ZR1 is built on the same aluminum chassis as the Corvette Z06 and features similar independent front and rear suspensions, using wishbones with aluminum upper and lower control arms, transverse composite leaf springs, electronically adjustable Monotube shock absorbers and anti-roll bars. The ZR1 differs in the way the suspension is tuned and optimized for its massively wide front and rear tires. Magnetic Selective Ride Control is standard and tuned specifically for the ZR1. This provides a comfortable and compliant ride at normal speeds while at the same time enabling the dampers to be firmed up instantaneously when required, so that in vigorous cornering, the ZR1 can exceed a lateral 1g.

With such massive performance potential, stopping power is vital, which is why the ZR1 boasts vented and cross-drilled carbon-ceramic discs that are 15½ in / 394 mm in diameter at the front and 15 in / 380 mm in diameter at the rear – the largest on any production vehicle.

The ZR1 is instantly recognizable, thanks to its raised carbon-fibre bonnet. This incorporates a clear, polycarbonate window so that onlookers can see the top of the engine, which has the legend 'LS9 SUPERCHARGED' embossed on its sides and the Corvette crossed flags logo on the front. Carbon fibre is widely used to reduce weight, on the roof, front splitter, front bumpers and full-width, body-coloured rear spoiler. The theme continues in the cockpit with its lightweight seats.

The result is a car with a power-to-weight ratio of 420 bhp per tonne. That's better than that of the Porsche 911 GT2, the Ferrari 599 GTB Fiorano and the Lamborghini LP640 Murcielago. This is reflected in astonishing raw performance figures: a 0–60 mph acceleration time of 3.4 seconds – even quicker than the Ferrari Enzo's – and a 0–100 mph time of 7.8 seconds. Its maximum speed of more than 205 mph / 330 km/h can be reached from a standstill in a little over 30 seconds. In June 2008, Corvette development engineer Jim Nero set a lap time of 7 minutes 26.4 seconds on the famous 12.9-mile Nürburgring race track in Germany, driving a standard production ZR1. At the time, this was the fastest lap ever recorded for a production car. Indeed, only a handful of cars are faster. One such is the Bugatti Veyron, but then it also costs more than $1,000,000 more to buy.

At launch, GM executives said they planned to build around 3,000 Corvette ZR1s a year. That means the ZR1 will remain a relatively rare sight – and the most likely view of it will be a glimpse of its rear end fast disappearing towards the horizon.

CHEVROLET CORVETTE ZR-1 2009

ENGINE: 6,162 cc V8

MAXIMUM POWER: 638 bhp at 6,500 rpm

MAXIMUM TORQUE: 819 Nm at 3,800 rpm

MAXIMUM SPEED: 205 mph / 330 km/h

0–60 MPH ACCELERATION: 3.4 secs

TRANSMISSION: 6-speed manual

LENGTH: 176¼ in / 4,476 mm

WIDTH: 76 in / 1,928 mm

HEIGHT: 49 in / 1,244 mm

WHEELBASE: 105¾ in / 2,685 mm

MANUFACTURE DATE: 2009–present

BRAKES: disc (f and r)

SUSPENSION: wishbone (f and r)

WHEELS: alloy, 19 in (f), 20 in (r)

TIRES: 285/30 ZR-19 (f), 335/25 ZR-20 (r)

De Tomaso Pantera

'The finest Italian automotive engineering and design. With an engine American mechanics know and respect!' That was how Ford launched the De Tomaso Pantera in 1971. But why was Ford advertising a mid-engined Italian supercar?

The Pantera ('Panther' in Italian) had been unveiled at the 1970 New York Auto Show as the replacement for the De Tomaso Mangusta. Its chassis was very similar to that of the earlier Mangusta, though it had a brand new body designed by Tom Tjaarda at Ghia and a Ford V8 under its engine cover. Alejandro De Tomaso was aware that Ford was looking for a follow-up for its GT40 model, so he suggested that the Pantera should be built in larger quantities and that Ford should look after distribution in the USA while he himself would be responsible for sales elsewhere. Ford assented to the idea, and also agreed to part-fund the expansion in production facilities required by the significant added volumes.

At first it looked like a masterstroke. Costing around $10,000, the Pantera had the looks and kudos of a Maserati or Ferrari at a fraction of the cost, even if it was still twice the price of a Corvette. It was highly specified, too, with air conditioning, die-cast magnesium wheels and power windows as standard. Better still, the well-proven Ford 5,763 cc 351 cu in four-barrel V8 was not only far more reliable than any highly stressed Italian engine, but could also be serviced just about anywhere. The 'Cleveland' V8 produced 310 bhp in the USA and 330 bhp at 5,400 rpm in Europe, where emissions regulations were less severe. With the V8 positioned behind the driver and just in front of the rear axle, weight distribution was optimized, and with fully independent coil-spring suspension and the same ZF transaxle used in the Maserati Bora, the Pantera's handling should have been good.

Early road testers found it quite a handful, however, with a tendency to oversteer first and then snap into an oversteer spin. Apparently, tire pressures were critical to the handling, but not all buyers were informed of this. Early road tests also suggest that the early cars were not all built to the same standards: 0–60 mph acceleration times, for example, varied between 5.5 and 6.8 seconds, while top speeds were reported at between 129 mph / 208 km/h and 159 mph / 256 km/h.

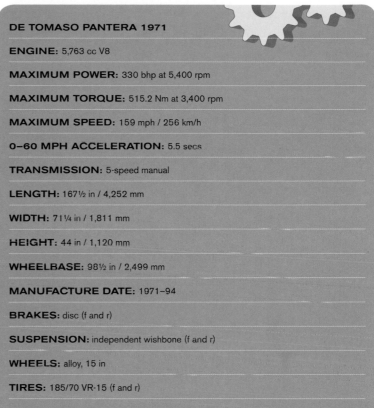

DE TOMASO PANTERA 1971	
ENGINE:	5,763 cc V8
MAXIMUM POWER:	330 bhp at 5,400 rpm
MAXIMUM TORQUE:	515.2 Nm at 3,400 rpm
MAXIMUM SPEED:	159 mph / 256 km/h
0–60 MPH ACCELERATION:	5.5 secs
TRANSMISSION:	5-speed manual
LENGTH:	167½ in / 4,252 mm
WIDTH:	71¼ in / 1,811 mm
HEIGHT:	44 in / 1,120 mm
WHEELBASE:	98½ in / 2,499 mm
MANUFACTURE DATE:	1971–94
BRAKES:	disc (f and r)
SUSPENSION:	independent wishbone (f and r)
WHEELS:	alloy, 15 in
TIRES:	185/70 VR-15 (f and r)

One explanation is that the earliest cars had lower gearing than later cars and so accelerated faster. And the difference in top speeds could be because the cars were to either US or European specification.

Sadly, there were other more serious problems with the Pantera. Despite Ford's claim in early adverts that the Pantera was 'A car so carefully built (it is virtually handmade) there will only be 2,500 made in the first year', build quality was questionable, rustproofing was minimal, its cockpit was cramped and poorly designed, its engine tended to overheat and its performance wasn't all that had been hoped for in its emasculated USA specification. Famously, Elvis Presley put two bullets into his Pantera in 1974 when it refused to start one day.

In 1974, ugly bumpers were fitted to comply with tougher new US safety regulations. In 1975, the regulations changed again, and would have required a complete redesign of the car and probably a new powertrain too, but Ford pulled the plug. It stopped importing the Pantera in 1974, by which time some 6,000 units had been sold. De Tomaso continued making the car for years in Europe, however, and it was actually re-imported into the USA in 1981 by motor traders in Santa Monica, California. It's estimated that between 1971 and 1994, when the Pantera finally went out of production, a total of 7,260 were manufactured.

Dodge Challenger SRT8

'King of the asphalt', booms the advertising material. 'Flawlessly sculpted design packing serious Hemi muscle with track-ready suspension and legendary styling.' Dodge could be describing its 1970s Challenger muscle car, but in fact it's praising an all-new 2008 Challenger, built some 35 years after the original.

The new Challenger looks, sounds and performs like a muscle car. What Dodge has so successfully created is a design that remains faithful to the Challenger heritage while incorporating a host of modern technologies. What is also encouraging is that the production Challenger remains pretty faithful to the concept car originally shown at the 2006 Detroit Auto Show. It's bold and aggressive in appearance and clearly harks back to the 1970s Challenger without becoming a dull retro design.

The latest Dodge Challenger SRT8 was engineered with a focus on the five pillars of every SRT vehicle: bold exterior design that resonates with the brand image, a race-inspired interior, precise ride and handling, an outstanding powertrain and benchmark braking. Under the long bonnet is a 6.1-liter Hemi V8 producing 425 bhp at 6,200 rpm and 569 Nm of torque at 4,800 rpm which translates into tire-smoking 0–60 mph acceleration in 5.0 seconds and a top speed of some 170 mph / 274 km/h – all for a shade under $38,000.

Unlike smaller-engined versions of the Challenger, the SRT8 is recognizable by its much deeper front spoiler, a rear spoiler and large brake-cooling ducts. Inside the cabin, the driver settles into a deep leather bucket seat and is faced with an array of dials and

DODGE CHALLENGER SRT8 2008

ENGINE: 6,059 cc V8

MAXIMUM POWER: 425 bhp at 6,200 rpm

MAXIMUM TORQUE: 569 Nm at 4,800 rpm

MAXIMUM SPEED: 170 mph / 274 km/h

0–60 MPH ACCELERATION: 5.0 secs

TRANSMISSION: 5-speed automatic or 6-speed manual

LENGTH: 197¾ in / 5,022 mm

WIDTH: 75¾ in / 1,923 mm

HEIGHT: 57 in / 1,448 mm

WHEELBASE: 76½ in / 1,946 mm

MANUFACTURE DATE: 2008–present

BRAKES: disc (f and r)

SUSPENSION: A-arm (f), 5-link (r)

WHEELS: alloy, 20 in

TIRES: 245/45 R-20 (f), 255/45 R-20 (r)

in-class interior space, but in truth, the rear is so cramped that this is best considered a very spacious two-seater.

The Challenger SRT8 comes with either a five-speed automatic box or a six-speed manual with dual clutch that has been lifted from the Dodge Viper – this is the first time a modern Hemi-engined car has had a manual gearbox option. A limited slip rear diff, a traction-control system, a more direct steering ratio, those upgraded Brembo brakes and a sophisticated multi-link suspension system are all part of the SRT8's comprehensive specification.

On the open road, the SRT8 handles like a dream, while the rorty growl of its Hemi V8 makes just the sort of noises that might be expected of a latter-day muscle car. And its overall performance makes this just as desirable in its own way as the original 1970s Challenger was. No wonder, then, that 4,300 customers placed orders on the very first day the Challenger SRT8 was announced. A year later, the Challenger range was extended to include a second Hemi engine – a 370 bhp 5.7-liter version – and a 250 bhp V6. It means Challenger prices start as low as $23,000.

But if the flagship ST8 is exciting, there's the distinct possibility of more to come. In late 2008, Dodge revealed a Challenger SRT10 Concept with a 600 bhp V10 crammed under its bonnet. Officially, this is just a concept car; unofficially, it could well be ready for production as a 2010 model. It seems the muscle car is enjoying a second coming.

computer read-outs set into carbon-fibre trim materials. The on-board computer, incidentally, records not only fuel consumption and current speed but also 0–60 mph acceleration, standing quarter-mile times, and even g-forces (0.88 g on the skid plan) and braking performance from the massive Brembo discs. (For the record, 0–60 mph takes just 110 ft / 33.5 m.)

Also standard is a 13-speaker Kicker audio system with a 322-watt amplifier and 200-watt subwoofer, a satellite radio and a MyGig infotainment system. Dodge asserts that there's seating for five in what it claims is the best-

Dodge Charger 500 Daytona

DODGE CHARGER 500 DAYTONA 1969	
ENGINE:	6,891 cc V8
MAXIMUM POWER:	425 bhp at 5,000 rpm
MAXIMUM TORQUE:	640 Nm at 4,000 rpm
MAXIMUM SPEED:	200 mph / 322 km/h
0–60 MPH ACCELERATION:	5.7 secs
TRANSMISSION:	3-speed automatic or 4-speed manual
LENGTH:	229¼ in / 5,821 mm
WIDTH:	76½ in / 1,946 mm
HEIGHT:	53½ in / 1,358 mm
WHEELBASE:	117 in / 2,972 mm
MANUFACTURE DATE:	1969
BRAKES:	disc (f), drum (r)
SUSPENSION:	upper and lower control arm (f), live axle (r)
WHEELS:	alloy, 14 in
TIRES:	F70–14 (f and r)

One of the most bizarre and extreme muscle cars of the late 1960s came about because of poor aerodynamics on the track and the fact that Ford was winning too many races. The 1968 Dodge Charger was quick but not quick enough. Quite simply, it generated far too much drag to compete on the banked NASCAR circuits, which the leading cars were lapping at close to 200 mph / 322 km/h.

To improve the car's chances, a closed front nose was fitted to smooth airflow at the front, and the rear window, whose shape had generated a vacuum and therefore loads of drag, was changed to a flush-mounted unit. This was the Charger 500, of which Dodge built just enough to qualify the car for NASCAR.

In a sense, the Charger 500 was a great success, in that it won 18 NASCAR races in the 1969 season. Unfortunately, however, the Ford Torino won 30. Returning to the drawing board, Dodge's aerodynamicists came up with some further tweaks. The nose was extended forwards by 18 in / 457 mm to reduce drag and increase downforce, and a massive rear tail wing was fitted to cut out rear-end lift at high speeds. Overall, the airflow was some 20 per cent more efficient than before, and this was enough to give the car a decisive edge over its Ford and Mercury competitors.

The new model was called the Charger 500 Daytona, and just over 500 examples were built and sold for homologation

Like its cousin the Plymouth Road Runner Superbird, the Charger 500 Daytona created loads of interest but generated few sales. Dodge had to produce 505 examples in order to race, but many were initially unsold in Dodge dealerships. In later years, the popular TV series *The Dukes of Hazzard* gave the Dodge Charger a massive publicity boost as the dukes' orange 1969 model, dubbed *The General Lee*, allowed them to outrun the sheriff in most episodes.

Today, all Chargers are sought after, with the Daytona – most especially one of the rare 75 Hemi-engined examples – being the most desirable of all. Costing around $3,993 when they were launched, they are valued well into six figures today, and the very finest examples can sell for as much as $750,000.

purposes. In fact, the car wasn't ready to race until very late in the 1969 season, but it made a huge impact on the roads, not least because every one came with red, black or white stripes down the sides bearing the name 'Daytona' in large letters. Another outstanding feature was the headlights, which were hidden in the front nosecone and flipped up when switched on.

The road cars were fitted with GM's 7,210 cc 375 bhp Magnum V8 as standard, though the 6,981 cc Hemi V8 engine was also available, producing 425 bhp at 5,000 rpm and 640 Nm of torque at 4,000 rpm. Transmissions were either four-speed manual or three-speed TorqueFlite automatic. The suspension arrangement was little changed from the standard Charger R/T chassis, with torsion bars at the front and leaf springs at the rear. However, the standard Charger's drum brakes were upgraded for the Daytona, with discs fitted at the front and a brake booster added to the rear drums.

Interestingly, although the road-going 500 Daytona looked quick even when it was standing still, it was actually slower to accelerate than the standard Dodge Charger 500 and had a lower top speed – simply because the new nose and tailfin added some 300 lb / 136 kg to the weight. On the racetrack it was a different story, however. The improved airflow made the Charger 500 Daytona decisively quicker than its rivals. So much faster, that US driver Buddy Baker recorded the first ever 200 mph / 322 km/h lap at the Talladega circuit in Alabama in March 1970.

Dodge Viper SRT-10

In the late 1980s, Chrysler was a company desperately in need of a shot in the arm. Its chairman Lee Iacocca had put in place a new model programme, but the new cars aimed at restoring the fortunes of the struggling company wouldn't be ready for launch until at least 1992. What Chrysler needed was something to excite the car-buying public right now. A small team was put together to create something at low cost – Chrysler didn't have much money to throw around then – but with an enormous 'Wow!' factor.

Fortunately, the perfect engine was available. The company had already developed an 8-liter V10 for its largest pick-up truck and this was shoehorned into an outrageously long and low two-seater sports car. The bonnet was enormous, to emphasize the power and potential of its engine, while the sharply cut-off rear resembled the haunches of a crouching beast. Massive side exhausts and enormous air vents completed the package.

In tribute to the Shelby Cobra, which was the initial inspiration for the project, the concept car that was revealed at the 1989 Detroit Motor Show was called the Dodge Viper. It was received with such enthusiasm that Chrysler put a small team of just 85 people to work on turning the Viper into a production car. Their collaboration was so successful that the first customer deliveries began in 1992.

The production car remained very true to the concept in appearance, though a huge amount of work behind the scenes was required. For example, although it would have produced loads of power, the weight of the engine in its cast-iron form

DODGE VIPER SRT-10 2008

ENGINE: 8,382 cc V10

MAXIMUM POWER: 600 bhp at 6,100 rpm

MAXIMUM TORQUE: 760 Nm at 5,000 rpm

MAXIMUM SPEED: 193 mph / 311 km/h

0–60 MPH ACCELERATION: 3.5 secs

TRANSMISSION: 6-speed manual

LENGTH: 175½ in / 4,459 mm

WIDTH: 75¼ in / 1,911 mm

HEIGHT: 47½ in / 1,210 mm

WHEELBASE: 98¾ in / 2,510 mm

MANUFACTURE DATE: 2008–present

BRAKES: disc (f and r)

SUSPENSION: double wishbone (f and r)

WHEELS: alloy, 18 in (f), 19 in (r)

TIRES: 275/35 ZR-18 (f), 345/30 ZR-19 (r)

torque at 5,000 rpm thanks to input from both McLaren Automotive and consultant engineers Ricardo in the UK. That monstrous output translates into 0–60 acceleration in 3.5 seconds and a top speed of 193 mph / 311 km/h for the Roadster and 202 mph / 325 km/h for the more aerodynamic Coupé.

Since its initial launch, the Viper has changed a great deal, developing from a fast but relatively unrefined sports car into a truly great supercar, whose performance, handling and speed is at least as good as those of competitors such as the Audi R8, Ford GT and Porsche 911 Turbo. What has not changed is the Viper's 'Bad Boy on the Block' attitude. And all credit to Chrysler for that!

would have badly affected the handling of a light sports car. As a result, a new aluminium-alloy version was created with the help of Lamborghini. This 7,990 cc V10 produced 400 bhp but was 100 lb / 50 kg lighter than the original truck engine. It also had lots of torque – 630 Nm at 3,600 rpm – which allowed the six-speed manual transmission to be long-geared to provide fast acceleration and reasonable fuel economy at the same time.

The Dodge Viper's performance was outstanding – 0–60 mph in 4.5 seconds and a top speed of 165 mph / 266 km/h – but its appearance was even more incredible. Here was a genuine supercar, with head-turning presence on the street, that had been conceived and created on a shoestring budget. It was a triumph for Chrysler, not only because of the interest it created but also because it demonstrated that a small team working closely together could achieve great things. Chrysler learnt the lesson: from then on, each new model was created by a dedicated 'Platform Team'.

A hard-topped coupé, the GTS, was added to the range in 1996, and at the same time, the chassis was strengthened, the suspension and brakes were refined and the engine output was boosted to 450 bhp, which pushed the top speed up to 192 mph / 309 km/h. Since then, the Viper and its GTS stablemate have been steadily improved and enhanced. The very latest 2008 Viper SRT-10 now produces 600 bhp at 6,100 rpm and 760 Nm of

Ferrari Enzo

Back in 1998, Ferrari boss, Luca Cordero di Montezemolo, had a big problem on his hands. The company had a history of producing supercars that set new standards. This started with the 250L in 1963, a road-legal racecar that became Ferrari's first supercar. Next came the GTO, launched in 1984 to massive critical acclaim, then the F40 in 1987 and the F50 in 1995. The company now had to come up with a successor to the fabulous F50, yet how was it going to create something even better than the supercar that had been designed to celebrate Ferrari's 50th birthday?

Montezemolo gave his engineers and the designers at Pininfarina three orders: make the car 'really impressive', employ the most radical technologies, and give it a clear association with the F1 racecars, which at the time were all conquering. Apparently, more than 20 proposals were considered, but the one that was ultimately chosen – and that became the Ferrari Enzo – was an aggressive silhouette with a nose resembling that of an F1 car and a body shape that was determined more by aerodynamic needs than by aesthetics. In short, the Enzo was never meant to look beautiful, just purposeful.

A brand-new V12 engine was commissioned, a 5,998 cc unit producing 660 bhp. Like Ferrari's F1 engine, it had a variable-length induction system and continuously variable exhaust-valve timing – a first for Ferrari. The engine and six-speed gearbox was bolted to the rear of the car's carbon-fibre tub.

Now came the 'radical technologies'. With the Enzo, Ferrari became the world's first manufacturer to integrate all the car's electronic control systems so that they could instantly communicate with each other and allow the central 'brain' to choose the optimum settings in all road conditions.

This connected the suspension (which had adaptive dampers that could be adjusted to provide more comfort or more body control) with the engine, transmission, traction control, ABS, aerodynamics and even the brakes. The brakes were carbon fibre, which produces immense stopping power. As in an F1 car, the driver could adjust the brake balance between front and rear.

The carbon-fibre bodywork was designed to optimize the car's aerodynamic performance. That's why it has a long front overhang and why, under the floor, there's a sophisticated venturi arrangement that speeds up the airflow, thereby increasing the downforce. It's so effective that at speeds over 180 mph / 290 km/h, the downforce is more than 1,764 lb / 800 kg. The resulting appearance is far from elegant, but it works.

The Enzo's 0–62 mph acceleration is a tire-shredding 3.6 seconds, it can achieve 0–125 mph in 9.5 seconds and it has a maximum speed of 217 mph / 350 km/h. Like the F1, the Enzo has a 'Launch Control' incorporated into the transmission, which provides the fastest possible start by 'dropping' the clutch at the optimum engine speed.

Launched in 2002 at the Paris Motor Show, the Enzo would inevitably be compared with two other supercars introduced at about the same time: the Porsche Carrera GT and the Mercedes-Benz SLR McLaren. It's possible to argue about which is the best-looking, the most practical or even the best all-rounder. But there's no doubt at all that the Ferrari Enzo is both the quickest and the most technically advanced vehicle in the world.

Ferrari had originally planned to produce just 349 Enzos, at a list price of £450,000, but because of demand from existing F40 and F50 customers, this number was upped to 399. Later, one more car was built, numbered 400, and was auctioned for nearly twice the list price, for the benefit of survivors of the 2004 Tsunami in Southeast Asia.

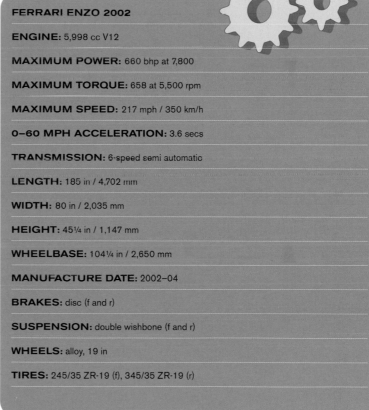

FERRARI ENZO 2002

ENGINE: 5,998 cc V12

MAXIMUM POWER: 660 bhp at 7,800

MAXIMUM TORQUE: 658 at 5,500 rpm

MAXIMUM SPEED: 217 mph / 350 km/h

0–60 MPH ACCELERATION: 3.6 secs

TRANSMISSION: 6-speed semi automatic

LENGTH: 185 in / 4,702 mm

WIDTH: 80 in / 2,035 mm

HEIGHT: 45¼ in / 1,147 mm

WHEELBASE: 104¼ in / 2,650 mm

MANUFACTURE DATE: 2002–04

BRAKES: disc (f and r)

SUSPENSION: double wishbone (f and r)

WHEELS: alloy, 19 in

TIRES: 245/35 ZR-19 (f), 345/35 ZR-19 (r)

Ferrari F40

'I asked my engineers to build me the best car in the world. And now it is here.' That is how Enzo Ferrari introduced the F40 model, the car launched to celebrate Ferrari's 40th anniversary in 1988. This was a truly special Ferrari, not least because it was the very last launched before the death, that same year, of the company's founder, Enzo himself. It was the very epitome of the 1980s supercar: its styling was aggressive and raw, its performance was head-and-shoulders above any other car of its time, and its handling was so good that only a truly skilled racing driver could extract the very maximum from its awesome potential.

The F40, designed like so many Ferraris by Pininfarina, was not beautiful, yet it looked so right. It certainly wasn't comfortable, yet none of its owners complained about that. And it wasn't particularly sophisticated in its engineering, yet its performance was all that really mattered. A top speed of 202 mph / 325 km/h was truly special back in 1988. The F40 was built just like a racing car, yet Ferrari never officially raced. However, it did provide assistance to privateers who wanted to extract the ultimate performance on the track – and some modified racecars eventually pushed out as much as 700 bhp.

Its suspension closely followed contemporary racing car design, with double wishbones front and rear, coil springs and

FERRARI F40 1988

ENGINE: 2,936 cc V8

MAXIMUM POWER: 478 bhp at 7,000 rpm

MAXIMUM TORQUE: 576 Nm at 4,500 rpm

MAXIMUM SPEED: 202 mph / 325 km/h

0–60 MPH ACCELERATION: 3.5 secs

TRANSMISSION: 5-speed manual

LENGTH: 174½ in / 4,430 mm

WIDTH: 78 in / 1,980 mm

HEIGHT: 44½ in / 1,130 mm

WHEELBASE: 96½ in / 2,450 mm

MANUFACTURE DATE: 1988–91

BRAKES: disc (f and r)

SUSPENSION: independent double wishbone (f and r)

WHEELS: alloy, 17 in

TIRES: 245/40 ZR-17 (f), 335/35 ZR-17 (r)

There were few concessions to creature comforts in the cockpit either. There were no carpets, no stereo, and not even any interior panelling – the doors and other panels were simply exposed carbon fibre. The one item that was included was air conditioning, but only because the Middle East was an important market for Ferrari and it realized that this really was essential there.

When it first announced the F40, Ferrari said it would produce just 400. But faced with an order bank that initially exceeded 3,000, the production line was kept rolling, and in the end, more than 1,300 examples were produced between 1988 and 1991. Even today, the F40 still looks fresh. It was conceived as an uncompromising sports car, one that would offer levels of performance previously unheard of in a road car. It was, and remains, a classic Ferrari, and it stands as a homage to the man who created it: the 'Old Man' himself, Enzo Ferrari.

dampers and anti-roll bars front and rear. Ventilated discs were standard to ensure adequate braking, which was important, because the F40's performance was truly stunning for its day. It was entirely possible, in dry conditions, to spin the wheels when accelerating in first, second and third gears and, despite the massive tires (335/35 ZR17 at the rear and 245/40 ZR17 at the front), it took a highly skilled driver to balance the massive power delivery with the available grip.

That power came from an engine that was not directly linked to the current Ferrari F1 powerplant, but it was a V8 instead of the usual Ferrari high-revving V12. The F40's V8 was a twin-turbo, twin-turbocharged double overhead cam design that pushed 478 bhp through a five-speed manual transmission to the rear wheels. It achieved 0–60 mph in a tire-shredding 3.8 seconds, 0–100 mph took just 8.2 seconds. It's not certain whether the magic 200 mph / 322 km/h figure was actually achievable, but what was important at the time was that Ferrari claimed it for the F40.

Like the 288 GTO, to which the F40 was the spiritual successor, it had a tubular-steel chassis. But unlike the 288, the F40 made extensive use of Kevlar and carbon-fibre composites on the floorpan, fascia and bulkhead. In addition, its body panels were composed of composite materials, its side windows and rear screen were made of plexiglass, and even the seats were made from carbon fibre, all to save weight.

Ford GT

It all started in 2002, when Ford decided it should make a massive statement to celebrate its forthcoming centenary. And what better way to pay heritage to the past, while at the same time looking confidently to the future, than to create a successor to the legendary 1960s Le Mans-winning GT40?

The concept car, which was unveiled at the 2002 Detroit Auto Show, shared the silhouette of the original GT40 and was obviously inspired by it. Some purists saw it as a weak retro pastiche, but most were enthused by the latter-day supercar project, and in general, it received such a favourable reception that Ford gave it the green light for production. The team with the task of turning what was no more than a show car into a street-legal production was given a deadline: the car had to be ready for the centenary celebrations in June 2003.

The exterior styling might hark back to the 1960s, but underneath, the Ford GT is all 21st century. Its aluminium body sits on an immensely strong aluminium spaceframe chassis. The 5.4-liter supercharged V8 engine is mid-mounted behind the passenger cabin and drives the rear wheels via a six-speed manual transmission and a limited slip differential. The suspension is all independent, with double wishbones front and rear.

On the road, the grip provided by the massive Goodyear Eagle tires is immense, helped in the downforce produced at higher speeds by the venturi tunnel designed into the floorpan. As with the McLaren F1, the Ford GT's designers chose to fit neither traction control nor an electronic stability control system, leaving it to the driver to harness the power of the V8 engine.

And what power! The all-aluminium V8 was already in use in different Ford trucks and SUVs, but for the GT40, a Lysholm supercharger was added, together with revised cylinder heads and hotter high-lift camshafts. The result is 550 bhp and 678 Nm of torque – more than enough to offer 0–60 mph acceleration in 3.7 seconds, 0–100 mph in 7.4 seconds and a top speed of 204 mph / 328 km/h.

Despite its awesome performance, the Ford GT is actually a reasonably practical proposition. Though it can be driven as fast as any Ferrari or Lamborghini, its massive torque and tractability means it can be cruised with ease – it can be left in third gear, for example, all the way from 30 mph / 48 km/h to 120 mph / 93 km/h.

The cabin is larger, more comfortable and more practical than that of the original GT40, which was hampered by being so low – the '40' of its name derived from its height, which was just 40 in / 1,016 mm. Thanks, too, to modern legislation, the latest Ford GT is longer, wider and higher than the original, and this allows more space for the driver and passenger to get comfortable. Like the original, however, the GT has no luggage space.

Ford announced a production run of just 4,500 examples of the GT and was immediately inundated with enquiries and orders. However, although early customers were even willing to pay premiums of $100,000 or more above the list price of $203,599, in the end, only 4,038 were built before production was stopped in 2006.

The Ford GT is one of the great supercars of the 21st century, one that more than achieved the ambitions of its designers to create a car that would combine all the performance, brilliance and image of a Ferrari 360 with the practicality, reliability, build quality and ease of driving of a Honda NSX. It was the perfect 100th birthday present for Ford.

FORD GT 2003

ENGINE: 5,409 cc V8

MAXIMUM POWER: 550 bhp at 6,500 rpm

MAXIMUM TORQUE: 678 Nm at 3,750 rpm

MAXIMUM SPEED: 204 mph / 328 km/h

0–60 MPH ACCELERATION: 3.7 secs

TRANSMISSION: 6-speed manual

LENGTH: 182¾ in / 4,643 mm

WIDTH: 77 in / 1,953 mm

HEIGHT: 44¼ in / 1,125 mm

WHEELBASE: 106¾ in / 2,710 mm

MANUFACTURE DATE: 2003–06

BRAKES: disc (f and r)

SUSPENSION: upper A-arm and lower L-arm (f and r)

WHEELS: alloy, 18 in (f), 19 in (r)

TIRES: 235/45 ZR-18 (f), 315/40 ZR-19 (r)

Gumpert Apollo

The Gumpert Apollo is not pretty, but it's a technological tour de force. It was developed by former Audi Director of Motorsport Roland Gumpert and, perhaps not surprisingly, uses many Audi parts in its construction. Chief among these Audi parts is the twin turbo-charged 4.2-liter V8 that sits at the heart of the Apollo, mated to a six-speed sequential transmission. It's tuned to produce either 650 bhp in the 'base' Apollo, 690 bhp in the sportier Apollo S and an awesome 789 bhp in the Apollo R. Figures for the Apollo S show that peak power comes in at 6,300 rpm and maximum torque is 850 Nm at 4,000 rpm. The sheer volume of power, combined with the relative light weight of the car, gives it a power-to-weight ratio that's superior even to that of the McLaren F1, and its claimed performance is 0–60 mph in three seconds and a top speed of 220 mph / 354 km/h.

The Apollo's design is supercar conventional – like many others, it's a mid-engined, rear-wheel drive two-seater. Underpinning the car is a tubular frame, with either fibreglass body panels or, in the lightweight Apollo R, carbon-fibre panels. Suspension is by double wishbones front and rear with inboard adjustable dampers. The ventilated disc brakes are also mounted inboard, with six-piston calipers both front and rear.

What's special is the car's aerodynamics. As well as the huge rear spoiler, it has an undertray consisting of two massive venturis extending the whole length of the car, which speed up the airflow under the car the faster it travels. This increase in air speed in turn lowers the pressure, with the result that the Apollo is claimed to have as much downforce as a DTM racecar. In fact, Gumpert goes further, suggesting that if driven at around 200 mph / 322 km/h, the car has so much downforce – some 2,646 lb / 5,833 kg – that it could actually be driven upside down in a tunnel!

And yet despite all this extreme high-tech engineering, the Apollo doesn't require a driving superstar at the wheel. It can be driven gently with little effort, thanks to the relatively light clutch, power-assisted steering and tractable power delivery from the Audi V8. But it's at higher speeds that the Apollo is transformed, and it really needs a racetrack to explore the limits of its astonishing performance. It has massive grip, neck-breaking

acceleration and stunning stopping power.

In truth, the Gumpert Apollo is a racing car, just one that has been made street legal and been given a small boot to carry a modicum of luggage. The upward-swinging gullwing doors look sensational, but getting in and out over the wide side pods is far from easy. Once inside, the cabin is reasonably spacious for the driver and passenger, but the four-point harnesses indicate this is a car with serious intent.

Of course, none of this comes cheap. The price of the base Apollo is just over €300,000, with the Apollo S costing €378,000 and the Apollo R no less than €427,000. Gumpert remains a small, highly specialized company, but it plans production of some 30 cars a year. Those numbers won't frighten the likes of Ferrari, Lamborghini or Porsche, but the Apollo's sheer performance and all-round capability might give them something to think about, particularly as it seems there is more to come. Gumpert has already created a hybrid-powered Apollo, which was raced in 2008 at the 24 Hours Nürburgring race. And at the 2009 Geneva Motor Show, it unveiled the 800 bhp Apollo Speed, which has an even more aerodynamic body, lower ride weight, carbon-fibre wheels and a claimed 0–62 mph time of three seconds, 0–124 mph time of 8.9 seconds and a top speed of 224 mph / 360 km/h.

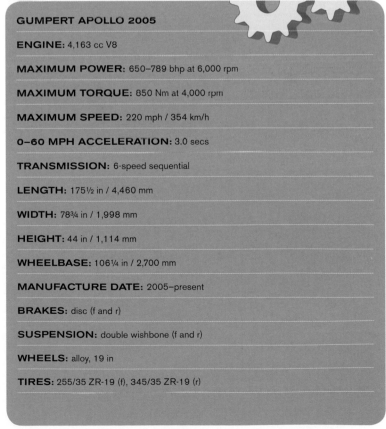

GUMPERT APOLLO 2005

ENGINE: 4,163 cc V8

MAXIMUM POWER: 650–789 bhp at 6,000 rpm

MAXIMUM TORQUE: 850 Nm at 4,000 rpm

MAXIMUM SPEED: 220 mph / 354 km/h

0–60 MPH ACCELERATION: 3.0 secs

TRANSMISSION: 6-speed sequential

LENGTH: 175½ in / 4,460 mm

WIDTH: 78¾ in / 1,998 mm

HEIGHT: 44 in / 1,114 mm

WHEELBASE: 106¼ in / 2,700 mm

MANUFACTURE DATE: 2005–present

BRAKES: disc (f and r)

SUSPENSION: double wishbone (f and r)

WHEELS: alloy, 19 in

TIRES: 255/35 ZR-19 (f), 345/35 ZR-19 (r)

Honda NSX

HONDA NSX 1995

ENGINE: 2,997 cc V6

MAXIMUM POWER: 280 bhp at 7,300 rpm

MAXIMUM TORQUE: 294 Nm at 5,400 rpm

MAXIMUM SPEED: 170 mph / 274 km/h

0–62 MPH ACCELERATION: 5.7 secs

TRANSMISSION: 5-speed manual

LENGTH: 174½ in / 4,430 mm

WIDTH: 71¼ in / 1,811 mm

HEIGHT: 46 in / 1,171 mm

WHEELBASE: 99½ in / 2,530 mm

MANUFACTURE DATE: 1990–2005

BRAKES: disc (f and r)

SUSPENSION: independent double wishbone (f and r)

WHEELS: alloy, 15 in (f), 16 in (r)

TIRES: 205/50 ZR-15 (f), 225/50 ZR-16 (r)

Of all Japanese motor manufacturers, Honda has always shown the most interest in motor racing and has displayed the greatest engineering genius. It had won Grands Prix in the 1960s, and its engines dominated F1 in the 1980s, when it shared four Constructors' titles with Williams and McLaren. But what it had never done until the 1990s was produce a true supercar to challenge established manufacturers such as Porsche, Ferrari and Lamborghini. When the company decided to build such a car, it typically set its sights high: the new car would not only be able to match the performance of the best in the world at that time, but it would also be drivable by people of average ability and would be sold through Honda's existing dealer network.

The Honda NSX (New Sports Experimental) project was six years in the making. Starting with a completely clean sheet of paper, the design team led by Nobuhiko Kawamoto created a brand new engine, chassis and aluminium body. While competitors chose V8 or V12 engines for their flagships, Honda designed a lightweight 2,997 cc V6, incorporating double overhead cams, four valves per cylinder and variable valve timing. The thinking was that if the overall weight of the car could be kept as low as possible, a lightweight but highly tuned engine would provide the necessary performance, without the need for turbochargers or massive displacement. Amazingly, the result was truly outstanding performance – a top speed of around 170 mph / 274 km/h and acceleration from 0 to 62 mph in 5.7 seconds –

with an average fuel consumption of around 20 mpg / 7.8 km/l. No supercar had ever been so frugal.

The NSX's body was crafted from aluminium, a material that is far more difficult to work with than steel, but that is substantially lighter. Similarly, Honda opted for aluminium suspension units, which again reduced overall weight but which also crucially reduced the unsprung weight, significantly improving the handling. It was, in fact, the world's first-ever all-aluminium production car. Honda was fortunate in being able to call upon the services of F1 World Champion Ayrton Senna while it was developing the chassis, and the result is a car with safe, predictable and neutral handling, even at high speeds. Steering has speed-sensitive power assistance, and this, together with a light clutch, smooth gearchange and excellent visibility, makes the NSX very easy to drive.

When the Honda NSX went on sale in 1990 it was well equipped by supercar standards, with ABS, leather trim and air conditioning as standard. In 1995, the NSX-T was launched, with a T-bar targa-style roof. At the same time, an automatic gearbox, dubbed the F-Matic was offered for the first time. Later, in 1997, the engine was uprated to 3,179 cc, which delivered 290 bhp and 304 Nm of torque, and a six-speed transmission replaced the previous five-ratio box.

Production finally ended in 2005, and although Honda at that time promised it would be replaced by an all-new V10-powered NSX, that project was shelved. That decision may have been made, in part, because the NSX was extremely expensive to build, and Honda may never have seen a return on the capital it invested in the supercar, despite building some 15,000 examples.

The decision to abandon the new NSX is a pity because the only thing that held the original back was that it was a Honda, a marque that lacked the exclusivity of Ferrari or Lamborghini. But even if it shared a badge with thousands of small hatchbacks, the NSX was a superlative machine, beautifully built in one of the world's most modern factories. It was as fast as contemporary Ferraris and Lamborghinis, and it was more reliable, had a more comfortable ride, handled better and was far more practical for everyday use.

Jaguar XJ220

The outstanding star of the 1988 British Motor Show was a long, low, sleek mid-engined coupé that adorned the Jaguar stand. This was the XJ220, a stunning aluminium jewel powered by a massive V12 engine that produced over 500 bhp.

It featured four-wheel drive, an AP racing twin-plate clutch and a five-speed manual gearbox. It had a bonded-aluminium chassis with aluminium body panels, and the combination of massive power and relatively low weight promised blistering performance. Jaguar officials estimated a top speed of 220 mph / 354 km/h and acceleration from 0 to 60 mph in 3.5 seconds, figures that would have made the XJ220 the fastest car of its generation.

Wealthy enthusiasts queued up to place deposits for the car, even though no price had been mentioned and even though Jaguar insisted this was just a design study. But no-one was surprised when, just one year later, it was officially announced that the XJ220 would go into limited production in a joint venture

between Jaguar and Tom Walkinshaw Racing, the company responsible for Jaguar's recent successes at Le Mans.

At the time, the world was in the grip of a speculative supercar boom, with cars such as the Ferrari F40 and Porsche 959 commanding massive premiums over their already elevated list prices. Perhaps swept along on a tide of enthusiasm, Jaguar announced an initial production run of 220 examples, with the provision of increasing this to 350 if demand was high enough, despite an eventual price tag of £403,000. Jaguar collected 350 firm orders in a matter of days, and looked set for a serious commercial success, until the supercar bubble collapsed a few months later, and those who had placed deposits began clamouring to get their money back, claiming they had been misled.

The reason for this was that in place of the V12 and four-wheel drive that had graced the concept car, the production XJ220 had a V6 Turbo engine and two-wheel drive. It was the same engine that had powered the very fast XJR-10 and the Metro 6R4 rally car, and produced 542 bhp at 6,500 rpm – more than enough to offer a top speed of over 200 mph / 322 km/h and acceleration from 0 to 60 mph in 4.0 seconds, but according to the disgruntled potential buyers, it wasn't what had been promised. There was further dismay when, in 1990, JaguarSport

launched the XJR-15, which was fitted with the very same V12 that had originally been destined for the XJ220.

In the event, only 280 XJ220s were ever produced, and it took some years before the last of these found a good home. This was a pity, because the XJ220 had real potential. On the test track, it was timed at 217 mph / 349 km/h, so there was no doubting its performance, and indeed until the launch of the McLaren F1 in 1994, the XJ220 could claim to be the world's fastest car. In addition, it was a striking-looking design with impeccable build quality and incorporating the very latest manufacturing technology. It featured a bonded and riveted aluminium body/chassis with aluminium body panels, and though it lacked the concept's four-wheel drive system, it didn't need it for stability purposes, because it was the world's first road car to generate true ground effects. Thanks to a pair of underbody venturis, the XJ220 generated as much as 600 lb / 1,323 kg of downforce at 200 mph / 322 km/h.

Just how effective the XJ220's aerodynamics were can be judged by the car's 1993 win in the Grand Touring class at Le Mans, a track where the long Mulsanne Straight soon reveals any shortcomings of stability at high speeds.

Though Jaguar had created some stunning vehicles in the past – such as the one-off XJ13 – this was the company's first production supercar and it's unfortunate that its arrival coincided with the collapse of the supercar speculation bubble. Nevertheless it was an impressive machine.

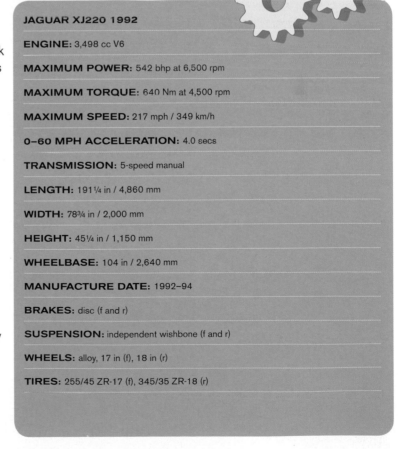

JAGUAR XJ220 1992

ENGINE: 3,498 cc V6

MAXIMUM POWER: 542 bhp at 6,500 rpm

MAXIMUM TORQUE: 640 Nm at 4,500 rpm

MAXIMUM SPEED: 217 mph / 349 km/h

0–60 MPH ACCELERATION: 4.0 secs

TRANSMISSION: 5-speed manual

LENGTH: 191¼ in / 4,860 mm

WIDTH: 78¾ in / 2,000 mm

HEIGHT: 45¼ in / 1,150 mm

WHEELBASE: 104 in / 2,640 mm

MANUFACTURE DATE: 1992–94

BRAKES: disc (f and r)

SUSPENSION: independent wishbone (f and r)

WHEELS: alloy, 17 in (f), 18 in (r)

TIRES: 255/45 ZR-17 (f), 345/35 ZR-18 (r)

Koenigsegg CCX

Back in 1994, wealthy Swedish businessman Christian von Koenigsegg had a dream: to create a world-beating road-legal supercar using Formula 1 technology. It's something many have aspired to, but the difference is that Koenigsegg actually achieved it. The first carbon-fibre concept appeared at the

Geneva Motor Show in 2000 and the first Koenigsegg CC 8S customer cars were delivered in 2002.

A new model, the CCR, was announced in 2004, and this gained international fame in 2005, when, at the massive Nardo test track in Southern Italy, it made it into the *Guinness Book of Records* as the fastest production car ever made. It was timed at 241.63 mph / 388.87 km/h as it took the crown from the McLaren F1. The Koenigsegg's record has since been eclipsed by the Bugatti Veyron (253.2 mph / 407.5 km/h), but it was still a massive achievement for what was, at the time, such a small company.

Koenigsegg's big move came in 2006 with the introduction of the CCX, a model designed from scratch to meet all US safety laws and even California's notoriously tough emissions legislation. The starting point was the engine. Previously, Koenigsegg had used Ford Modular V8 racing engines, but for the CCX, it developed and built its own engine at its factory on a military air base in Ängelhom, Sweden. It's a 4,719 cc all-aluminium V8 that has been subjected to a special heat treatment that strengthens the aluminium and thus allows thinner and lighter engine block to be employed. With the

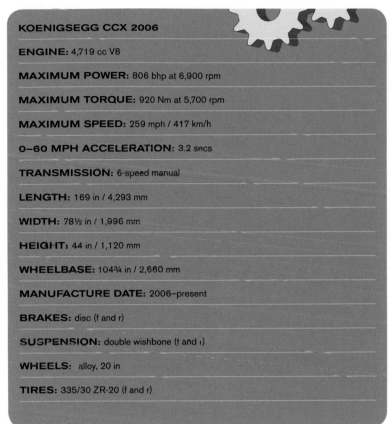

KOENIGSEGG CCX 2006

ENGINE: 4,719 cc V8

MAXIMUM POWER: 806 bhp at 6,900 rpm

MAXIMUM TORQUE: 920 Nm at 5,700 rpm

MAXIMUM SPEED: 259 mph / 417 km/h

0–60 MPH ACCELERATION: 3.2 secs

TRANSMISSION: 6-speed manual

LENGTH: 169 in / 4,293 mm

WIDTH: 78½ in / 1,996 mm

HEIGHT: 44 in / 1,120 mm

WHEELBASE: 104¾ in / 2,660 mm

MANUFACTURE DATE: 2006–present

BRAKES: disc (f and r)

SUSPENSION: double wishbone (f and r)

WHEELS: alloy, 20 in

TIRES: 335/30 ZR-20 (f and r)

Koenigsegg also produced an 'environmentally friendly' version of the CCX, the CCX-R, which was converted to run on ethanol biofuel as well as normal petrol. Incredibly, when running on biofuel it produces 1,018 bhp and 1,060 Nm of torque and improves acceleration from 0 to 62 mph to just 2.9 seconds. This is because biofuel has a higher octane value than the petrol sold at pumps and because it also has the effect of cooling the combustion chambers. The Koenigsegg CCX-R is the world's most powerful production car, overtaking the Bugatti Veyron (1,001 bhp).

Only two CCX Edition cars and four CCX-Rs were made, however, as Koenigsegg announced at the 2009 Geneva Motor Show that the company's future would lie in more environmentally sustainable products such as the Quant solar-electric sports car that it previewed at the Show.

help of a pair of centrifugal superchargers, it produces 806 bhp at 6,900 rpm and 920 Nm of torque at 5,700 rpm. Dry-sump lubrication is employed so the engine can sit lower in the chassis. This engine is mated to either a six-speed manual or a sequential transmission, driving the rear wheels through a limited slip differential. Unusually, Koenigsegg customers can choose the gear ratios that best suit their driving style.

The CCX's body is slightly larger than that of the earlier CCR and is made from carbon fibre and Kevlar. The doors open by rotating forwards and upwards in an impressive design known as dihedral synchro-helix. There's even an element of practicality about the car in that it has a removable targa top that can be stored under the bonnet. With such massive performance on tap, attention to aerodynamics is crucial. The CCX has a totally flat underside with venturi tunnels at the rear to speed up the airflow and therefore increase the downforce. A rear spoiler is also an option.

According to Koenigsegg, the performance of the CCX is 0–62 mph in 3.2 seconds, 0–124 mph in 9.8 seconds and it has a top speed of 259 mph / 417 km/h. And yet for some, this still wasn't enough, and so in 2008, Koenigsegg created a revised model called the CCX Edition, in which power was boosted to 888 bhp and torque to 921 Nm. It also featured a larger adjustable rear wing and a wholly carbon-fibre body.

Lamborghini Countach

LAMBORGHINI COUNTACH 25TH ANNIVERSARY 1988
ENGINE: 5,167 cc V12
MAXIMUM POWER: 455 bhp at 7,000 rpm
MAXIMUM TORQUE: 501 Nm at 5,200 rpm
MAXIMUM SPEED: 190 mph / 306 km/h
0–60 MPH ACCELERATION: 4.8 secs
TRANSMISSION: 5-speed manual
LENGTH: 163 in / 4,140 mm
WIDTH: 78¾ in / 2,000 mm
HEIGHT: 42¼ in / 1,070 mm
WHEELBASE: 98½ in / 2,500 mm
MANUFACTURE DATE: 1971–90
BRAKES: disc (f and r)
SUSPENSION: unequal double wishbone (f), lower wishbone (r)
WHEELS: alloy, 15 in
TIRES: 225/50 ZR-15 (f), 345/35 ZR-15 (r)

The Lamborghini Countach was probably the most stunning, shocking and ground-shaking design that the motor business has ever experienced. Its styling, when unveiled at the 1971 Geneva Motor Show, looked like something from outer space.

Lamborghini had proved itself a worthy adversary to Ferrari when it introduced its luscious Miura mid-engined supercar in 1966, but this latest model, again the work of stylist Marcello Gandini, abandoned the gentle curves of the Miura in favour of aggressive sharp edges and a wedge profile that no other manufacturer had dared offered before. If this wasn't enough, the Countach also sported outrageous 'scissor' doors and massive vents and scoops, some of which were needed for cooling purposes but all of which contributed to a truly over-the-top design. It was the new kid on the block, it was aggressive and self-confident, and it was determined to be noticed (the show car was painted a vivid yellow).

Three years later, the Countach went into production, by which time some changes had been made. The monocoque chassis of the show car had been replaced by a tubular frame, and the five-liter engine had been supplanted by a four-liter derivative, mainly because the five-liter had proved unreliable due to cooling problems – in fact, it had blown up during testing! But despite this, the production car was still an astonishing achievement.

What had not changed were the eye-catching lines that ran from the front to the back of the wedge-shaped car. Cooling remained an issue, which is why the distinctive vents remained, but it still looked like a car taken off the pages of sci-fi comic: it retained those magnificent scissor doors, guaranteed to draw a crowd whenever the Countach drew up outside a restaurant or theatre.

It also made a statement out on the open road. It had a mid-mounted V12 engine mounted longitudinally, with the gearbox at the front to improve weight distribution. Initially, six Weber carburetors provided the fuel, though later fuel injection was adopted. The original Countach produced 375 bhp at 8,000 rpm and 499 Nm of torque at 5,500 rpm, and achieved 0–60 mph in 5.6 seconds and a top speed of around 170 mph / 274 km/h, though that was a good way below the 200 mph / 322 km/h that had been hoped for from the planned five-liter. Incidentally, the Countach never achieved 200 mph / 322 km/h,

even in later years, when, in the 5000 QV model introduced in 1985, its engine was increased to five liters and power reached 455 bhp – more than the original prototype. The Countach looked magnificent, but its aerodynamics were never brilliant, and its coefficient of drag of around 0.4 meant even the final 25th Anniversary cars could only manage 190 mph / 306 km/h.

The Countach may have been outrageous, but it remained in production for 20 years, during which time it evolved and was improved but it never lost its ability to draw the crowds. It finally went out of production in 1991, by which time more than 2,000 examples had been built.

The most successful incarnation was the last, known as the Countach Anniversary, launched in 1988 to mark Lamborghini's 25th anniversary. It was mechanically identical to the 5000 QV but the body was substantially restyled. By this time, the company had been bought by Chrysler, which pushed for the addition of a few modern creature comforts, including air conditioning and electric windows. In all, 650 examples of this last model were sold, despite the car being by then close to 20 years old.

Lamborghini Gallardo

A new chapter at Lamborghini began in 1998, when Volkswagen Group's Audi subsidiary bought the company from Indonesian President Suharto's eldest son, Tommy, who had gained his majority interest in 1993, when he picked up Chrysler's stake in the company. At that time, the Italian supercar company was making only around 200 Diablo cars a year, but Audi had far greater plans for the legendary marque. Its first job in turning round the company was to create a new range of cars, and the first of these, the Murcielago, arrived in 2002. But the Gallardo,

which was launched in 2003, is significant as being the first Lamborghini developed wholly under Audi's ownership and control. It was an instant triumph, successfully marrying Audi's German engineering skills with the heart and soul of the Italian supercar manufacturer.

Like all Lamborghinis, the Gallardo has massive visual presence: this is not a car that is going to go unnoticed on the road. Its aluminium body design is sharp, angular, aggressive and low, with front lights like blades and gaping cooling inlets. The original design was the work of Italdesign-Giugiaro, with final tweaks by Lamborghini's own Styling Center. The aluminium body panels are mounted on a light but immensely strong aluminium spaceframe chassis that features double wishbone suspension front and rear, massive Brembo brakes and Pirelli Pzero tires.

At the heart of the Gallardo is a newly developed V10 engine, whose block and cylinder heads are manufactured by Cosworth, the British engineering company whose engines have won more Formula 1 victories than those of any other supplier. The 5.0-liter V10 produces 500 bhp at 7,800 rpm and 510 Nm of torque at 4,500 rpm. In true racing fashion, it has variable valve timing and dry-sump lubrication, with throttle control performed via a Drive-by-Wire system. The transmission is a six-speed manual unit operated by paddles on the steering wheel, though a Lamborghini e-gear unit is also available, which

LAMBORGHINI GALLARDO 2003

ENGINE: 4,961 cc V10

MAXIMUM POWER: 500 bhp at 7,800 rpm

MAXIMUM TORQUE: 510 Nm at 4,500 rpm

MAXIMUM SPEED: 197 mph / 317 km/h

0–60 MPH ACCELERATION: 3.9 secs

TRANSMISSION: 6-speed manual

LENGTH: 169¼ in / 4,300 mm

WIDTH: 74¾ in / 1,900 mm

HEIGHT: 45¾ in / 1,165 mm

WHEELBASE: 100¾ in / 2,560 mm

MANUFACTURE DATE: 2003–present

BRAKES: disc (f and r)

SUSPENSION: double wishbone (f and r)

WHEELS: alloy, 19 in

TIRES: 235/35 ZR-19 (f), 295/30 ZR-19 (r)

offers a sequential gearshifting system and the ability to choose between normal, sport and automatic modes.

The Gallardo is unusual in supercar territory in that it has a permanent four-wheel drive system that normally distributes the drive 70 per cent to the rear and 30 cent to the front. Viscous couplings change the ratios under hard acceleration, braking or cornering to provide the optimum traction in all road conditions. Special attention was paid to getting the optimum weight distribution of 42 per cent front and 58 per cent rear, reckoned by Lamborghini's engineers to be perfect for a sports car.

The Gallardo's magnificent engine makes it possible for it to accelerate from 0 to 62 mph in only 3.9 seconds and to reach a top speed of 197 mph / 317 km/h. And the combination of the superbly balanced four-wheel-drive system, the fantastically precise steering and the sublime handling means that the performance potential is achievable even by drivers who will never compete at the top levels of motor sport. By supercar standards, the Gallardo is reasonably practical too: its cabin is spacious and comfortable for two, the conventional doors open wide for easy access and there's reasonable luggage storage at the front.

Soon after the launch of the Gallardo, two other models were added to the range: a convertible and a Superleggera, or Superlight, which is not only some 220 lb / 91 kg lighter, but also squeezes an extra 10 bhp out of its V10, giving it even more neck-breaking acceleration. Lamborghini's badge is a raging bull, and it's from this heritage that the Gallardo gets its name – it's a breed of fighting bull. And the car proves that Lamborghini is fighting in the marketplace too: the year after its launch, more than 2,000 Lamborghini Gallardos were sold.

Lamborghini Murciélago

LAMBORGHINI MURCIÉLAGO 2002

ENGINE: 6,192 cc V12

MAXIMUM POWER: 580 bhp at 7,500 rpm

MAXIMUM TORQUE: 650 Nm at 5,400 rpm

MAXIMUM SPEED: 205 mph / 330 km/h

0–60 MPH ACCELERATION: 3.85 secs

TRANSMISSION: 6-speed manual

LENGTH: 180¼ in / 4,580 mm

WIDTH: 80½ in / 2,045 mm

HEIGHT: 44¾ in / 1,135 mm

WHEELBASE: 105 in / 2,665 mm

MANUFACTURE DATE: 2002–present

BRAKES: disc (f and r)

SUSPENSION: double wishbone (f and r)

WHEELS: alloy, 18 in

TIRES: 245/35 ZR-18 (f), 335/30 ZR-18 (r)

When Audi took over Lamborghini in 1998, a Bertone-designed successor to the Diablo was already quite close to production, but was abandoned by the new owners in favour of a design by Audi's chief designer, Luc Donckerwolke.

In 2002, this new model – named the Murciélago – was the subject of one of the most dramatic launches ever staged for a new car. Hundreds of journalists, owners, dealers and VIPs were flown to the slopes of Mount Etna in Sicily, where the car was unveiled in a spectacular *son et lumiére* show that included the eruption of artificial lava flows.

Back in the real world, there was some grumbling about the design of the new supercar, but that came mainly from Lamborghini die-hards, who struggled to accept that a Belgian could create an Italian masterpiece. The Murciélago was more angular than the Diablo it replaced, though it lacked the truly sharp edges of the original Countach. Its wedge-shaped body was created with angular lines at the front combined with more rounded curves elsewhere. Needless to say, the trademark Lamborghini air intakes and outlets were retained, as were the impressive scissors-opening doors.

The chassis was constructed from high-strength steel tubing with some structural elements, such as the floorpan, in carbon fibre. All the external body panels were fashioned from carbon fibre, with the exception of the roof and door panels, which were made from steel. The engine derived from the 30-year-old design that had powered the Countach for so long, but for the Murciélago

it was updated with the very latest sophisticated technology, including electronically controlled variable valve timing, drive by wire throttle, and a variable induction system. It also now had a dry-sump lubrication system, which allowed the engine to be mounted 2 in / 50 mm lower to reduce the center of gravity and improve handling. The capacity was stretched to 6,192 cc and the power output was boosted to 580 bhp at 7,500 rpm and torque to 650 Nm at 5,400 rpm. As for performance, it was as spectacular as the car's appearance – 0–62 mph in 3.85 seconds and a top speed of some 205 mph / 330 km/h.

Just as important as its outright performance was the Murciélago's driveability, which was much improved over that of earlier Lamborghinis. Its smoother torque curve and sophisticated electronic engine management system made it much more tractable in traffic, and its high-speed handling, stability and grip were also greatly improved, thanks to the rigidity of the structure, the lowered center of gravity, improved aerodynamics and superbly tuned suspension.

The Murciélago had an impressively low drag coefficient, though for the sake of stability it has an adjustable rear wing that increases downforce (and inevitably drag) at higher speeds. The rear wing sits completely flush with the bodywork until the car reaches 80 mph / 129 km/h, at which speed it rises to 50 degrees, then at around 135 mph / 217 km/h it rises again to 70 degrees, where it generates enough downforce for the car to remain extremely stable, even at speeds above 186 mph / 299 km/h.

Permanent four-wheel drive was standard, as was a six-speed manual transmission, though a year after the initial launch, a new e-gear sequential gearbox was offered as an option. The layout was typically Lamborghini, with a mid-mounted engine, the transmission mounted in front of the engine, with the rear differential integrated into the engine unit, and a central viscous coupling that adjusts the torque between the front and rear wheels as required to maintain optimum traction.

Lamborghini launched a convertible version of the Murciélago in 2004, and in 2006, introduced the uprated Murciélago LP640, in both hardtop and convertible versions, with a new 6,496 cc V12 engine, producing 640 bhp at 8,000 rpm and 660 Nm of torque at 6,000 rpm. By now, the 0–62 mph acceleration time had dropped to 3.4 seconds, though the official top speed remained at 205 mph / 330 km/h. At the time of its launch, the roadster was billed by Lamborghini as being the fastest convertible on the road.

Lancia Delta HF Integrale Evoluzione II

It may be a surprise to find a small Italian hatchback in a book dedicated to dream cars and supercars. The Lanci Delta Integrale was neither expensive nor exclusive, it didn't have a particularly impressive top speed, and its acceleration, while brisk, didn't put the car in the supercar bracket. Nevertheless, in its time, it was one of the fastest cars of all along winding roads.

In the 1980s, a number of motor manufacturers turned to four-wheel drive to improve high-speed handling and grip. Audi led the way with the original quattro, which was followed by Porsche's 959, Ford's Sierra XR4x4, VW's Rally Golf and Citroën's BX 4x4. Lancia also got involved, first with the Delta HF Turbo 4WD in 1986. Lancia and the Delta were simply unstoppable on the rally circuit, winning the World Rally Championship six times in a row between 1987 and 1992.

Ordinary drivers were able to associate themselves with the legend when the first Integrale was launched in 1988. It produced 185 bhp from its eight-valve 2.0-liter four-cylinder engine and cost only £15,455, at a time when a Porsche 911, which had a similar performance, cost more than twice that amount. It was a revelation, as never before had a road car offered the ability to be driven so fast over ordinary roads: 185 bhp in small and relatively light car gave it a very respectable power to weight ratio, but what made a difference was the amazing levels of traction and the astonishing grip in corners.

The Delta Integrale had a fixed 47:53 front to rear torque split in the transmission system, which featured an epicyclical center differential and torque splitter with a limited slip viscous coupling

LANCIA DELTA HF INTEGRALE EVOLUZIONE II 1993

ENGINE: 1,995 cc inline 4-cylinder

MAXIMUM POWER: 215 bhp at 5,750 rpm

MAXIMUM TORQUE: 308 Nm at 2,500 rpm

MAXIMUM SPEED: 137 mph / 220 km/h

0–60 MPH ACCELERATION: 5.5 secs

TRANSMISSION: 5-speed manual

LENGTH: 153½ in / 3,900 mm

WIDTH: 69¾ in / 1,770 mm

HEIGHT: 53¾ in / 1,365 mm

WHEELBASE: 97¾ in / 2,480 mm

MANUFACTURE DATE: 1988–94

BRAKES: disc (f and r)

SUSPENSION: MacPherson strut (f), double transverse arm (r)

WHEELS: alloy, 16 in

TIRES: 205/45 ZR-16 (f and r)

This was a car that cost much the same as a small executive saloon, and yet it was capable of out-running sports cars costing two or three times as much. There were many cars that could be driven faster in a straight line, and some that could pull more lateral g through smooth and dry corners, but none was quicker point to point on minor roads or in less than perfect conditions. Better still, the Integrale was a properly practical car with four seats and reasonable luggage space, too. No wonder that total sales reached 44,296 before production finally ceased in November 1994.

and a Torsion rear differential. The toughened-up suspension was tuned for performance rather than for comfort and featured MacPherson struts and lower wishbones at the front and MacPherson struts and transverse rods at the rear. Its 1,995 cc engine was fitted with a turbocharger to boost top-end power and provided 0–62 mph acceleration in 6.6 seconds and a top speed of 134 mph / 216 km/h.

Lancia continued to improve the car: in 1989, a four-valve version of the same engine was launched, which boosted power to 200 bhp, reduced 0–62 mph acceleration time to 5.7 seconds and increased the top speed to 137 mph / 220 km/h. Then in 1991, the Evoluzione was launched, with power up to 210 bhp and even better grip, thanks to a strengthened bodyshell and a widened track. It looked more aggressive too, thanks to the flared wheel arches. Though the bare performance figures were hardly changed – 0–62 mph in 5.5 seconds and the same 137 mph / 220 km/h top speed – the Evoluzione was a major step forward in terms of roadholding, handling and driveability. In short, it could be pushed even harder and driven even faster. The final incarnation was the Evoluzione II, which was even more powerful (215 bhp) and had bigger 16-inch wheels, a catalytic converter and air conditioning. Despite these power-sapping additions, the performance of the Evoluzione II was unchanged.

Lancia Stratos

LANCIA STRATOS 1973

ENGINE: 2,418 cc V6

MAXIMUM POWER: 187 bhp at 7,000 rpm

MAXIMUM TORQUE: 225 Nm at 4,000 Nm

MAXIMUM SPEED: 143 mph / 230 km/h

0–60 MPH ACCELERATION: 6.0 secs

TRANSMISSION: 5-speed manual

LENGTH: 146 in / 3,708 mm

WIDTH: 69 in / 1,750 mm

HEIGHT: 43¾ in / 1,110 mm

WHEELBASE: 85¼ in / 2,180 mm

MANUFACTURE DATE: 1973–78

BRAKES: disc (f and r)

SUSPENSION: double wishbone (f), MacPherson strut (r)

WHEELS: alloy, 14 in

TIRES: 205/70 VR-14 (f and r)

Three separate events contributed towards the development of the Lancia Stratos, one of the greatest rally cars of all time and one of the finest roadgoing supercars. First, Fiat acquired 50 per cent of Ferrari in 1969; second, Fiat rescued Lancia the same year, honouring all its debts and making it a wholly-owned subsidiary; and third, Bertone showed a stunning Lancia-engined concept car called the Stratos at the Turin Motor Show of 1970.

In rebuilding Lancia, Fiat wanted to return it to its roots as a successful competitions marque, and Bertone's wedge-shaped Stratos, with its 1.6-liter Lancia Fulvia HF engine mid-mounted behind the seats and driving the rear wheels, seemed to offer the possibility of producing a rally car that would be light, agile and competitive. The only weakness was the engine, which by this time was past its sell-by date and offered no real possibility of being further developed. A solution was found at Ferrari, whose 2.4-liter quad-cam V6 produced for the Dino 246 GT looked perfect. Bertone was brought back to restyle the car, both to accommodate the transverse V6 with its integral five-speed gearbox and transaxle and to make the Stratos a production reality. The world's first custom-built rally car duly appeared in 1973.

It had a central steel cage with a rear frame supporting the engine and strut suspension, while wishbones were specified at the front of the car. The fibreglass bodywork was unusually short and wide and featured the very distinctive crescent-shaped massive front windscreen. By contrast, rear visibility was close to non-existent, but this wouldn't matter in rallying. The 2,418 cc V6 with its bank of three Weber carburettors was tuned to produce 187 bhp at 7,000 rpm and 225 Nm of torque at 4,000 rpm, which gave it acceleration from 0 to 60 mph in 6.0 seconds and a top speed of 143 mph / 230 km/h.

International rallying regulations required that 400 examples were built for homologation purposes and this was not achieved until 1974, so in its first season, the Lancia Stratos raced as a prototype. Once it was homologated, it was just about invincible, winning the final Targa Florio in 1974, taking outright honours in the Monte Carlo Rally four times and clocking up hundreds of victories and

the World Rally Championship in 1974, 1975 and 1976, before it was finally retired in 1977.

Although the Stratos was homologated, and the official Lancia records show that 492 cars were actually built, there is some doubt as to whether this figure is accurate. The plan was for Bertone to build the first batch of 500 cars and then later, a second batch to take total production to 1,000. That second batch was certainly not built, and, in fact, as late as 1978, more than three years after Bertone built the last Stratos monocoque chassis, it was still possible to buy a new Stratos from the factory in Turin for 12 million lire, or around £7,500. It's likely that as few as 250 were actually sold, due to the oil crisis and an increase in tax rates on powerful cars in Italy from 18 per cent to 35 per cent, which took its toll on the top end of the car market.

The roadgoing cars were called Lancia Stratos Stradale, though few efforts were made to make them either comfortable or practical as everyday cars. The cabin was noisy and cramped and because the front of the car was used to house cooling fans and the spare tire, there was virtually no luggage space either. But the modest commercial success of the Lancia Stratos does nothing to dim its reputation as one of the most outstanding and iconic cars of its time.

Lotus Elise

The Lotus Elise is a small, light sports car with outstanding grip and handling, which, in typical Lotus tradition, was designed from the outset for enthusiastic drivers. Colin Chapman, who founded Lotus cars in 1952, was an engineering genius, whose primary obsession was reducing weight in order to improve performance.

In the mid-1990s, Lotus was struggling for survival in the hands of Italian entrepreneur Romano Artioli. Artioli was more interested in Bugatti, which he also owned, but to his credit, he signed off the Elise with plans for Lotus to build around 700 examples a year. In fact, the Elise was so successful that it not only exceeded its own sales targets, but also can be said to have single-handedly rescued Lotus from likely collapse.

The car was first shown at the 1995 Frankfurt Motor Show and was in full production at Lotus's Hethel plant in Norfolk, England, by the autumn of the following year. Its extremely light but massively rigid chassis was constructed from extruded and bonded aluminium, to which lightweight composite body panels were bonded. Lotus' motto is 'Performance through light weight' and the Elise is a classic example of this philosophy: it weighed just 1,598 lb / 725 kg, compared to the Porsche Boxster, for example, which tips the scales at 2,756 lb / 1,250 kg.

Its four-cylinder 1,796 cc engine produced a modest 120 bhp at 5,500 rpm, but because the Elise was less than half the weight of a normal saloon, its performance was outstanding –

0–60 mph in six seconds, 0–100 mph in 18 seconds and a top speed of 126 mph / 203 km/h. Although these figures in themselves do not qualify the Elise for supercar status, its handling and grip was such that it could be cornered at over 1g on standard road tires, which meant that virtually nothing could stay with it on winding roads.

Lotus continued developing and improving the Elise. In 1999, it launched the Elise 111S, which was fitted with a Rover K-Series engine that produced 143 bhp, then in 2000, it introduced a roofless 340R, with output boosted to 177 bhp. The weight was planned to be just 1,102 lb / 500 kg and the 340R got its name from the fact that this would have given it a power-to-weight ratio of 340 bhp per tonne. In the event, the weight crept up a little to 1,252 lb / 568 kg, so Lotus decided to limit production to 340 units instead. By 2000, more developments were introduced with the Series 2 Elise. Like previous models, this Elise initially had a Rover K-Series engine, but switched to the Toyota 1.8-liter unit in 2005. The latter produced 189 bhp, and mated to a six-speed close-ratio gearbox, it was good for 0–60 mph in 4.9 seconds, or an even quicker 4.7 seconds if the Sport package was chosen.

In 2008, Lotus launched a new supercharged Elise SC model, producing 218 bhp and reducing the 0–60 mph acceleration time to just 4.4 seconds – and this despite its considerable weight

gain, due to its adoption of ABS, airbags and extra comforts such as electric windows. Even so, at 1,986 lb / 901 kg, it's still one of the lightest cars on the market, and for that reason it remains one of the most nimble as well.

After more than 13 years in production, the Lotus Elise is still going strong, thanks to three vital ingredients: a lightweight body, high-revving engines and superb handling. Conceptually, it may be, in many ways, a very old-fashioned sort of sports car, despite the undoubted high-tech approach to its construction and design, but it's hard to think of any car that's more fun and more rewarding to drive, and at such an affordable price both to buy and to run. Lotus' founder, Colin Chapman, who died in 1982, would have been proud of the Elise.

LOTUS ELISE 1996	
ENGINE: 1796 cc inline 4-cylinder	**WIDTH:** 67 in / 1,701 mm
MAXIMUM POWER: 120 bhp at 5,500 rpm	**HEIGHT:** 47¼ in / 1,201 mm
MAXIMUM TORQUE: 165 Nm at 3,000 rpm	**WHEELBASE:** 90½ in / 2,301 mm
MAXIMUM SPEED: 126 mph / 203 km/h	**MANUFACTURE DATE:** 1996–present
0–60 MPH ACCELERATION: 6.0 secs	**BRAKES:** disc (f and r)
TRANSMISSION: 5-speed manual	**SUSPENSION:** double wishbone (f and r)
LENGTH: 146¾ in / 3,726 mm	**WHEELS:** alloy, 15 in (f), 16 in (r)
	TIRES: 185/55 R-15 (f), 205/50 R-16 (r)

Lotus Esprit Turbo

LOTUS ESPRIT TURBO 1980

ENGINE: 2,174 cc inline 4-cylinder

MAXIMUM POWER: 210 bhp at 6,250 rpm

MAXIMUM TORQUE: 271 Nm at 4,500 rpm

MAXIMUM SPEED: 150 mph / 241 km/h

0–60 MPH ACCELERATION: 5.6 secs

TRANSMISSION: 5-speed manual

LENGTH: 165 in / 4,191 mm

WIDTH: 73 in / 1,852 mm

HEIGHT: 44 in / 1,118 mm

WHEELBASE: 96 in / 2,438 mm

MANUFACTURE DATE: 1980–92

BRAKES: disc (f and r)

SUSPENSION: upper wishbone (f), double transverse link (r)

WHEELS: alloy, 15 in

TIRES: 195/60 VR-15 (f), 235/60 VR-15 (r)

The origins of the Lotus Esprit – the model that replaced the two-seat mid-engined Lotus Europa – go back as far as 1972, when Giorgio Giugiaro's ItalDesign showed a Silver Car concept based upon a Europa chassis. It was an astonishing, angular, 'folded-paper' design that used straight lines to create a visually stunning wedge shape. Lotus immediately started work on making it a production reality, and the M70 project was born. This in turn evolved into the Lotus Esprit, which was launched at the 1975 Paris Motor Show and went into production the following year.

It was fitted with a Lotus four-cylinder 2.0-liter engine producing 160 bhp, which drove the rear wheels via a five-speed manual transmission that formed part of the rear transaxle. It wasn't a huge amount of horsepower, but as the Esprit weighed less than 2, 205 lb / 1,000 kg and handled better than any previous Lotus model, its actual performance was outstanding. (The official Lotus figures of 6.8 seconds for 0–60 mph acceleration and top speed of 138 mph / 222 km/h may have been exaggerated, however; contemporary roadtests suggest that eight seconds and 133 mph / 214 km/h are nearer the mark.)

But more was to come. In 1980, Lotus held a party in London's Albert Hall, where it revealed a new turbocharged Esprit, resplendent in the colours of the Essex Lotus F1 team livery. Giugiaro had been commissioned to revise the bodywork

of this new Esprit Turbo, which concealed what was practically an all-new car. It had a new backbone chassis-frame, completely revised rear suspension and much improved aerodynamics. Most important was the engine: it was still a four-cylinder unit, now bored out to 2.2 liters, but with the addition of a turbocharger, its peak power was increased to 210 bhp at 6,250 rpm and peak torque 271 Nm at 4,500 rpm. Significantly, the engine was tuned to produce much of its torque low down, so the Esprit Turbo was extremely flexible and didn't suffer excessively from the turbo lag that blighted many early turbocharged cars. Very few other changes were necessary to cope with the extra power, which was a tribute to the original Esprit, but a larger clutch was fitted along with larger brake discs.

At £20,950, the Lotus Esprit Turbo was not cheap, but it was a real supercar. Its 0–60 mph acceleration was now down to 5.6 seconds and the top speed was 150 mph / 241 km/h. Better still, it handled beautifully, had enormous levels of grip and well-weighted steering. No wonder one contemporary road tester described it as 'the perfect driving machine'.

The first 100 cars off the production line all had that same F1-inspired Essex Lotus livery that had been seen on the first Turbo to be revealed. They also all had air conditioning, a sophisticated stereo system and a special scarlet leather interior trim. In 1980, a more usual range of colours was offered, and the price was dropped to £16,917, though the air conditioning and stereo then became optional extras.

The car also received a massive publicity boost that year when it was featured in the James Bond film *For Your Eyes Only*. (This was the second time the Esprit had found its way into an Bond film: in 1977, a normally aspirated Esprit had appeared in *The Spy Who Love Me*, during which it converted into a submarine.)

In 1986, the Esprit Turbo gained a power boost when the engine compression was raised. These High Compression (Esprit Turbo HC) models put out 215 bhp, but more importantly, the torque was raised to 300 Nm, which made the car even more tractable. The Esprit Turbo continued after 1987 in a far more rounded body designed by Peter Stevens, who went on to design the McLaren F1. For many, however, it's the original Giugiaro/ItalDesign style that remains the real thing.

Maserati Bora

There was only one star of the 1971 Geneva Motor Show – a stunning new mid-engined supercar on the Maserati stand whose beautiful bodywork had been penned by Giorgetto Giugiaro and whose mechanical design was by Maserati's engineering chief Giulio Alferi. The Maserati Bora was the first car produced by the Italian firm since it had been bought by Citroën in 1968 and it accurately reflected the way supercar design was moving – away from the traditional front-engine and towards the mid-engined concept. De Tomaso had its Mangusta and Lamborghini had its Miura. Now it was Maserati's turn.

The Bora had a steel monocoque with a separate steel rear subframe to which the engine and transmission was mounted. As well as reducing vibrations into the passenger compartment, this layout resulted in a 42:58 weight distribution front to rear, which in turn contributed to good handling characteristics. The steel body panels were produced for Maserati by Officine Padane of Modena in Italy. Though the suspension was conventional – wishbones with coil springs, shock absorbers and anti-roll bars front and rear – this was actually the first time that Maserati had offered fully independent rear suspension. The braking system

was also a first for Maserati, inherited from Citroën and employing high-pressure hydraulics to operate the ventilated disc brakes. Those same hydraulics also powered the clutch, the retractable headlights and, most interestingly, the pedal box, consisting of the clutch, brake and throttle assemblies, which could be moved forward and back in relation to the fixed driver's seat.

The mid-mounted engine was Maserati's 4,719 cc V8 with four Weber carburettors that was longitudinally mounted and drove the rear wheels via a five-speed ZF transaxle. Power output for cars destined for the European market was set at 310 bhp at 6,000 rpm with peak torque of 440 Nm at 4,200 rpm. The Bora's 0–60 mph time is usually quoted as 7.1 seconds, though the British magazine *Autocar* claimed it achieved 6.5 seconds to 60 mph and 15.3 seconds to 100 mph. Top speed was close to 170 mph / 274 km/h, with first gear being good for around 50 mph / 80 km/h, second up to at least 80 mph / 129 km/h, third to 120 mph / 193 km/h, fourth to 147 mph / 237 km/h and fifth to some 168 mph / 270 km/h. US-specification cars had a lower output because of emissions regulations and performance inevitably suffered somewhat.

If the Maserati Bora's performance was in the supercar category, then so were its looks. It was low, sleek and boasted a remarkably large glass area with a wide wraparound front screen and further large glass panels over the engine compartment and the long rear quarters. The stainless-steel roof and A-pillars added contrast to the body colour and were a unique feature of the Bora, whose overall design bore many of the hallmarks of the earlier Ghibli – perhaps no surprise as both were penned by Giugiaro. Also distinctive were the Bora's Campagnolo alloy wheels with their unusual polished stainless-steel hubcaps.

For a supercar, an unusual degree of attention was paid to comfort and luxury. For a start, the passenger cabin was insulated from engine noise by an extra removable carpeted aluminium panel and the rear window between the passengers and the engine was double glazed. The car was fitted with air conditioning and electric windows and the Bora also had a modicum of practicality that its rival lacked, including quite reasonable luggage space in the front boot.

Later on, in 1975, Maserati fitted the Bora with a larger 4.9-liter engine that raised the power output to 320 bhp at 5,500 rpm and increased the peak torque to 454 Nm at 4,000 rpm. By the time the Bora went out of production in 1979, 524 had been built. The Bora was also the basis of the 2+2 Maserati Merak that was sold between 1972 and 1983. The latter was powered by the physically smaller V6 – also used by the Citroën SM – in order to provide space for rudimentary rear seats.

MASERATI BORA 1973

ENGINE: 4,719 cc V8

MAXIMUM POWER: 310 bhp at 6,000 rpm

MAXIMUM TORQUE: 440 Nm at 4,200 rpm

MAXIMUM SPEED: 170 mph / 274 km/h

0–60 MPH ACCELERATION: 7.1 secs

TRANSMISSION: 5-speed manual

LENGTH: 96 in / 4,328 mm

WIDTH: 68 in / 1,730 mm

HEIGHT: 44½ in / 1,133 mm

WHEELBASE: 102¼ in / 2,596 mm

MANUFACTURE DATE: 1971–79

BRAKES: disc (f and r)

SUSPENSION: independent wishbone (f and r)

WHEELS: alloy, 15 in

TIRES: 215/70 VR-15

McLaren F1

MCLAREN F1 1994

ENGINE: 6,064 cc V12

MAXIMUM POWER: 627 bhp at 7,400 rpm

MAXIMUM TORQUE: 649 Nm at 5,600 rpm

MAXIMUM SPEED: 231 mph / 372 km/h

0–60 MPH ACCELERATION: 3.2 secs

TRANSMISSION: 6-speed manual

LENGTH: 168¾ in / 4,288 mm

WIDTH: 76¾ in / 1,820 mm

HEIGHT: 45 in / 1,140 mm

WHEELBASE: 107 in / 2,718 mm

MANUFACTURE DATE: 1994–97

BRAKES: disc (f and r)

SUSPENSION: double wishbone (f and r)

WHEELS: alloy, 17 in

TIRES: 235/45 ZR-17 (f), 315/45 ZR-17 (r)

From the very outset, the McLaren F1 was planned to be the greatest supercar ever built. That didn't just mean it would be the fastest, though it certainly was. And it didn't just mean it should be the most expensive and exclusive, though it most certainly was. It meant it should be conceived, designed and engineered absolutely without compromise. So if gold was the best reflector of heat, gold would be used in the engine bay. If supercharging and turbocharging would result in even minute delays between the driver pushing the throttle and the engine responding, then an all-new naturally aspirated engine would be commissioned. And if the strongest and lightest material for the structure of the car was carbon fibre, then that would be specified, whatever the cost and however difficult it made the manufacturing process.

The F1 was conceived by Gordon Murray, a brilliant South African engineer who had made his name at the Brabham Formula 1 team, creating a series of innovative designs that pushed the boundaries of both current technology and current regulations. The design was by Peter Stevens, who worked alongside Murray to create a car that was both elegant and superbly packaged. Both men wanted to avoid aesthetically ugly large spoilers, so to ensure high-speed stability, the F1 was designed to incorporate Formula 1-style ground-effect aerodynamics, which meant that the faster it was driven, the more downforce was applied to the wheels.

Low weight was an obsession for Murray, whose ambition was that the F1 should weigh no more than 2,205 lb / 1,000 kg . In the event, that was unachievable (it ended up at 2,513 lb / 1,140 kg), but the quest for low weight meant, among other things, that the car had to be extremely compact. To provide decent interior space, Murray specified a central driving position, with passenger seats on either side and just behind the driver. It made getting in and out a bit of a struggle for the driver, but once in place, he or she was perfectly positioned to enjoy an unrivalled driving experience.

Behind the passenger cabin was the mid-mounted six-liter V12 that BMW built to Murray's specifications. It was a lightweight, all-alloy design, driving the rear wheels via a six-speed manual transmission. Because of the need to save

weight, and because Murray wanted this to be a true drivers' car, there was no four-wheel drive, no power assistance for the brakes, no traction control and not even an ABS system. But because the chassis was so finely engineered, and because the aerodynamics were so perfectly tuned, the F1 was more than capable of handling the 627 bhp that the V12 churned out at 7,400 rpm. It was also capable of handling the highest speed any road car had achieved up till then – 231 mph / 372 km/h.

A few cars were built for racing, and the McLaren F1 was extremely successful at Le Mans, winning outright despite having been originally conceived as a road car. But more important was its performance on the road: quite simply, the McLaren F1 remains the greatest supercar ever devised. Performance figures are truly staggering: 0–60 mph in just over 3 seconds, 0–100 mph in 6.5 seconds, 0–125 mph in 9.8 seconds and 0–200 mph in under 30 seconds. The McLaren F1 not only set new standards, it raised the bar so high that it would take years before any other manufacturer produced a car with a higher top speed or better acceleration.

And yet, paradoxically, the F1 was not a commercial success. It was launched in 1992 at a time of economic turmoil, and although the original plan was to sell 350 examples, only around 100 roadgoing cars were delivered before production finally ceased in 1997. The price of £634,500 reflected the 'money no object' style of the development programme, and yet it's estimated that McLaren still lost money on the project.

Mercedes-Benz SLR McLaren Roadster

The Mercedes-Benz SLR McLaren came about in 2003 when Mercedes-Benz and its Formula 1 partner McLaren decided to combine their experience to create a new supercar for the road. The 'SLR' part of the name is important because it unites the legend of the highly successful SLR racing models of the 1950s with the cutting-edge technology of modern Formula 1 vehicles from the Vodafone–McLaren–Mercedes team.

Stylistic elements such as the arrow-shape tip of the F1 Silver Arrow establish a visual link with the modern racing cars, while the 1950s SLR legend lives on stylistically in the distinctive lateral louvres, side pipes behind the front wheels and the wide-opening gullwing doors. Mercedes-Benz and McLaren produced a Coupé version of the SLR first in 2004, and the convertible Roadster followed in 2007.

With the exception of the two aluminium engine frames, the body of the SLR Roadster is made entirely from carbon-fibre-reinforced plastic, which offers extremely low weight, incredible strength – and therefore passenger safety in the event of an accident – and a degree of torsional stiffness that no other open-topped car has yet achieved. Its fabric roof can be opened or closed in less than ten seconds to ensure the car remains practicable in all weathers, and the design has been fine-tuned in a wind tunnel to ensure that high-speed handling and aerodynamics are optimized. Interestingly, attention was also paid to aeroacoustics, so, Mercedes claim, it's still possible to carry on a normal conversation at 124 mph / 200 km/h with the top down!

But what the SLR is really all about is performance. Its five-liter AMG V8 supercharged powerplant is positioned front-mid-engine for optimum weight distribution and is mated

MERCEDES-BENZ SLR MCLAREN ROADSTER 2007

ENGINE: 5,439 cc V8

MAXIMUM POWER: 617 bhp at 6,500 rpm

MAXIMUM TORQUE: 780 Nm at 3,250–5,000 rpm

MAXIMUM SPEED: 201 mph / 323 km/h

0–60 MPH ACCELERATION: 3.8 secs

TRANSMISSION: 5-speed automatic

LENGTH: 183¼ in / 4,656 mm

WIDTH: 75 in / 1,908 mm

HEIGHT: 49¾ in / 1,261 mm

WHEELBASE: 106¼ in / 2,700 mm

MANUFACTURE DATE: 2007–present

BRAKES: disc (f and r)

SUSPENSION: double wishbone (f and r)

WHEELS: alloy, 18 in

TIRES: 245/40 ZR-18 (f), 295/35 ZR-18 (r)

controls, a starter button that glows red when the key is in, and lots of aluminium and fine leather. Though it shares its basic concept with the Coupé, the SLR Roadster has more than 500 components that are either new or uprated. Obviously the soft top is new, but there are also changes to the boot lid, windscreen, doors, rear wings and roll-over bars.

The Mercedes-Benz SLR Roadster, like the Coupé before it, was produced at McLaren's Formula 1 factory in Woking, England, and it's not just the fastest convertible ever to wear a Mercedes-Benz badge, it's also the most expensive, at an eye-watering £350,000 – a little more than the £333,000 cost of the Coupé. But for the fortunate few, the SLR Roadster is the ultimate stimulation for the senses. It offers all the driving performance, technology and design of the SLR Coupé with the additional joy to be had from open-top motoring, and that makes it a unique supercar.

to an AMG Speedshift R five-speed automatic transmission with steering-wheel-mounted paddle shifters. Maximum power is a healthy 617 bhp at 6,500 rpm and its maximum torque of 780 Nm at 3,250 rpm ensures that acceleration is neck-breaking, 3.8 seconds from 0 to 62 mph, while the top speed is 201 mph / 323 km/h. Remarkably, and despite its extra weight, the Roadster is only marginally slower than the Coupé, which can reach a speed of 207 mph / 333 km/h.

To ensure the SLR Roadster stops as well as it goes, it is fitted with an advanced electro-hydraulic braking system that employs carbon-fibre-reinforced lightweight ceramic brakes. A high degree of safety is ensured by unique carbon-fibre crash elements, steel-reinforced A-pillars and two fixed roll-over bars. The comprehensive specification also features adaptive airbags, knee and side airbags as well as seat-belt tensioners and a tire-pressure monitoring system.

The SLR Roadster's styling closely resembles that of the Coupé: it has a long bonnet and short tapered tail, the eye-catching front-opening scissor doors, the massive side vents and the side exhaust pipes, and the active aerodynamics, including a spoiler mounted on the rear air brake. As the spoiler's angle is altered, so the amount of downforce it provides is increased. Inside the cabin there are body-contoured carbon-fibre sports seats, a sport steering wheel with fingertip gearshift

Mercedes-Benz SLR McLaren Stirling Moss

It has no roof and no windscreen, it's the ultimate SLR, aimed at providing unadulterated high-speed excitement, and it's named after one of the greatest Mercedes-Benz SLR drivers ever. Stirling Moss, with his navigator Denis Jenkinson, won the Mille Miglia in 1955, a race run over normal roads, through towns and villages in central Italy, at an average speed of over 100 mph / 161 km/h. He covered more than 1,000 miles / 1,610 km in 10 hours, 7 minutes and 48 seconds and he still holds the Mille Miglia record.

It was an awesome achievement, and the car that now bears his name is equally incredible. For a start, the SLR Stirling Moss accelerates from 0 to 62 mph in a scorching 3.5 seconds and runs on to a top speed of 217 mph / 349 km/h, powered by a supercharged V8 engine churning out a massive 650 bhp.

According to Mercedes-Benz, the new SLR Stirling Moss unites the character of the current SLR models with the fascination of the SLR of 1955. The core values of both the historical and the present-day SLR models are married with an exciting new design, innovative technology, high-class materials displaying perfect craftsmanship and, above all, a unique driving experience for all the senses. To ensure the lightest possible weight, the entire bodywork is created from carbon fibre. The arrow-shaped design has a strikingly long bonnet and a compactly muscular rear, where two air scoops behind the driver and passenger hide additional roll bars. Powerfully contoured wings with black-painted ventilation slats provide a reminder of the 300 SLR of the 1950s, and, like the original

car, the SLR Stirling Moss has high side skirts. It was these that lead the designers to incorporate dramatic folding swing doors that open forwards.

Inside, the cockpit is reduced to bare essentials, sculpted from carbon fibre and aluminium, and there's an aluminium plate engraved with the signature of Stirling Moss around the gear lever. Fine-quality leather seats are just about the only concession made to creature comforts. This Spartan theme extends even to protection from the elements – there is no roof and there are no side windows, just a pair of wind deflectors a couple of centimeters high to direct the airflow over the heads of the occupants. If the car has to be parked outside, it can be closed by two tonneau covers, which are carried in the boot.

Though it looks radically different to the 'standard' Mercedes-Benz SLR McLaren, this car clearly derives from that model. One common feature is the aerodynamic concept that combines a closed underbody with a diffuser in the rear bumper for maximum possible downforce at the rear, though in the Stirling Moss, this difffuser is much larger than that of the Coupé and Roadster. And when, at the highest speeds, even the downforce generated by the diffuser needs a little help, there's a manually operated airbrake that further increases the contact pressure. It can also be raised during powerful braking at speeds above 75 mph / 121 km/h to ensure maximum stability.

Yet despite the lack of standard creature comforts and the extremely high performance potential of this latest supercar

from the Mercedes-Benz stable, the SLR Stirling Moss is not aimed at the racetrack, but rather at 'individuals who have exquisite requirements and nurture very special dreams'. It might be mentioned, too, that this car is also aimed at extremely wealthy individuals, as the price is €750,000. And that it's also aimed exclusively at existing Mercedes-Benz SLR McLaren customers: they alone will be offered the opportunity to buy one of just 75 examples that are being built. For the fortunate few, this supercar looks likely to become a serious collector's item, because it is planned that it will be the final SLR to be built: these SLR Stirling Moss cars, bearing chassis numbers one to 75, will bring the SLR era to an end.

MERCEDES-BENZ SLR MCLAREN STIRLING MOSS 2009

ENGINE: 5,439 cc V8

MAXIMUM POWER: 650 bhp at 6,500 rpm

MAXIMUM TORQUE: 820 Nm at 4,000 rpm

MAXIMUM SPEED: 217 mph / 349 km/h

0–60 MPH ACCELERATION: 3.5 secs

TRANSMISSION: 5-speed automatic

LENGTH: 189¾ in / 4,820 mm

WIDTH: 86½ in / 2,194 mm

HEIGHT: 48 in / 1,220 mm

WHEELBASE: 106¼ in / 2,700 mm

MANUFACTURE DATE: 2009–present

BRAKES: disc (f and r)

SUSPENSION: double wishbone (f and r)

WHEELS: alloy, 19in

TIRES: 255/35 ZR-19 (f), 295/30 ZR-19 (r)

Mitsubishi Lancer Evolution X

MITSUBISHI LANCER EVOLUTION X 2008

ENGINE: 1,998 cc inline 4-cylinder

MAXIMUM POWER: 354 bhp at 6,500 rpm

MAXIMUM TORQUE: 492 Nm at 3,500 rpm

MAXIMUM SPEED: 155 mph / 259 km/h

0–62 MPH ACCELERATION: 4.1 secs

TRANSMISSION: 5-speed manual

LENGTH: 177 in / 4,495 mm

WIDTH: 71¼ in / 1,810 mm

HEIGHT: 58¼ in / 1,480 mm

WHEELBASE: 104¼ in / 2,650 mm

MANUFACTURE DATE: 2008–present

BRAKES: disc (f and r)

SUSPENSION: MacPherson strut (f), multi-link (r)

WHEELS: alloy, 18 in

TIRES: 245/40 R-18 (f and r)

The first Mitsubishi Lancer Evolution was produced by the Japanese company to allow it to enter the 1992 World Rally Championships. The car combined the four-wheel-drive system from the Galant model with the smaller Lancer chassis and Mitsubishi's four-cylinder 244 bhp turbocharged engine. Because, as a road car, this was something rather special, Mitsubishi had no trouble shifting 5,000 examples in Japan to fulfill its homologation requirements, and so, initially at least, there were no official exports of the car.

Over the next few years, the Evolution was further developed: in fact, a new version was produced almost annually, so that by 1998, the eighth generation, or Evolution VIII, had appeared. Some earlier Evolution cars had been sold outside Japan as grey imports, but the Evo VIII was the first to be exported by Mitsubishi to the UK and other European markets.

At that time, the Japanese Evo VIII was producing 276 bhp according to official figures, but regulations in Mitsubishi's home market banned any advertising of power outputs over that figure, and the car's true power output was undoubtedly greater. Its real potential became clear only when cars were prepared for the UK market: in fact, the FQ400 Evolution VIII, as marketed for Mitsubishi by Ralliart UK, produced 405 bhp thanks to special tuning. That translated into 0–60 mph acceleration in 3.5 seconds, 0–100 mph in 9.1 seconds and a maximum speed of 176 mph / 283 km/h. That made it one of the fastest cars on the road, not least because its permanent four-wheel drive gave it massive traction and race-bred handling.

In 2005, the Evolution IX was launched simultaneously in Japan and Europe, a clear indication of the importance of the latter market in maintaining the Evo's image, and once again, it raised the bar in terms of performance. There was therefore a real sense of excitement when Mitsubishi revealed the Concept-X car at the Tokyo Motor Show later that year, a design study that foreshadowed the Evolution X, which would appear in 2008.

Like all Lancer Evolutions before it, the Evo X has permanent four-wheel drive and a four-cylinder turbocharged 2.0-liter engine. But there the similarity ends, because, despite its name, the Evolution X is no mere evolution, but a wholly new model that boasts an incredible display of technologies.

Three engine outputs were available at launch, ranging from 290 bhp in the entry-level Evolution X FQ300 to 354 bhp in the flagship FQ360. Torque was equally impressive, ranging from 402 Nm to 492 Nm. That translated in the quickest Evo to 0–62 mph acceleration in 4.1 seconds and a top speed electronically limited to 155 mph / 259 km/h.

But even that wasn't sufficient performance for the Evo's most hardcore devotees, so Mitsubishi introduced the FQ400 model, with peak power boosted to 403 bhp at 6,500 rpm and peak torque to 525 Nm at 3,500 rpm. Acceleration time for 0 to 62 mph is down to 3.8 seconds, though the top speed remains firmly limited to 155 mph / 259 km/h.

Ensuring all the FQ400's power is put to good use is Mitsubishi's Super-All Wheel Control (S-AWC) four-wheel-drive system, which adjusts the torque according to which wheels have the best grip, giving the FQ400 sensational performance. The S-AWC system combines a number of electronic systems,

including Active Stability Control and Active Center Differential, Active Yaw Control and Sport ABS, giving the FQ400 optimum cornering ability, traction and grip. In a nod towards the Evo's rallying heritage, the driver can select the most suitable set-up for the S-AWC system – Tarmac, Gravel or Snow – via a wheel-mounted button.

To produce 403 bhp from a 2.0-liter engine, high-flow fuel injectors are fitted to the aluminium cylinder head, and a new hybrid intercooled turbocharger with increased response and reduced turbo lag is also specified. In addition, a remapped Engine Control Unit allows incredible output, excellent driveability and sensational acceleration, depending on demand. The Evo X can move through town traffic as easily as it can take on a rally special stage – and all with the convenience of a standard saloon car offering seating for five as well as useful luggage space. It's a perfect example of practicality with explosive performance potential.

Morgan Aero 8

Morgan, the most traditional of all British sports car makers, tends to launch a new model about once every 30 years, so there was a frisson of excitement in the air at the 2000 Geneva Motor Show when chief executive Peter Morgan prepared to unveil the Aero 8. As the wraps came off, there was a stunned silence, because the new car, while clearly a Morgan, had a closed cabin, aerodynamic bodywork and very strange headlights. It polarized opinion: onlookers – and presumably Morgan customers too – either loved it or hated it. It was a design about which it was impossible to be indifferent.

This was a big risk for a small family-owned company like Morgan to take. It had tried once before to persuade its customers into a more modern design. Its Plus Four Plus, launched in 1964, was an elegant coupé with styling rather similar to the MGA. It was far more comfortable than the traditional Morgan, and had far better aerodynamics, but it was a commercial disaster because Morgan's customers simply preferred the older, pre-war design.

The most radical aspect of the Aero 8 lies in its construction. Gone is the traditional Morgan wooden frame, which is replaced by an aluminium alloy chassis with aluminium body panels mounted upon it. At the time, this was not just radical for Morgan, it was also leading the industry: Morgan was using formed aluminium panels significantly earlier than either Aston Martin or Bentley, and its chassis used the same technology that Lotus employed in the Elise.

A further innovation for Morgan was the fully independent suspension with a cantilever upper arm and lower wishbone with inboard coil springs and shocks at the front, and transverse wishbones with cantilever mounted inboard coils springs and shocks at the rear. In the original 2002 version, power came from a BMW-sourced 4,398 cc V8, producing 286 bhp at 5,400 rpm and 440 Nm of torque at 3,600 rpm, mated to a six-speed manual transmission driving the rear wheels. That was more than enough to offer 0–62 mph acceleration in 4.5 seconds and a top speed of just under 160 mph / 256 km/h.

MORGAN AERO 8 2002		WIDTH: 69¾ in / 1,770 mm
ENGINE: 4,398 cc V8		HEIGHT: 47¼ in / 1,200 mm
MAXIMUM POWER: 286 mph at 5,400 rpm		WHEELBASE: 99½ in / 2,525 mm
MAXIMUM TORQUE: 440 Nm at 3,600 rpm		MANUFACTURE DATE: 2000–present
MAXIMUM SPEED: 160 mph / 256 km/h		BRAKES: disc (f and r)
0–62 MPH ACCELERATION: 4.5 secs		SUSPENSION: independent lower wishbone (f), independent transverse wishbone (r)
TRANSMISSION: 6-speed manual		WHEELS: alloy, 18 in
LENGTH: 162¼ in / 4,120 mm		TIRES: 255/40 ZR-18

The Aero 8 is ferociously fast, but the whole car has been designed to cope with this. It has massive disc brakes, all with ABS, electronic brakeforce distribution and drag torque control to prevent lock-up. It has an electro-hydraulic power steering system to provide assistance at low speeds without interfering with the accuracy of the steering at higher velocities. And despite the lack of anti-roll bars, it corners without any body roll, thanks to the Morgan-designed suspension, which offers both a reasonable ride and outstanding grip and poise.

In many ways, the Aero 8 is a great car. The only problem, for some people, were those weird cross-eyed headlamps. This aspect was addressed in 2007, when the front end was redesigned to incorporate more conventional xenon lights. At the same time, some minor changes were made at the rear, including the addition of a small ducktail to improve stability. Then, in 2008, BMW's bigger 4.8-liter V8 was fitted, along with the option of either manual

or automatic transmission. This boosted the power output to 368 bhp and the top speed to 170 mph. While 0–62 mph acceleration for the manual car remains at 4.5 seconds, the auto is actually quicker, recording 4.2 seconds.

Unlike the earlier Morgan Plus Four Plus, the Aero 8 has been a major commercial success for the company: more than 600 examples of the bespoke hand-built sports car have been delivered to customers so far. Interest may have been boosted by the car's successes at Le Mans and in the FIA GT3 European Championship, but the main reason customers add their names to Morgan's long waiting lists is that the Aero 8 provides all the performance of a Porsche 911 in a car that's both instantly recognizable and yet rare.

Morgan Plus 8

The Morgan Plus 8 was first launched in 1968 and it remained in production for a full 36 years. But then Morgan is a very traditional British sportscar manufacturer, for which change comes rarely. The company has remained in family ownership ever since H.F.S. Morgan founded it in 1909 to produce three-wheeled sports cars. It took the company until 1935 to build its first four-wheel car – the 4/4 – and virtually every car Morgan has

launched since then has been a variation on that original theme. Indeed, the Plus 8 looks very similar to the Plus 4 model that was launched in 1950 and is still in production today.

But the Plus 8 was special in its day because it was fitted with a 3.5-liter V8 engine that gave it massive performance. The engine was the 3,528 cc Rover V8, itself a development of a Buick V8 design, and its 168 bhp at 5,200 rpm gave the Plus 8

MORGAN PLUS 8 1992

ENGINE: 3,946 cc V8

MAXIMUM POWER: 190 bhp at 4,750 rpm

MAXIMUM TORQUE: 312 Nm at 2,600 rpm

MAXIMUM SPEED: 130 mph / 209 km/h

0–62 MPH ACCELERATION: 6.1 secs

TRANSMISSION: 5-speed manual

LENGTH: 156 in / 3,962 mm

WIDTH: 63 in / 1,600 mm

HEIGHT: 48 in / 1,219 mm

WHEELBASE: 98 in / 2,489 mm

MANUFACTURE DATE: 1968–2004

BRAKES: disc (f), drum (r)

SUSPENSION: sliding pillar (f), live axle (r)

WHEELS: alloy, 15 in

TIRES: 205/60 VR-15

1997, the capacity of the Rover V8 was increased to 4.6 liters, which boosted the power output to 220 bhp and brought the 0–60 mph acceleration time down to around five seconds.

But the Morgan Plus 8 was never really about mere performance – it was about the whole experience of owning and driving a bespoke sports car with a heritage stretching back nearly 100 years. There's no doubting that was an automotive throwback, with its 1930s-style long fluted bonnet, flat windscreen, wings and spare wheel bolted on the back. But that's the whole point of a Morgan; it's not another anodyne and rather soulless modern car, instead it's a piece of genuine craftsmanship with a character that is totally unique.

In all, 3,506 of these handbuilt sports cars were produced before the Plus 8 went out of production in 2004, the victim of European emission regulations. However, in the same year, Morgan launched a very similar-looking car. It has a 3.0-liter Ford V6 under its bonnet, it's called the Morgan Roadster and it continues the long and honourable Morgan sportscar tradition.

a spirited 0–60 mph acceleration of 6.7 seconds, though its top speed was limited to 124 mph / 200 km/h by the car's archaic aerodynamics. Like all Morgans before it, the Plus 8 was built on a wooden, ash frame, to which the body panels were attached. If that sounds old-fashioned, then the suspension was even more so – it still used sliding pillars at the front and a live axle with leaf springs at the rear. The rather agricultural steering was by worm and nut, which resulted in 2.4 turns lock to lock and heavy steering, even at higher speeds. Discs at the front were complemented by drum brakes at the rear.

It sounds a disastrous specification, but on the road, the Plus 8 was unique. The suspension was set so hard that it was said that if you drove over a coin, you could feel whether it was heads or tails uppermost. It tended to understeer in corners, though a dab of power could swiftly change this into opposite-lock oversteer. However, although the car required all the driver's attention, the payback was sheer, exhilarating joy, with all the pleasures that a quick open-topped sports car can provide. And in 1968, all that was available for £5,417.

Over the years, the Plus 8 evolved: in 1990, the V8 was bored out to 3,946 cc, so that it now produced 190 bhp at 4,750 rpm and 312 Nm of torque at 2,600 rpm. Its 0–60 mph acceleration improved a little to 6.1 seconds, but the 0–100 mph time, at 18.4 seconds, was a full two seconds quicker than before. In

Nissan 370Z

Nissan's Z line of sports cars was launched in 1969, the same year as the Datsun 240Z. Over the years, the famous letter was appended to a succession of models, continuing after Datsun changed its name to Nissan in the 1980s with the 300Z launched

in 1989 and the 350Z in 2003. Through its many incarnations, the Nissan Z has become not only a massive commercial success but also an iconic Japanese sports car.

The latest in this long and honourable lineage is the 370Z, first revealed at the 2008 Los Angeles Motor Show and going on sale in 2009. It's based upon the 350Z that preceded it, but is sharper, more agile and more powerful. In terms of its styling, the 370Z is also meaner and more aggressive looking, with a widened track and shortened wheelbase to improve roadholding and handling. It's ½ in / 10 mm lower, 1¼ in / 33 mm wider and 2½ in / 65 mm shorter than the 350Z, though it retains its predecessor's silhouette, incorporating a long bonnet, short overhangs and aggressive rear haunches.

Lightweight materials, including aluminium bonnet, tailgate and doors, which save some 71 lb / 32 kg of kerb weight, also contribute to the car's fine handling. In addition, the front-midships rear-wheel-drive platform has been re-engineered to move the engine as far back as possible, thus optimizing the weight balance, which is now 53:47 front to rear. A further bonus comes from an increase of some 30 per cent in the torsional

NISSAN 370Z 2009

ENGINE: 3,699 cc V6

MAXIMUM POWER: 331 bhp at 7,000 rpm

MAXIMUM TORQUE: 366 Nm at 5,200 rpm

MAXIMUM SPEED: 155 mph / 249 km/h

0–62 MPH ACCELERATION: 5.3 secs

TRANSMISSION: 6-speed manual or 7-speed automatic

LENGTH: 167¼ in / 4,250 mm

WIDTH: 72¾ in / 1,845 mm

HEIGHT: 51¾ in / 1,315 mm

WHEELBASE: 100½ in / 2,550 mm

MANUFACTURE DATE: 2009–present

BRAKES: disc (f and r)

SUSPENSION: double wishbone (f) multi-link (r)

WHEELS: alloy, 19 in

TIRES: 245/45 R19 (f) 275/35 R19 (r)

traction and stability systems that can either reduce engine torque or brake individual wheels according to need.

Inside, the cockpit features a deep fascia and prominent center console with the important gauges attached to the steering column to ensure they are always highly visible. Like its predecessor, the 370Z is a true two-seater, and no effort has been made to incorporate the vestigial rear seats that are fitted to many sports cars. Figure-hugging supportive seats, aluminium pedals and a prominent stop/start button on the fascia all hint at the car's sporting lineage.

In essence, the 370Z shares the DNA of the original 240Z, a car that in its time shook up the sportscar sector with its appealing blend of high performance and high style. The 370Z displays that same philosophy in its combination of effortless performance, pin-sharp handling and cutting-edge design.

rigidity of the body, thanks in part to an additional bracing bar on top of the front suspension turrets. The suspension remains a double wishbone arrangement at the front and multi-link at the rear, but the increased use of forged aluminium makes it lighter and stiffer, which benefits the car's handling and ride.

Power comes from Nissan's 3.7-liter V6 with variable valve timing and lift, which boosts low-end power, raises the high-end torque and improves efficiency over the whole range. Its output is 331 bhp at 7,000 rpm, some 18 bhp more than the 350Z produced. With torque also increased from 358 Nm to 366 Nm at 5,200 rpm, the 370Z can accelerate from 0 to 62 mph in 5.3 seconds while its top speed is electronically limited to 155 mph / 259 km/h.

As well as less weight, more power and sharper handling, the 370Z also boasts a unique six-speed manual transmission, which incorporates what's called Synchro Rev Control (SRC). This is the world's first such gearshift control system, which automatically synchronizes both up and down gear changes, allowing drivers of all abilities to achieve perfectly smooth gear changes every time without resorting to the old-fashioned 'heel-and-toe' or double-declutching methods. Interestingly, the alternative seven-speed automatic transmission also incorporates a feature that 'blips' the throttle on downshifts to synchronize the input and output shaft speeds. To aid traction and stability, the 370Z is fitted with a viscous limited slip differential and electronically controlled

Nissan GT-R

NISSAN GT-R 2009

ENGINE: 3,799 cc V6

MAXIMUM POWER: 485 bhp at 6,400 rpm

MAXIMUM TORQUE: 588 Nm at 3,200 rpm

MAXIMUM SPEED: 194 mph / 312 km/h

0–62 MPH ACCELERATION: 3.5 secs

TRANSMISSION: 6-speed dual clutch

LENGTH: 183 in / 4,650 mm

WIDTH: 74½ in / 1,895 mm

HEIGHT: 54 in / 1,370 mm

WHEELBASE: 109½ in / 2,780 mm

MANUFACTURE DATE: 2007–present

BRAKES: disc (f and r)

SUSPENSION: double wishbone (f) multi-link (r)

WHEELS: alloy, 20 in

TIRES: 255/40 ZRF20 (f) 285/35 ZRF20 (r)

The Nissan GT-R enjoys a long and extremely rich heritage that stretches back as far as 1969. That was when Nissan first used the name GT-R (standing for Grand Turismo Racing) on the Skyline PGC10 model. To be frank, it was an ugly, angular and ill-proportioned car, but it had a relatively powerful six-cylinder 2.0-liter engine, it handled well, and it responded well to being driven fast. It was successful in competition, and yet it was also a practical four-seater saloon.

In the years that followed, the Skyline GT-R's reputation grew and grew as successive models gained even greater motorsport success and started to become a proving ground for the very latest technological innovations. Four-wheel drive and four-wheel steer were introduced with the 1989 GT-R, a model that was more than a match for the very best sports cars around the world – which was just as well, because this was the first Skyline GT-R to be exported from Japan, albeit in very limited numbers. Twin ceramic turbochargers helped boost power of the 2.6-liter straight six engine to over 300 bhp, giving it a top speed of 160 mph / 257 km/h and 0–60 mph acceleration in under five

seconds. And what really brought it to the world's notice is that this relatively unknown Japanese car broke the production-car lap record at the Nürburgring. The GT-R that appeared in 1995 was a relatively modest evolution of the 1989 car, but 1999 saw the launch of a radically new model that claimed to have 280 bhp on tap. In reality, it produced significantly more, as was proved when a GT-R again took the Nürburgring production-car lap record.

Nissan's problem in 2007 was how to improve on a car that had become something of a legend. Its solution was unveiled at that year's Tokyo Motor Show: the all-new GT-R was powered by a 3.8-liter twin-turbo V6 producing an awesome 485 bhp at 6,400 rpm and 588 Nm of torque at 3,200 rpm. That was good enough to offer 0–62 mph acceleration in 3.5 seconds and a top speed of 194 mph / 312 km/h. Once again, Nissan's engineers had produced a dynamic marvel, and once again, they showcased technologies that had never been seen before. In particular, the car's unique driveline consisted of the world's first rear transaxle with a dual-clutch, paddle-shift six-speed transmission and permanent four-wheel drive.

Fascia-mounted switches allow the driver to adapt a whole range of settings, including the gearshift pattern, the damper settings and the stability control settings, depending on the conditions and driving style. The car can be changed in an instant from a raw, race-mode supercar requiring full driver involvement to a soft and comfortable coupé complete with automatic transmission. Like earlier GT-R models, it puts enormous performance potential into the hands of the driver, but at the same time, it is a car that can be driven safely and swiftly by people who would never aspire to be racing drivers. Very few other cars offer such speed with such ease of driving.

While the cockpit's deep front seats are contoured for high performance driving, the overall ambiance is one of understated luxury, with full leather upholstery, dual-zone air conditioning, a high-quality stereo system with a hard drive for downloading favourite music, and a multi-function LCD screen, which was developed in conjunction with the designers of the Sony Playstation Gran Turismo game.

Although the new GT-R is now exported around the world, production is limited to around 1,000 units a month simply because that is the maximum the specialist build process can cope with: every engine and transmission is individually assembled by a team of craftsmen in a special clean room area of Nissan's Yokohama plant.

Noble M15

Noble cars are for those who love to drive. The British company, founded by Lee Noble in 1999, has a simple outlook, which itself is expressed quite simply: 'Designed and engineered with a purity that rewards driver skill, our cars are neither dictated to nor hindered by unnecessary computer assistance. Noble puts you back in the driving seat'.

In his suspicion of computer-controlled systems, Noble's thinking is very similar to that of Gordon Murray, designer of the legendary McLaren F1, who also felt that everything possible should be done to provide an authentic driving experience.

Noble's first car was launched in 1999 – the two-seater convertible M10 model, powered by a 2.5-liter naturally aspirated Ford engine. Thanks to its lightweight glass-reinforced plastic body, the Noble M10 was seriously fast, capable of reaching 60 mph from standstill in around 3.5 seconds and had a top speed of 170 mph / 274 km/h.

The M10 was soon replaced by the mid-engined M12, which was fitted with a far more powerful turbocharged Ford engine – either a 2.5-liter V6 producing 310 bhp or a 3.0-liter V6 producing 325 bhp. The M12 was a no-compromise car, in many respects a racecar that was road legal. Lee Noble therefore set about designing a new model that would be more practical in everyday use, more comfortable and more refined,

but that would nevertheless retain all the performance potential of the earlier M12.

The M15 duly appeared in 2006, and was road tested by various magazine and TV journalists, all of whom gave it rave reviews. First of all, they were astonished by its sheer performance – the 3.0-liter twin turbocharged Ford Duratec engine had been tuned to produce 455 bhp at 6,800 rpm and 617 Nm of torque at 4,800 rpm, which made the car devastatingly fast – it could reach from 060 mph in 3.4 seconds, 0–100 mph in under eight seconds and a top speed of 185 mph / 298 km/h. According to Noble, 200 mph / 322 km/h is attainable, but it chose to gear the car for rapid acceleration throughout the range rather than outright top speed.

To improve weight distribution, the engine is installed longitudinally, in contrast to all previous Nobles, in which it was mounted transversely. This change also improves cooling, facilitates access for servicing and allows the use of the same sort of transaxle that Ferrari and Lamborghini employ. There was also critical acclaim for the M15's confidence-inspiring chassis. The spaceframe chassis with integral rollcage is 57 per cent stiffer than that of the M12 and improves handling still further. Suspension is a development of the earlier Noble system, with double wishbones, coil springs and gas-pressurized dampers front and rear.

Better still, in addition to this breathtaking performance, the M15 offers a civilized, comfortable and reasonably spacious cabin that provides creature comforts previously unheard of at Noble, including electric windows, satellite navigation and even traction control and ABS. The interior is beautifully trimmed with high-grade leather and there's even some 872 gallons / 3,300 liters of luggage space in compartments in the front and rear.

In 2006, the Noble M15 was quoted with a list price of £74,950, considerably less than the Ferrari F430 or Audi R8. It also boasts a power-to-weight ratio of 370 bhp per ton, which exceeds either the Ferrari F430 at 342 bhp per ton or the Lamborghini Gallardo at 343 bhp per ton.

And yet the car never went into volume production. According to Noble, the car that had been loaned for those early road tests was a pre-production prototype, which an in-house review decided was not good enough – not fast enough, not stiff enough and not beautiful enough. So the company went back to the drawing board and has rethought and re-engineered virtually every component of the car. The result will be two new cars – the M600 and the M15C – that will share many features but remain very different in feel and appearance. If they are to be better than the M15, they are going to be very good indeed.

NOBLE M15 2006

ENGINE: 2,968 cc V6

MAXIMUM POWER: 455 bhp at 6,800 rpm

MAXIMUM TORQUE: 617 Nm at 4,800 rpm

MAXIMUM SPEED: 185 mph / 298 km/h

0–60 MPH ACCELERATION: 3.4 secs

TRANSMISSION: 6-speed manual

LENGTH: 168 in / 4,270 mm

WIDTH: 72¾ in / 1,850 mm

HEIGHT: 44 in / 1,116 mm

WHEELBASE: 96 in / 2,438 mm

MANUFACTURE DATE: 2006–present

BRAKES: disc (f and r)

SUSPENSION: wishbone (f and r)

WHEELS: alloy, 18 in (f), 19 in (r)

TIRES: 225/40 ZR-18 (f), 285/40 ZR-19 (r)

Pagani Zonda

Horacio Pagani spent his childhood modelling supercars out of wood and clay and later found himself a job as a junior mechanic at Lamborghini. Specializing in carbon-fibre manufacturing techniques, he found himself working on the development of the Countach Evoluzione, the world's first car with a carbon-fibre chassis. He left in 1988 to set up his own consultancy, which was immediately contracted by Lamborghini to help develop the composites for the Diablo and Countach Anniversary models.

But in the meantime, he started working on his own pet project – the development of a supercar codenamed the 'C8 Project', which Pagani planned to call the Fangio F1 in honour of his motor-racing hero. A major breakthrough came in 1994, when Mercedes-Benz agreed to supply him with its V12 engine, but it took five more years of hard work before the first car was ready to be unveiled at the 1999 Geneva Motor Show. Because Fangio had died by then, the car's name was changed to the C12 Zonda, after a wind that blows in the Andes mountains in South America.

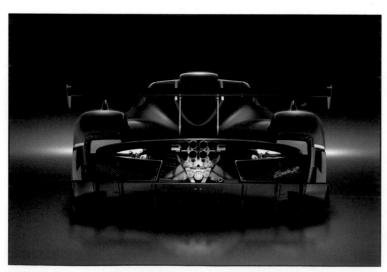

That first Pagani Zonda, like all Zondas since, had its engine mounted behind the passenger cockpit driving the rear wheels. Its AMG-tuned Mercedes V12 produced 542 bhp and provided sparkling performance – a 0–60 mph acceleration time of 3.7 seconds, a 0–100 mph time of 7.5 seconds and a top speed of around 220 mph / 354 km/h, which made it one of the fastest cars in the world. It looked the part, too, thanks to its carbon-fibre bodywork and squat, aerodynamic lines. With a price tag of $320,000, it was never intended to be a mass-produced car, but the company has sold an average of about ten cars a year since.

Because the cars are hand-built, it's relatively easy to make changes to the specification, and Pagani was offering a slightly faster C12 S model by 2001. For the first time, a convertible version of the model was offered, as well as a coupé. In 2002, the output of the engine was dramatically increased with the installation of a new 7,291cc V12, which produced 547 bhp, pushed the top speed up to 224 mph / 360 km/h and reduced the 0–60 mph acceleration to 3.5 seconds. Another model was added to the range in 2004 – the Zonda C12 S Monza. With more than 600 bhp on tap, a lighter body and modified aerodynamics, it offered a whole new level of performance. Next up, in 2005, was the Zonda F, which, again, was available in both roadster and coupé formats and produced in excess of 600 bhp. And yet, astonishingly, there was still more to come.

The 2009 Zonda R produces 750 bhp at 7,500 rpm and 710 Nm of torque at 5,000 rpm from its 5,987 cc dry-sump bi-turbo Mercedes-Benz AMG V12, powering the rear wheel via a six-speed sequential transmission. To help in transmitting so much power to the road, a 12-stage Bosch Motorsport traction-control system is standard, while to ensure adequate stopping power, massive ventilated Brembo brakes are fitted, with six-piston callipers at the front and four-piston callipers at the rear. The suspension system uses double A-arms with forged suspension arms, pull-rod helical springs and Ohlins adjustable

PAGANI ZONDA R 2009

ENGINE: 5,987 cc V12

MAXIMUM POWER: 750 bhp at 7,500 rpm

MAXIMUM TORQUE: 710 Nm at 5,000 rpm

MAXIMUM SPEED: 217 mph / 349 km/h

0–62 MPH ACCELERATION: 2.7 secs

TRANSMISSION: 6-speed sequential

LENGTH: 188 in / 4,775 mm

WIDTH: 81 in / 2,055 mm

HEIGHT: 45 in / 1,140 mm

WHEELBASE: 109½ in / 2,780 mm

MANUFACTURE DATE: 2009–present

BRAKES: disc (f and r)

SUSPENSION: independent double A-arm (f and r)

WHEELS: alloy, 19 in (f), 20 in (r)

TIRES: 255/35 19 (f), 335/30 20 (r)

shock absorbers. It has a carbon-titanium chassis and carbon-fibre body panels, and weight-saving extends even to the cabin, where the seats – designed to accommodate the F1 HANS safety device – are also constructed from carbon fibre. If there's any doubt as to the car's motorsport capability, it's also fitted with an integral roll cage. As to performance, according to Zonda, the R's acceleration from 0 to 62 mph is 2.7 seconds – an absolutely incredible achievement. And for good measure, top speed is recorded as over 217 mph. All Zondas have been true supercars, but the Zonda R could be said to be in a league of its own.

Porsche 911

Ferdinand Porsche was an automotive genius. His CV includes credits for designing the V16 Auto Union P-Wagen racing car in 1934 – one of the legendary Silver Arrows that dominated Grand Prix racing until the outbreak of World War II, the Tiger Tank during hostilities and, perhaps most especially, the Volkswagen Beetle. But he also put his own name to a small, nimble and lightweight sports car that he developed and launched in 1948 with the help of his son Ferry – the Porsche 356.

Like the Beetle, the Porsche 356 had a rear-mounted air-cooled four-cylinder engine, trailing link front suspension, and was constructed on a unitary floorpan and body design. Although the first few bodies were crafted in aluminium, later ones were all made out of steel. Power from the original 1.1-liter overhead-valve engine was just 40 bhp, and yet the Porsche 356 was soon to be found on the racetrack because of its good aerodynamics and handling. It stayed in production until 1965 and its successor followed many of its design and engineering leads.

The new car, the Porsche 901, was shown at the 1963 Frankfurt Motor Show, but failed to make a spectacular impression, not least because its 130 bhp was the same output as that of the final series of 2.0-liter 356 Carreras. Nevertheless,

PORSCHE 911 2003	**WIDTH:** 66.9 in / 1,770 mm
ENGINE: 3,596 cc Flat 6	**HEIGHT:** 51.2 in / 1,305 mm
MAXIMUM POWER: 320 bhp at 6,800 rpm	**WHEELBASE:** 92½ in / 2,350 mm
MAXIMUM TORQUE: 370 Nm at 4,250 rpm	**MANUFACTURE DATE:** 1964 to present
MAXIMUM SPEED: 177 mph / 285 km/h	**BRAKES:** Discs (f and r)
0–62 MPH ACCELERATION: 5.0 secs	**SUSPENSION:** Independent MacPherson strut (f), independent trailing arm (r)
TRANSMISSION: 6-speed manual or 5-speed Tiptronic	**WHEELS:** alloy, 17 in (f) 18 in (r)
LENGTH: 174.4 in / 4,430 mm	**TIRES:** 205/50 R 17 (f) 225/40 R 18 (r)

production started in 1964, the only major change being the car's name, because it transpired that Peugeot held the rights to all three-digit car names with a zero in the middle. Thus it was that the first Porsche 911 came into being, fitted with a 2.0-liter air-cooled flat-six engine with chain driven overhead camshafts producing 128 bhp at 6,200 rpm and 174 Nm of torque. It was basically a two-seater, but because rudimentary rear seats were fitted, it was described as a 2+2. At the time, its performance was truly sporting: 0–60 mph took 8.3 seconds and its top speed was 132 mph / 212 km/h.

Almost immediately after the 911's launch, Porsche started developing the car, and a higher-performance 911 S appeared in 1966, with power up to 158 bhp, torque up to 179 Nm and top speed up to 137 mph / 220 km/h. Interestingly, Porsche also produced a lower-powered version at around that time, using the four-cylinder engine from the 356 in a 911 body and calling it the Porsche 912. Apart from that aberration, the power and performance of the 911 went inexorably upwards over the years – and there were many, many years, because the 911 remains in production to this day, ranking alongside the Chevrolet Corvette and the Nissan Skyline as one of the longest-surviving sports cars in the world.

As an indication of just how far Porsche has traveled since 1964, the very latest 'basic' 911 Carrera produces 345 bhp at 6,500 rpm from its 3,614 six-cylinder boxer engine, which gives it a 0–62 mph acceleration time of 4.9 seconds and a top speed of 180 mph / 290 km/h. But that performance pales into insignificance compared to that of the 911 Turbo, however, which churns out 480 bhp and reaches 62 mph from a standstill in 3.9 seconds and a top speed of 193 mph / 311 km/h. And the Turbo is not even the fastest 911 on the market: the GT2 model produces 530 bhp from its 3,600 cc flat-six, accelerates from 0 to 62 mph in a tire-blistering 3.7 seconds and has a top speed of 204 mph / 328 km/h.

Such performance is a very far cry from that of the original, and in engineering and technical terms, the 1964 and the 2009 911s have nothing whatsoever in common. And yet in terms of their basic shape, design philosophy and sheer charisma,

it's abundantly clear that the first and most recent 911s share the same DNA. The Porsche 911 has been one of the most successful racing cars of all time – it has competed at Le Mans every year since 1964, for example, and taken numerous class wins – and one of the most enduring and successful road cars of all time, too. It is one of the automotive world's real classics – and, amazingly, it's still going strong.

Porsche 911 GT3

PORSCHE 911 GT3 2006

ENGINE: 3,800 cc flat four-cylinder

MAXIMUM POWER: 435 bhp at 7,600 rpm

MAXIMUM TORQUE: 430 Nm at 5,500 rpm

MAXIMUM SPEED: 194 mph / 312 km/h

0–62 MPH ACCELERATION: 4.1 secs

TRANSMISSION: 6-speed manual

LENGTH: 176 in / 4,465 mm

WIDTH: 71¼ in / 1,808 mm

HEIGHT: 50½ in / 1,280 mm

WHEELBASE: 92¾ in / 2,355 mm

MANUFACTURE DATE: 1999–present

BRAKES: disc (f and r)

SUSPENSION: independent MacPherson strut (f), independent trailing arm (r)

WHEELS: alloy, 19 in

TIRES: 235/35 ZR19 (f) 305/30 ZR 19 (r)

The latest Porsche 911 GT3, which was unveiled at the 2009 Geneva Motor, is the more recent evolution of what has become, in a very short while, an iconic sports car, one that's road legal but in its element on a track.

The first GT3 was introduced in 1999, based on the 996 model of the Porsche 911, the first of those rear-engined sports cars to be water cooled rather than air cooled. The GT3 differed radically from the standard production car, not least because its engine was a normally aspirated derivative of the turbocharged engine used in the Porsche 962 racing car. It produced 355 bhp (compared to 296 bhp of the standard 911), and thanks to that and its lower weight, it was substantially faster, recording 62 mph from standstill in around five seconds. More was to come in 2004, with a power upgrade to 381 bhp, which enabled the GT3 to reach 60 mph in 4.5 seconds, but the big news came in 2006, when the all-new 997 Porsche 911 was launched. In due course, a GT3 version was introduced, now with 415 bhp on tap and with a 0–62 mph acceleration time of just a fraction over four seconds.

Porsche continued development and introduced a second generation of the Type 997 911 GT3 in 2009. Porsche engineers' intention with this latest GT3 was simple: to offer even higher performance and driving dynamics. Its flat-six engine was increased in capacity to 3.8 liters and tuned to develop 435 bhp at 7,600 rpm, making it one of the world's most powerful naturally aspirated engines. The torque is also increased to 430 Nm at 5,500 rpm. Because this is unashamedly a driver's car, the only transmission that's fitted is Porsche's six-speed manual box, which is a full 66 lb / 30 kg lighter than the double-clutch manual transmission fitted to standard 911 road cars.

According to Porsche's official figures, the latest GT3 has a 0–62 mph acceleration time of 4.1 seconds and a maximum speed of 194 mph / 312 km/h. However, as the company is notorious for understating its cars' performance figures, it is highly probable that the 911 GT3 is capable of yet more, despite the fact that the engine has been made cleaner and easily conforms to EU5 emissions standards. In fact, former racing driver and Porsche development driver Walter Röhrl claims to

have lapped Germany's Nürburgring race track five seconds a lap faster than in the previous model.

So the engineers certainly seem to have succeeded in their first task, that of boosting performance, but what of handling and overall dynamic balance? The car looks very similar to the previous model, but hours in the wind tunnel have resulted in a shape that manages to increases downforce – to 243 lb / 110 kg at 196 mph / 315 km/h – without increasing the drag. The result is far more stability at high speed. Porsche has also managed to induce a slight reduction in understeer and to increase the rear stability by tweaking the suspension system and stiffening the springs and anti-roll bars.

The 911 GT3 is fitted as standard with the Porsche Stability Management (PSM) system, which helps the driver keep control of the car whatever the circumstances. But as this is a barely disguised racer, the driver can choose to deactivate both the Stability Control and Traction Control components in separate steps. This gives the driver absolute control, because, unlike in some other

supercars, these functions are not reactivated automatically even under the most extreme conditions, but only when manually switched back on.

Although it can be said that just about all Porsche 911s look the same, the new 'Aerodynamics Package' gives the latest GT3 its own distinctive appearance, enhanced by its new Bi-Xenon headlights, LED rear light clusters, and modified air intakes and outlets. All Porsche 911s are special, but some are quite definitely more special than others. The 911 GT3 is one of them.

Porsche 959

In 1983, Porsche unveiled a new Group B racing prototype at the Frankfurt Motor Show that looked something like a standard 911 on steroids. Two years later, again at Frankfurt, the company announced that it was putting the car into production as a road car, building just 200 examples for homologation purposes. A further two years later, in 1987, the 959 finally saw the light of day, by which time every one of the 200 was pre-ordered, despite a price tag of $225,000.

The 959 was clearly related to the 911 but it was also very different – longer, lower, wider, and sporting a massive wide tail with an enormous spoiler. With it vents and ducts to control the airflow over the body, it was clear that much work had gone into the aerodynamics, and the end result was a Cd of 0.31. But far more important than that drag co-efficient was the fact that the body created zero lift at higher speeds.

Like the 911, the 959 sported a six-cylinder horizontally opposed Boxer engine, but there the similarity ended. For the 959, Porsche's engineers created a 2.8-liter sequentially turbocharged masterpiece with twin overhead cams and four valves per cylinder. At lower speeds, only the left-hand turbo operated, while when top-end power was needed, the other turbo kicked in, too. This meant that the 959 could be driven around town without sacrificing its performance potential.

And what performance! With 450 bhp on tap, racing up through the six-speed gearbox, the 959 accelerated from 0 to 60 mph in 3.6 seconds, 0–100 mph in 8.8 seconds and on to a top speed of 195 mph / 314 km/h.

To achieve this level of performance, and to allow all of the 450 bhp to be safely transmitted to the road through the massive low-profile tires that Bridgestone created specially for this car, Porsche specified a full-time four-wheel-drive system that allowed the driver to adjust the level of torque transmitted to the front and rear wheels. Most, sensibly, Porsche also left the system in automatic mode and programmed the 959's computers to choose the optimum setting.

The 959's engineers also radically changed the suspension from that of the standard 911. The 959 had double wishbones front and rear, with twin dampers and concentric coil springs at each corner. The dampers were controllable to allow for standard or sports settings to be selected and for the ride height of the 959 to be lowered automatically at higher speeds for aerodynamic stability.

In addition, the 959 was actually sold in two forms, Sport and Comfort. The Sport model had no air conditioning, electric windows or rear seats and so was around 132 lb / 60 kg lighter than the Comfort.

Production started in 1987, though the 959 tested even the genius of Porsche's best engineers. It was so complex and so revolutionary that it proved impossible to build on standard production lines and so Porsche had to create a new facility to build the cars virtually by hand. It was also rumoured at the time that although the $225,000 price tag was enormous by the standards of the day, it actually cost Porsche nearly double that to build each one.

The new 959s were available only to existing Porsche owners, and, to deter speculators, purchasers had to agree not to sell them for at least six months. The car was never homologated for the USA market because Porsche refused to supply four examples for crash-testing purposes, so it could never be driven on public roads there. Wealthy collectors, including Microsoft founder Bill Gates, did import 959s, but not without severe difficulties with the authorities.

In the end, production continued until 1990 – far longer than Porsche had ever anticipated – by which time, 226 examples had been delivered to customers in Europe and perhaps 100 more had been built for racing.

The 959 was truly a one-off, but the lessons learnt in its development soon found their way onto 'standard' 911s. This was most notably evidenced in the launch of the four-wheel-drive Carrera 4 model, and four-wheel drive subsequently became standard on 911 Turbo models.

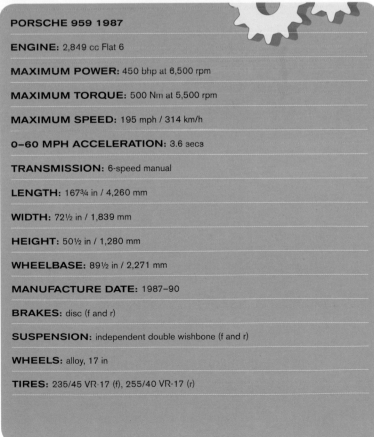

PORSCHE 959 1987

ENGINE: 2,849 cc Flat 6

MAXIMUM POWER: 450 bhp at 6,500 rpm

MAXIMUM TORQUE: 500 Nm at 5,500 rpm

MAXIMUM SPEED: 195 mph / 314 km/h

0–60 MPH ACCELERATION: 3.6 secs

TRANSMISSION: 6-speed manual

LENGTH: 167¾ in / 4,260 mm

WIDTH: 72½ in / 1,839 mm

HEIGHT: 50½ in / 1,280 mm

WHEELBASE: 89½ in / 2,271 mm

MANUFACTURE DATE: 1987–90

BRAKES: disc (f and r)

SUSPENSION: independent double wishbone (f and r)

WHEELS: alloy, 17 in

TIRES: 235/45 VR-17 (f), 255/40 VR-17 (r)

Porsche Carrera GT

The Porsche Carrera GT – one the finest supercars the company ever made – had a muddled start to its life. The basis of the car lay in a prototype built in preparation for Le Mans in 1999 but later abandoned because, for various reasons, Porsche chose not to compete against the Audi R8. Its engine, meanwhile, can be traced back to a V10 that Porsche designed in secret for the Footwork F1 team in the early 1990s. The two were brought together in a concept car unveiled at the Geneva Motor Show in 2000, where enough people offered to put down deposits to encourage Porsche to sign it off as a limited-edition road car.

From the very outset, the plan was to produce a racing car modified just enough to make it road legal, and at first glance, it was clear that the car's appearance owed more to the design of Porsche racing cars than its road cars. It is aerodynamic and muscular looking, with the mid-engined layout pushing the cockpit towards the front of the car. Large air scoops cool the engine and brakes while providing some raw visual clues to the

PORSCHE CARRERA GT 2003

ENGINE: 5,700 cc V10

MAXIMUM POWER: 612 bhp at 8,000 rpm

MAXIMUM TORQUE: 590 Nm at 5,750 rpm

MAXIMUM SPEED: 205 mph / 330 km/h

0–62 MPH ACCELERATION: 3.9 secs

TRANSMISSION: 6-speed manual

LENGTH: 181½ in / 4,610 mm

WIDTH: 75½ in / 1,920 mm

HEIGHT: 45¾ in / 1,160 mm

WHEELBASE: 107½ in / 2,730 mm

MANUFACTURE DATE: 2004–06

BRAKES: disc (f and r)

SUSPENSION: double wishbone (f and r)

WHEELS: alloy, 19 in (f) 20 in (r)

TIRES: 265/35 ZR19 (f) 335/30 ZR 20 (r)

The engine was the same V10 that had been used in the concept car, but its capacity was increased from 5.5 to 5.7 liters. The output was monumental – 612 bhp at 8,000 rpm and 590 Nm of torque at 5,750 rpm – as was the performance: the Carrera GT was good for 0–62 mph acceleration in 3.9 seconds, 0–124 mph in 9.9 seconds and a top speed of 205 mph / 330 km/h. A six-speed manual gearbox designed specially for the Carrera GT was fitted, operated via the world's first ceramic clutch. For good measure, the ventilated disc brakes were also constructed from ceramic materials.

The Porsche Carrera GT really only had one rival when production started in 2004 and that was the Ferrari Enzo. Both offered blistering acceleration and the sort of top speeds that could only ever be attained on a racetrack, but they were very different cars in conception and execution. The Ferrari was an expression of pure automotive emotion while the Porsche was perhaps a little more rational and a little less extrovert. Porsche originally announced it would built a run of 1,500 Carrera GTs but in the end had built only 1,270 by the time production was brought to a halt in 2006.

GT's ultimate potential. Meanwhile, the perforated stainless-steel powerdomes extending back over the engine ensure the mighty powerplant is clearly displayed.

The Carrera GT is essentially an open two-seater, but it was supplied with a pair of lightweight carbon shells weighing just 5¼ lb / 2.4 kg each, creating a roof to provide protection from the elements. Its construction owed much to race technologies, too, as this was the world's first production car to boast a monocoque chassis and modular frame constructed entirely in carbon fibre. Because a top speed of over 200 mph / 322 km/h was envisaged, good aerodynamics were crucial, and to ensure sufficient downforce, the underbody of the Carrera GT contains diffusers and venturis. With the added help of a large rear wing that is deployed when the speed of the car exceeds 75 mph / 121 km/h, the Carrera GT produced some 882 lb / 400 kg of total downforce at its top speed.

Other motorsport elements included lightweight forged magnesium wheels, magnesium and carbon-fibre seats, and a suspension set-up in which the spring/damper units were operated by stainless-steel pushrods and pivot levers attached directly to the chassis structure for absolute rigidity. The basic configuration of double wishbone pushrods front and rear, instead of the normal Porsche MacPherson struts, provides safer and more consistent handling.

Shelby Mustang GT350

Ford had launched the Mustang in 1964 very successfully. It looked good, it was relatively inexpensive and it sold in huge numbers. The only trouble was that it had been designed for style rather than true performance.

Ford itself started to put this right just a year later, when it offered the Cobra 4.7-liter V8 engine in the Mustang. With 271 bhp available, and with uprated suspension, wider tires and broad stripes, the car's performance was greatly improved.

More interesting, however, was the work of former racing driver Carroll Shelby, the man who had brought Ford together with British sports car company AC to produce the legendary Cobra. Shelby took a standard Mustang into his workshops in Los Angeles and set about making it perform, handle and brake far better than the original. By working on the manifolds of the 289 Cobra engine and fitting a Holley carburettor, he managed to extract 306 bhp from the sturdy V8. For racing, this was boosted to 360 bhp, and this car, the GT350R, immediately made its mark on the tracks, winning in its class first time out and running away with the SCCA B-Production road-racing series in 1965, 1966 and 1967.

Shelby's Mustang was fitted with a four-speed transmission as standard, though some cars that were built for the rental market through Hertz were fitted with three-speed auto boxes. There were no rear seats because the SCCA B-Production regulations stipulated a two-seater car. Instead, there was a shelf under the rear window that housed the spare wheel.

The suspension was uprated to cope with the extra power, with wishbones, coil springs, Koni shocks and an anti-roll bar at the front. Ford's live rear axle was retained at the back, along with trailing arms, semi-elliptic leaf springs and Koni shock absorbers. Braking was by discs at the front and drums at the rear.

SHELBY MUSTANG GT350 1965		
ENGINE: 4,727 cc V8		**WIDTH:** 68 ¼ in / 1,732 mm
MAXIMUM POWER: 306 bhp at 6,000 rpm		**HEIGHT:** 55 in / 1,397 mm
MAXIMUM TORQUE: 446 Nm at 4,200 rpm		**WHEELBASE:** 108 in / 2,743 mm
MAXIMUM SPEED: 149 mph / 240 km/h		**MANUFACTURE DATE:** 1965
0–62 MPH ACCELERATION: 6.5 secs		**BRAKES:** disc (f), drum (r)
TRANSMISSION: 4-speed manual		**SUSPENSION:** independent wishbone (f), live axle (r)
LENGTH: 181½ in / 4,613 mm		**WHEELS:** alloy, 15 in
		TIRES: 205/60 R-15 (f), 225/60 R-15 (r)

Side exhausts and extravagant stripes completed the visual package. With 306 bhp at 6,000 rpm and a massive 446 Nm of torque at 4,200 rpm on tap, the Shelby Mustang GT350 promised real performance, and it didn't disappoint: it raced from 0 to 60 mph in 6.5 seconds and had a top speed of 149 mph / 240 km/h. The Mustang had become a true performance car, a true 'muscle car'.

By 1967, the Shelby Mustang GT350, which remained in production, was joined by a second model, the GT500. This was fitted with Ford's very latest 7,014 cc V8, known as the Police Interceptor, and with its 355 bhp on tap, it was much quicker than the GT350, accelerating from 0 to 60 mph in around six seconds and with a top speed of over 150 mph / 241 km/h.

For some, this still wasn't enough, and a very few GT500s were converted to produce 425 bhp. It's not certain how many of these were sold, perhaps between 20 and 50, but these 'Shelby Super Snakes' are both extremely rare and extremely desirable.

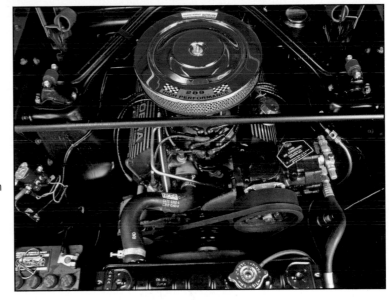

Many enthusiasts consider that real Shelby Mustangs were built only until 1967, the year in which production was shifted from Shelby's works in Los Angeles to one of Ford's many factories in Michigan. Certainly, the 1968 model seemed to be far more Ford than Shelby: it was bigger, heavier and significantly more comfortable, with higher trim levels, including power-sapping air conditioning and power steering, which had never been features of the earlier raw street racers that Shelby had designed.

It was clear that Ford wanted to move the Shelby Mustang upmarket, and each year, the finished product moved further away from Carroll Shelby's brilliant original concept.

Today, the Shelby Mustang is one of the most desirable of all muscle cars, and can fetch prices well into six figures at auction. The rarest competition GT350Rs – only 37 were built – have been auctioned at more than $500,000, which is not bad considering that the list price, when new, was $4,547 for the street version and $5,995 for the competition GT350R.

Subaru Impreza WRX STI

Subaru's Tecnica International (STI) division was originally established to develop entries for the World Rally Championship based on the company's Impreza mid-range saloon car. By adding a permanent four-wheel drive system, and turbocharging the flat-four engine to boost its output, STI created a highly successful competitor that won the World Rally Championship for Manufacturers titles three years in a row, from 1995 to 1997.

What STI also did was spearhead the development of a series of high-performance road cars that shared a lot of the rally car's technical features and most of its appearance too. In short, the Subaru Impreza WRX STI – initially sold only in Japan but soon exported to other markets too – was one of the fastest saloons of its size. It looked the part too: with its wings and air scoops, it could never be mistaken for the far more humble and decidedly ordinary standard Subaru Impreza.

The first Impreza WRX STI remained in production until 2001, during which time a number of versions and special editions were introduced. Similarly, the second generation WRX STI, which was in production from 2000 to 2008, was revised nearly every year, reaching a point where the engine was producing 320 bhp and 450 Nm of torque and offering 0–62 mph acceleration in 5.4 seconds and a top speed approaching 257 km/h / 160 mph.

So when the third generation Impreza WRX STI was announced late in 2007, hopes were high. No one was disappointed: the

new car had a new platform and suspension system, and made greater use of lightweight aluminium components to differentiate it from the 'normal' WRX. The new WRX STI has a longer wheelbase, despite being 50 mm / 2in shorter overall, and is wider too, broadening the track for improved grip. To demonstrate its potential, it has deep front bumpers, flared wheelarches, side air vents to feed the intercooler, side skirts, a roof spoiler and a diffuser integrated into the rear bumper to reduce lift.

The engine remains Subaru's trusty 2.5-liter flat-four unit, but it's been tuned to produce 300 bhp at 6,000 rpm and 407 Nm of torque at 4,000 rpm. As before, drive is taken to all four wheels via a six-speed manual gearbox to the all-wheel-drive system, which incorporates a torque-sensing electromagnetic center differential as well as front and rear limited slip differentials. The driver can manually select the ratio of drive taken to the front and the rear of the car via a switch on the center console.

Straight-line performance is sparkling – 0-62 mph comes up in just 4.8 seconds, while the top speed is electronically limited to 259 km/h / 155 mph – but what those figures can't reveal is just how quick the WRX STI is from point to point. Thanks to its four-wheel drive, there's so much grip, and thanks to the clever electronics, there's so much traction, that on winding roads, it can be driven as fast as just about any car on the market. Drivers can fiddle with all those controls that allow them to adjust the throttle response, the power settings, the torque ratios and even the traction control system, and no doubt these things make a difference to top-notch drivers on a rally stage, but on the road, the car's best left in Auto mode. For all but a tiny handful of experts, changing the settings won't make a blind bit of difference, and it's better to relax and enjoy the harsher, tauter and noticeably higher performance that differentiates the Subaru Impreza WRX STI from its lesser brethren.

SUBARU IMPREZA WRX STI 2009

ENGINE: 2,457 cc flat four-cylinder

MAXIMUM POWER: 300 bhp at 6,000 rpm

MAXIMUM TORQUE: 407 Nm at 4,000 rpm

MAXIMUM SPEED: 155 mph / 259 km/h

0-62 MPH ACCELERATION: 4.8 secs

TRANSMISSION: 6-speed manual

LENGTH: 173¾ in / 4,415 mm

WIDTH: 70¾ in / 1,795 mm

HEIGHT: 58 in / 1,475 mm

WHEELBASE: 103¼ in / 2,625 mm

MANUFACTURE DATE: 2007–present

BRAKES: disc (f and r)

SUSPENSION: A-arms (f and r)

WHEELS: alloy, 18 in

TIRES: 245/40 R18 (f and r)

Toyota 2000GT

Prestige motor manufacturers like Jaguar and Aston Martin pay millions to get their cars featured in the latest James Bond movies. So how did a humble Toyota get star billing in *You Only Live Twice*? Quite simply, the film's producer 'Cubby' Broccoli had seen the Toyota 2000GT when it was the undoubted star of the 1965 Tokyo Motor Show and he reckoned it would make the perfect set of wheels for Bond's Japanese associate Aki. Toyota was so keen to get involved that it went to the trouble of creating a pair of open-topped convertibles especially for the film.

Even without the James Bond publicity, it was clear that the 2000GT was something special. Toyota had been very successfully making mass-market cars for 30 years and felt it was time to make a statement of future intent. It would create a world-class GT car that would not only showcase the company's engineering skills, but would also boost the image of a company that, until then, had been known only for reliable and well-built, but basically plodding and soulless small cars. At the time of its launch, the 2000GT was described admiringly as a 'Japanese E-Type'. Not bad for a car that was originally intended to carry Nissan badges. Bizarrely, the car had been conceived by another Japanese company, Yamaha, on behalf of Nissan. Nissan, however, decided it wasn't right for them, so Yamaha sold the design to Toyota, who made some changes of its own then gave the car pride of place at the Tokyo Show in 1965.

It was beautifully proportioned. Much of the design work had been carried out by Count Albrecht von Goertz, the genius responsible for the earlier BMW 507, and he created the elegant aluminium body that sat on top of a steel backbone chassis with independent suspension in a set-up highly reminiscent of the Lotus Elan. It had sharp and responsive rack-and pinion steering and excellent brakes, thanks to its four-wheel disc brakes – the first time any Japanese production car had boasted such a

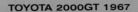

TOYOTA 2000GT 1967

ENGINE: 1,988 cc inline 6-cylinder

MAXIMUM POWER: 150 bhp at 6,600 rpm

MAXIMUM TORQUE: 175 Nm at 5,000 rpm

MAXIMUM SPEED: 131 mph / 211 km/h

0–60 MPH ACCELERATION: 10 secs

TRANSMISSION: 5-speed manual

LENGTH: 164½ in / 4,176 mm

WIDTH: 63 in / 1,600 mm

HEIGHT: 45¾ in / 1,161 mm

WHEELBASE: 91¾ in / 2,329 mm

MANUFACTURE DATE: 1967–70

BRAKES: disc (f and r)

SUSPENSION: independent coil spring (f and r)

WHEELS: alloy, 15 in

TIRES: 165/41 HR-15 (f and r)

specification. A five-speed manual transmission took the drive via a limited slip differential to the rear wheels. Under the bonnet was a 2.0-liter DOHC in-line six-cylinder engine, fuelled via three Mikuni-Solex side-draft carburettors that produced 150 bhp at 6,600 rpm and 175 Nm of torque at 5,000 rpm, enough to provide 0–60 mph acceleration in 10 seconds and a top speed of 131 mph / 211 km/h, which was highly respectable at the time. Contemporary road tests raved about the 2000GT's performance, and especially its vice-free handling. Its ride, cornering and levels of grip were praised, as was the car's near-perfect balance, thanks to the low center of gravity, 48:52 weight distribution and Lotus-inspired suspension. This truly was the first Japanese car that could challenge the best that Europe and the USA could offer in terms of both style and driving dynamics.

Production of the Toyota 2000GT started in 1967 but came to an end in 1970, by which time only 351 examples had been built. It wasn't the fastest car on the road, but that probably wasn't the reason sales were so hard to come by. More likely, car buyers found it hard to stomach the idea of spending $7,230 on a Japanese car when at that time a Chevy Corvette cost $4,663 and an E-Type Jaguar $5,559. But for those who did choose to buy one, the rewards were high. They not only enjoyed driving one of the most interesting and technically advanced cars of the time, but those that kept hold of it could now be looking at an asset worth between $100,000 and $200,000.

TVR Griffith

The British sports car manufacturer TVR was founded in 1946 by Trevor Wilkinson, who very early on started making two-seaters with glass-reinforced-plastic bodies over tubular-steel chassis. The company's first production car, launched in 1954, was the Grantura, and it was superseded in 1980 by the very angular, wedge-shaped Tasmin. In the meantime, an American dealer had been experimenting with fitting a big-bore AC Cobra engine into his TVR Grantura. His name was Jack Griffith, and when, many years later, TVR first put a big V8 into one of its production cars, it named the car TVR Griffith in his honour.

The car was first unveiled as a prototype at the 1990 British Motor Show, where it was an instant success. It had the appearance of a traditional British sports car, with clear influences of both the Jaguar E-Type and the AC Cobra in its smooth and curvaceous composite body. The style was clean and uncluttered – the door handles and boot catch were concealed to avoid interrupting the fluid design, for example. Its appearance was both aggressive and elegant, and its proportions were near perfect.

The original plan had been to modify the existing chassis of the TVR V8S, but it simply wasn't stiff enough for the performance TVR had in mind for the Griffith, so instead, TVR adapted the much tauter chassis of the TVR Tuscan Racer. All-independent suspension was essential, and TVR chose unequal-length twin wishbones, with coil-over adjustable telescopic shock absorbers with anti-roll bars front and rear. With its wide track and massive tires, the Griffith offered excellent grip

and viceless handling in the dry (though it could be more than a handful in the wet) that was well capable of transmitting the V8 engine's power to the road. Reassuringly, the huge ventilated disc brakes front and rear performed as if they had been designed for the racetrack.

At first, TVR used the Rover 3.9-liter V8 engine in the Griffith, though over the years this was uprated to 4.0 liters and later to 4.3 liters. Later still, in 1993, TVR developed its own 5.0-liter version of the Rover V8 – the Griffith 500 – and by this time it was producing 335 bhp at 6,000 rpm and 475 Nm of torque at 4,000 rpm. The power output was later

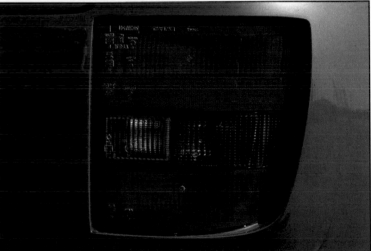

reduced to 320 bhp to provide smoother idling and to make the car more driveable at lower speeds. Even the earliest Griffiths had a top speed of just under 150 mph / 241 km/h and acceleration from 0 to 60 mph in under five seconds, which made them faster in terms of acceleration than either the Porsche 911 Turbo or the Ferrari Testarossa, two of the Griffith's contemporary competitors. The Griffith 500 was even quicker, taking just 4.1 seconds to accelerate from 0 to 60 mph and continuing to a top speed of 167 mph / 269 km/h.

Quite apart from its out-and-out performance, what was special about the Griffith was its carefully tuned big-bore stainless-steel exhaust system, which did more than just

optimize performance, it also emphasized the magnificent roar of the V8 engine, which became one of the car's hallmarks. The Griffith stayed in production until 2002. The final 100 examples were badged SE (Special Edition), and these had a different fascia and rear lights and new door mirrors, and each was individually numbered.

The Griffith was very successful, despite it being an uncompromising prospect. For those who wanted a little more practicality – a bigger boot and softer, more compliant suspension – TVR developed the Chimaera, a model that was just as fast as the Griffith but a little less brutal. But the Griffith remains, meanwhile, a wonderful, timeless classic.

Picture Credits

The publisher would like to thank the following for permission to reproduce the following copyright material:

Index

AC
Ace 160
Cobra 427 160-63
Alfa Giulia 12
Alfa Romeo
8C Competizione 10-11
Montreal 12-13
RZ 14
SZ 14-15
Alferi, Giulio 248
Artioli, Romano 44, 244
Ascari
Ecosse 164
KZ1 164-5
Aston Martin
DB4 Zagato 16
DB5 166-7
DB7 Vantage Zagato Coupé
16-17
DB9 18-21
DB9 Volante 20
DBAR1 17
V8 Vantage 168-9
Audi 157, 234
quattro 170-73
R8 174-5
S8 22-3

Baker, Buddy 199
Baur 178
Bentley 148
Arnage 26
Arnage Drophead Coupé 24
Azure 26
Azure T 24-5
Brooklands 26-9
Continental Supersports 176-7
R-Type Continental 30-33
Bertone 100, 116, 242, 243
Bez, Ulrich 16
Bizzarrini, Giotto 74, 100, 116
BMW 34-5, 84, 148, 156, 157
3.0 CS 13
7-Series saloons 34, 35
507 Roadster 36
Hydrogen 34-5
M1 178-9
M3 CSL 180-81
M5 23, 37, 182-5
Z8 36-9
Braeckel, Dirk van 176
Broccoli, 'Cubby' 296
Brosnan, Pierce 37
Brown, David 166
Bugatti 244
EB 16/4 Veyron 40-43, 226,
227
EB110 44-5
EB110 SS 44-5
Type 35 46-9
Bugatti, Ettore 44, 45

Cadillac Allante 540-51
De Ville 51
Eldorado Convertible 52-3
XLR-V 54-5
Caine, Michael 117
Castriota, Jason 126
Caterham
Caterham 7 186
Superlight R300 186-7
Chapman, Colin 186, 244, 245
Charreton, Jacques 65
Chevrolet
Camaro SS 188-9
Camaro Z28 56-9
Corvette 54
Corvette Sting Ray 60-63
Corvette ZR-1 190-93
Chrysler 202, 203, 231, 234
Citroën 248
DS 64, 65
SM 64-5
Traction Avant 64
Cosworth 234

DaimlerChrysler 132
Dallara, Gianpaolo 116
Datsun 268
De Lorean, John Z 66, 68
De Lorean DMC-12 66-9
De Tomaso, Alejandro 194
De Tomaso Pantera 194-5
Dodge
Challenger SRT8 196-7
Charger 500 Daytona 138,
198-201
Viper SRT-10 202-5
Donckerwolke, Luc 236
Donohue, Mark 59

Egger, Wolfgang 10
Elf 45

Facel Vega 130
Ferrari 88, 126
246 GT Dino 70-73
246 GTS Spyder 73
250 GTO 74-7
365 GTB/4 Daytona 78-9
California 80-83
Enzo 206-9
F40 210-13
F430 11
Ferrari, Enzo 70, 88, 107, 210,
211
Fiat 70, 126, 242
Fisker, Henrik 84
Fisker Karma 84-7
Forghieri, Mauro 44
Ford
Falcon 92
Fastback 92
GT 214-17
GT40 Mk I Production 88-91

Mustang 56, 92-3, 188, 189,
290
Premier Automotive Group 20
Thunderbird 94-7
Ford, Henry, II 88
Frua 130

Gandini, Marcello 12, 44, 116,
130, 230
Gates, Bill 285
General Motors (GM) 52, 56,
59, 60, 94, 160
188, 199
Corvette 94
Giugiaro, Giorgio 66, 100, 178,
246-7, 248
Goertz, Count Albrecht von 36,
296
Griffith, Jack 300
Gumpert, Roland 218
Gumpert Apollo 218-19

Hoffman, Maxi 134
Honda
FCX Clarity 35
NSX 179, 220-21

Iacocca, Lee 92, 202
Ickx, Jacky 174
Infiniti
FX35 98
FX50 98-9
Iso Grifo 100-101
Issigonis, Alec 116

Jaguar 20
C-Type 102
D-Type 102-5
E-Type 61, 102, 106-9, 167
XFR 110-13
XJ220 222-5
XKSS 104
James Bond movies 37, 166,
247, 296
Jenkinson, Denis 258
Jensen FF 114-15

Kawamoto, Nobuhiko 220
Koenigsegg, Christian von 226
Koenigsegg CCX 226-9
Kristensen, Tom 174

Lagonda Rapide 130
Lamborghini 22, 23, 178
Countach 44, 103, 179,
230-33
Gallardo 22, 234-5
Miura P400 116-19
Murciélago 236-9
Lamborghini, Ferrucio 78, 116
Lancia
Delta HF Intregrale Evoluzione
II 240-41

Stratos 73, 242-3
Thema 23
Land Rover 20
Range Rover 120-21
Lexus
LS 400 122-3
LS 460 122-3
Lincoln Continental Mark IV
124-5
Lola 88
Lotus 45
Elise 244-5
Esprit 66, 68
Esprit Turbo 246-7
Lotus 7 186

McLaren F1 252-5
Mako Shark 60
Maserati 11, 64
Bora 248-51
Coupé 11
GranTurismo 11, 126-9
Khamsin 65
Merak 64, 65, 250
Quattroporte 23, 142, 130-31
Maybach, Wilhelm 132
Maybach 62 132-3
Mercedes-Benz 84, 156, 157
300 SL 134-5
350 SL 13
S55 AMG 23
S65 AMG 136-7
SLR McLaren Roadster 256-7
SLR McLaren Stirling Moss
258-61
Michelin 40, 45
Mitchell, Bill 60
Mitsubishi Lancer Evolution X
262-3
Montezemolo, Luca Cordero di
206
Morgan
Aero 8 264-5
Plus 8 266-7
Roadster 267
Morgan, H.F.S. 266
Morgan, Peter 264
Moss, Stirling 258
Mouton, Michele 170
Muller, Victor 152
Mulliner, H.J. 32
Murray, Gordon 252, 253, 274

Nissan
370Z 268-71
GT-R 272-3
Noble, Lee 164, 274
Noble M15 274-5

Operon, Robert 65

Pagani, Horacio 276
Pagani Zonda 276-7

Penske, Roger 59
Peugeot 65, 66
Piech, Ferdinand 40, 170, 171
Pininfarina 50, 79, 80, 126,
206
Plymouth Superbird 138-9
Pontiac
Firebird 56, 66, 188
GTO 66
Porsche 86
911 278-81
911 GT3 282-3
959 284-5
Carrera GT 286-9
Panamera 140-43
Porsche, Ferdinand 170, 278
Presley, Elvis 195

Ralliart UK 262
Renault 66
Rivolta, Renzo 100
Röhrl, Walter 282-3
Rolls Royce 30, 32
Phantom 148-51
Phantom Drophead Coupé
144-7
Silver Dawn 32

Saab 86
Sayer, Malcolm 107
Scaglietti 79
Shelby, Carroll 160, 162, 290,
291
Shelby Mustang GT350
290-91
Sinatra, Frank 117
Spyker C8 Laviolette 152-5
Stevens, Peter 247, 252
Subaru Impreza WRX STI
292-5
Suharto, Tommy 234

Tjaarda, Tom 194
Tom Walkinshaw Racing 224
Toyoda, Eiji 123
Toyota 122, 123
2000GT 296-9
TVR Griffith 300-302

Valmet Automobile 86
Vickers Group 148
Volkswagen Group 40, 45,
148, 170, 176, 234
Volkswagen Phaeton W12 4
Motion 156-7
Volvo 20, 66

Wilkinson, Trevor 300

Zagato 14, 16
Zagato, Andrea 16
Zwart, Klaas 164, 165